Archdiocese of Chicago
Celebrating 150 Years

This year marks the 150th anniversary of the creation of the Diocese of Chicago, an event that had profound consequences for the history of the Catholic Church in the Midwest. When the diocese was established on November 28, 1843, it embraced the entire state of Illinois, a vast territory covering 56,560 square miles. Although it was divided five times in its history, the Chicago diocese nevertheless continued to increase in population. Raised to the status of an archdiocese in 1880, it is now the second largest Roman Catholic diocese in the United States.

Few Americans living in the middle nineteenth century could have predicted the phenomenal growth of the diocese or its tremendous impact on the city of Chicago. In the 1840s, Catholics were scattered in small settlements throughout the state, and their efforts to establish parishes and build churches and schools were hampered by the lack of finances and clergy. Nowhere was the situation more desperate than in Chicago, a frontier town on the shore of Lake Michigan.

When Bishop William J. Quarter arrived in May 1844, he found a single Catholic church in the city—Saint Mary's at Wabash Avenue and Madison Street. Not only was the cathedral still under construction, it was also saddled with a large debt. Yet within a few years, Catholic institutions dotted the landscape, powerful symbols of the progress—and promise—of Catholicism in Chicago. How was all this possible? The authors of *Catholicism, Chicago Style* suggest that for more than a century, Catholics in this diocese have shared a belief that their institutions contributed to the well-being of society. An idea of the magnitude of this accomplishment is the fact that from a single parish in 1833, the Archdiocese of Chicago has expanded to include 800 Catholic institutions in Cook and Lake Counties. With an enrollment of nearly 150,000 students, its Catholic school system is the ninth largest system of any kind in the United States, public or private. Catholic Charities of the Archdiocese of Chicago is the largest private social services agency in the Midwest.

The essays in this volume make a convincing case that parochial institutions did more than preserve the ancestral faith of wave after wave of immigrants and their American-born children and grandchildren. Catholic parishes and schools also created community in the urban metropolis and its surrounding settlements. One of the results of all this church-building, suggest the authors, was an intensification of Catholic identity and confidence. But the process was not an easy one. *Catholicism, Chicago Style* reminds us that Catholics have been challenged from with[?] [...] as from within by such forces as nativism, ethnicity, nationalism, [...]

Far from being the monolithic structure depicted by [...] the Catholic Church in metropolitan Chicago has been [...] tion, touching the lives of millions. For more that 150 [...] have contributed to the growth and vitality of the Chica[...] on the accomplishments of earlier generations who created parishes and schools in industrial slums, "bungalow belts," and suburban residential districts, Catholics in the twentieth century have been enthusiastic supporters of social justice programs, Catholic action movements, and ecumenical endeavors. Few dioceses anywhere in the United States have been as blessed as Chicago. Her people represent a wide range of ethnic, racial, linguistic, cultural, economic, and educational backgrounds, continuing witness to the inclusivity of the universal church.

The challenges confronting us in the 1990s are as formidable as those faced by Catholics in the Chicago diocese 150 years ago. In his last pastoral letter written shortly before he died in 1848, Bishop William Quarter expressed his confidence in the future of Catholicism in the Midwest, and he pledged that "We shall use our best efforts" to ensure that Catholics "everywhere in the diocese" can participate fully in the local Church. Recently, the Archdiocese of Chicago initiated a strategic planning process that will shape the future direction of our Church as it enters the twenty-first century. Focusing on two of the most critical issues facing the archdiocese—evangelization and education and ministerial leadership—the plan will involve all parishes and institutions through a broad-ranging consultation process. Only by identifying the needs as well as the resources of Catholics in metropolitan Chicago will we be able to plan for our future.

The 150th anniversary of the Archdiocese of Chicago provides us with a unique opportunity to examine our history and celebrate our unity as a Catholic community. A fine starting place is *Catholicism, Chicago Style.* Written by three Chicago natives, handsomely illustrated with photographs from *The New World* and the archives of the archdiocese, and published by Loyola University Press, this book documents the richness of our collective past.

Finally, I would like to thank Fr. Raymond Baumhart, Jac Treanor, and the Sesquicentennial History/Lecture Committee for spearheading this important endeavor. It gives us a fine perspective on how we are "rooted in faith and rising to our call." I am grateful for their work and the effort of all those involved in our 150th celebration.

Joseph Card. Bernardin

Joseph Cardinal Bernardin
Archbishop of Chicago
November 28, 1993

Catholicism, Chicago Style

by Ellen Skerrett, Edward R. Kantowicz, and Steven M. Avella

A Campion Book

Loyola University Press
Chicago

Loyola University Press
3441 North Ashland Avenue
Chicago, Illinois 60657

Cover and interior design by Nancy Gruenke

Library of Congress Cataloging-in-Publication Data

Skerrett, Ellen.
    Catholicism, Chicago Style/by Ellen Skerrett, Edward R. Kantowicz, and Steven M. Avella.
        p. cm.
    Includes bibliographical references and index.
    ISBN 0-8294-0774-X
    1. Catholic Church—Illinois Region—History.   2. Chicago Region (Ill.)—Church history.
3. Catholic Church. Archdiocese of Chicago (Ill.)—History.   I. Kantowicz, Edward R.
II. Avella, Steven M.   Ill. Title
BX1418.C4S44 1993
282′.77311—dc20   93-31229
                                                                                                      CIP

To Jac Treanor, archivist extraordinaire

Contents

Illustrations

Photographs

Maps

Tables

Foreword

Catholicism, Chicago Style is published to mark the beginning of the sesquicentennial celebration of the archdiocese of Chicago. It is a collection of historical essays chosen to reflect the distinctive characteristics of one of the world's largest Roman Catholic archdioceses. These characteristics include: ethnic diversity; a close identification between parish and neighborhood; outstanding episcopal, clerical, and lay leadership; social and political liberalism; and a soaring self-confidence.

Although the collection contains some previously published work, the sesquicentennial planners are encouraging new scholarship that will further explore the rich traditions and successful innovations of Chicago's Catholic community. To stimulate budding authors, the sesquicentennial committee has announced plans for a major academic symposium November 4–5, 1994, at Loyola University Chicago. The symposium, entitled "Chicago and the American Catholic Experience," will bring together religious and lay leaders as well as leading scholars in an academic forum to investigate the historical legacy of Catholics in Chicago, and thereby contribute to the renewal of the faithful within the archdiocese and throughout the United States.

It is the hope of sesquicentennial planners that the symposium will explore many significant aspects of the Catholic experience, including labor relations, lay leadership, education, the arts, architecture, health care, and popular culture. Special attention will be given to the role of African-Americans, Hispanic-Americans, and women religious as well as the interplay of racial and ethnic interaction within the community. The outcome of the effort will be a series of essays that we hope to publish as a sequel to this volume.

Rev. Raymond C. Baumhart, S.J.
Loyola University
Chicago

Acknowledgments

"The Ethnic Church" by Edward R. Kantowicz was originally published in *Ethnic Chicago*, edited by Melvin G. Holli and Peter d'A. Jones (Grand Rapids, Mich.: William B. Eerdmans Publishing, 1994; 3rd ed.), and is reprinted with permission.

"The Irish in Chicago: The Catholic Dimension" by Ellen Skerrett was originally published in *The Irish in Chicago* by Lawrence J. McCaffrey, Ellen Skerrett, Michael F. Funchion, and Charles Fanning (Urbana, Ill.: University of Illinois Press, 1987), and is reprinted with permission.

"Cardinal Mundelein of Chicago and the Shaping of Twentieth-Century American Catholicism" by Edward R. Kantowicz was originally published in *The Journal of American History* 68 (June 1981), and is reprinted with permission.

"Reynold Hillenbrand and Chicago Catholicism" by Steven M. Avella was originally published in *U.S. Catholic Historian* 9 (Fall 1990), and is reprinted with permission.

"The Rise and Fall of Bernard Sheil" by Steven M. Avella was originally published in *The Critic* 44 (Spring 1990), and is reprinted with permission.

"Cardinal Meyer and the Era of Confidence" by Steven M. Avella was originally published in *U.S. Catholic Historian* 7 (Winter 1988), and is reprinted with permission.

"The Beginning and the End of an Era: George William Mundelein and John Patrick Cody in Chicago" by Edward R. Kantowicz was originally published in *Patterns of Episcopal Leadership*, edited by Gerald P. Fogarty, S.J., and copyright 1988 by the U.S. Catholic Conference, and is reprinted with permission of Macmillan Publishing Company, New York.

The authors were encouraged to publish these historical essays in book form by the History/Lecture Committee for the Archdiocese of Chicago's Sesquicentennial celebration:

Co-Chairs
  Rev. Raymond C. Baumhart, S.J.
  John J. Treanor

Members
  Judith Arnold
  Steven M. Avella
  Mary Ann Bamburger
  Conrad Borntrager, O.S.M.
  Joy Clough, R.S.M.
  Edward R. Kantowicz
  Ted Karamanski
  Mary Adolphine Ksioszk, C.S.S.F.
  Wayne Magdziarz
  Edward Marciniak
  Patricia Mooney-Melvin
  Steven Rosswurm
  Ellen Skerrett
  Mark Sorvillo
  David Wright, O.P.

Introduction

What Has Made Chicago Catholicism Distinctive?

Years ago, the parishioners of St. Leo's parish on the South Side threw a party for their long-time pastor, Msgr. Patrick J. Molloy, on the fortieth anniversary of his ordination. After numerous testimonials from prelates and politicians, Msgr. Molloy rose and addressed his parishioners. "I have seen the great boulevards of the world," the pastor orated. "The boulevards of Rome. The boulevards of Rio de Janeiro. The boulevards of Tokyo. They are all grand. But I would rather have an alley in Chicago than any one of them."[1]

Chicago Catholics have long shared Msgr. Molloy's sentiments. Closely identifying with the city and its neighborhoods, they walk its streets and alleys with a distinctive swagger. Confident that Chicago is a "Catholic town," they carry themselves with an "easy arrogance" that seems not to bother non-Catholics in Chicago but often irritates their Catholic coreligionists elsewhere in the United States. To outsiders it must seem that Chicago Catholics expect the Second Coming and the Last Judgment to take place on the shores of Lake Michigan.

For most of the twentieth century, Chicago has been the largest Catholic archdiocese in the United States, though it recently lost this numerical supremacy to Los Angeles.[2] Yet more than large numbers have set Chicago Catholics apart from (and in their own eyes, above) other American Catholics. Indeed Chicago Catholicism displays a distinctive style all its own.

Chicago-style Catholicism flows from at least five historical sources: ethnic diversity; a close identification between parish and neighborhood; able episcopal, clerical, and lay leadership; social and political liberalism; and, finally, as a result of all these other factors, a soaring self-confidence.

The first two marks of Chicago Catholicism, ethnic diversity and the close identification between parish and neighborhood, hark back to the very beginnings of Chicago in the mid-nineteenth century. Whereas most other American dioceses were dominated by either the Irish or the Germans, Chicago welcomed large numbers of both. The city's first resident bishop, the Irishman William J. Quarter, dedicated two German parishes, St. Peter's and St. Joseph's, in 1846, just two years after his arrival in the city. Catholic immigrants from Eastern and Southern Europe swiftly followed the Germans to Chicago. The Poles opened their first Chicago parish, St. Stanislaus Kostka, in 1867, just two years after the Bohemian parish of St. Wenceslaus. Lithuanians, Slovaks, Italians, and French-Canadians all founded their own parishes before 1900, followed in the twentieth century by Croatians, Slovenians, Hungarians, Dutch, Belgians, African-Americans, and Mexicans.

Certainly European immigrants settled in many other cities of the Northeast and the Midwest in the late nineteenth and early twentieth centuries, but in no other city did such a wide range of Catholic groups make their homes. A glance at the 1916 *Catholic Directory,* for example, reveals that over 75 percent of the parishes in Boston and Philadelphia were Irish. Even in polyglot New York and Brooklyn, the Irish dominated about two-thirds of the parishes; but in Chicago, by way of contrast, the Irish share fell below 50 percent. In other cities, one additional group of Catholic immigrants, such as the Italians in New York, might be numerous enough to challenge the Irish or German complexion of a city, but in Chicago the Irish, the Poles, and the Germans enjoyed roughly equal numbers. Four other ethnic groups established enough parishes throughout the city that they did not feel isolated. Indeed, as the first two chapters of this book detail, Chicago Catholics organized into separate "ethnic leagues" that were virtually subdioceses in their own right.

Roman authorities have recognized Chicago's pluralism by alternating Irish and non-Irish archbishops at the head of the see throughout the entire twentieth century. Today the city's archbishop, Joseph Cardinal Bernardin, is of Italian origin, and his auxiliary bishops are Irish, Polish, Mexican, and African-American.

No matter what their ethnic group, Catholic Chicagoans have traditionally taken much of their sense of neighborhood from their parishes. Poles, for instance, called the area around their mother church of St. Stanislaus Kostka the *Stanislawowo,* and they readily turned any parish name into a neighborhood name by adding the suffix *-owo* to the parish saint. The English-speaking Irish Catholics simply told friends that they lived in St. Gertrude's or Christ the King.

The Catholic Church is geographically organized, with each diocese carved into territorial parishes. Unlike many Protestants, who may travel across the city for Sunday services, a Catholic usually worships near where he or she lives. Theoretically, the national parishes for non-English speaking Catholics form an exception to this rule, for according to canon law a national parish is defined by language not territory, and a parishioner could come from a great distance to worship at the parish of his or her nationality. This is probably the way it works in many other cities, where a smaller nationality may have only one church. In Chicago, however, national parishes are numerous, and each one is really just an alternative neighborhood parish.

Early in this century, Archbishop James Quigley formulated a policy of organizing one territorial parish per square mile, and his successors followed this general rule within the city limits. In the inner city, however, numerous national parishes for non-English speaking Catholics also clustered within these square-mile quadrants so that many Chicago neighborhoods counted two, three, or as many as seven Catholic churches.

The concluding chapter of this book explores some of the intimate connections between parish and neighborhood. Catholic parishes humanized the harsh condition of urban life for newcomers to the city, or perhaps even sacralized it. Bricks and mortar played a key role in this process of turning neighborhoods into sacred space. In older, poorer sections of the city, dominated by the twin spires of church steeple and factory smokestack, the Catholic church might well provide the only place of beauty and tranquility. And since the churches were built through the generosity and hard work of the parishioners themselves, they proved that even poor people had control over at least one important aspect of their lives. In the suburbs, where individuals can easily be lost in a faceless anonymity, parishes have proven just as important in fostering a sense of community and belonging. Whether in city or suburbs, therefore, a Chicago-area parish helps Catholics answer the crucial questions: Who are you? Where are you from?

The other keynotes of Chicago Catholicism do not date back so far as its immigrant diversity and its neighborhood consciousness. During the nineteenth century the city's Catholics were neither ably led, politically liberal, nor exceptionally self-confident. In fact, Rome considered Chicago an ecclesiastical disaster area. The earliest bishops took one look at this muddy frontier town and started making plans to leave. One bishop literally went insane and had to be removed by Rome. At the turn of the century, a cabal of Irish-born pastors mounted a challenge to Archbishop Patrick Feehan and his American-born advisors, resulting in a schism and excommunication that broke the archbishop's heart and hastened his death.

This turbulent history led to one consequence that still lasts. The Vatican, endowed with the world's longest memory, has never entrusted the archdiocese to a native Chicagoan but has always appointed an outsider. This stands in sharp contrast to New York, where nearly all ruling bishops have been natives and even an archbishop from New Jersey is considered a foreigner.

One of the outsiders sent by Rome, from New York of all places, was George William Mundelein. From his arrival in 1916 until his death in 1939, he closely identified with his adopted city, turned around Chicago's ecclesiastical reputation, and established the tradition of outstanding leadership that has marked it

throughout the rest of the century. The third chapter in this book characterizes Mundelein as a "consolidating bishop," who centralized the administration of the archdiocese, set it on a firm financial footing, and tied it more closely to headquarters in Rome. He also trumpeted his 100 percent Americanism and forged close political ties with local Democratic politicians and with President Franklin Delano Roosevelt. In all these ways, Mundelein "put Chicago Catholicism on the map."

Mundelein also chose inspired associates, such as the seminary rector Msgr. Reynold Hillenbrand and Auxiliary Bishop Bernard J. Sheil, whom chapters 4 and 5 discuss. Though both were commanding individuals who earned a loyal and devoted following, Hillenbrand and Sheil had very different styles and personalities. Hillenbrand was Germanic, reserved, and deeply intellectual, whereas Sheil was Irish, gregarious, and warmhearted. They both applied Catholic teachings to the social and political realms, but they worked in very different ways. This diversity of approaches reflected Mundelein's, or any good manager's, ability to delegate authority and let a creative tension reign. The leadership of Mundelein, Hillenbrand, Sheil, and the numerous priests and laypeople they inspired earned Chicago Catholicism a reputation for social and political liberalism.

The two archbishops who succeeded Mundelein, Samuel A. Stritch and Albert G. Meyer, were more typical products of mid-century Catholicism than their predecessor. Mundelein was a towering individual who would have risen to the top in any line of work. Indeed his lay admirers used to tell him: "There was a great mistake in making you a bishop instead of a financier, for in the latter case Mr. Morgan would not be without a rival on Wall Street." No one would have said this to Stritch or Meyer, for as products of a well-developed clerical culture, it would be hard to imagine either as anything other than a priest or bishop. Nevertheless, each in his own way helped establish the twentieth century Chicago tradition of Catholic leadership.

Cardinal Stritch was a beloved figure, with a self-effacing smile and a pleasant southern lilt to his voice. He gained a reputation as the "bishop who said Yes," a permissive, tolerant figurehead who allowed "a thousand flowers to bloom." While Stritch was archbishop, the followers of Reynold Hillenbrand, such as Msgrs. John Egan and Daniel Cantwell, and lay leaders Patrick and Patricia Crowley, started many new social action organizations, including the Christian Family Movement, the Young Christian Workers, and the Catholic Interracial Council.

Albert Meyer, on the other hand, projected a colder public image and the scholarly manner of the seminary rector he used to be. Yet he too permitted priests and laypeople to address controversial social and political issues in Chicago, and as chapter 6 of this book explains, he himself emerged as an unlikely hero of the Catholic civil rights movement. Meyer seemingly reasoned himself into a liberal in a thoroughly medieval, syllogistic fashion: All people are equal in the sight of God, Negroes are people, ergo Negroes must be treated equally. End of argument. Cardinal Meyer also played a crucial role at the Second Vatican Council, particularly in the passage of the council's declaration on religious liberty. In a way, the Second Vatican Council, which was such a monumental achievement of church reform, proved to be something of a misfortune for Chicago since it took

Cardinal Meyer's leadership away from the city for long periods of time and then hastened his early death in 1965.

Meyer's successor, John Cardinal Cody, became a controversial figure due to his frequent disagreements with the Association of Chicago Priests and to newspaper charges of personal impropriety. Chapter 7 of this book points out that Cody came at the very end of an era in Catholic history, when priests and laypeople no longer accepted a bishop's directives unquestioningly, and he had a hard time adjusting. Nevertheless, in some ways, he continued the Chicago style of liberal leadership. Cody embraced and implemented many of the reforms of the Second Vatican Council, including the restoration of the permanent diaconate. Cody and his successor, the present archbishop, have ordained so many married men as deacons that Chicago now enjoys, along with its other distinctions, the largest corps of married clergy (deacons are ordained clergy) in the world. Cody also took a leadership role in race relations, and when the *Chicago Sun-Times* leveled a number of personal allegations against him in 1981 the first group to defend him was the black clergy caucus.

In his first decade as head of the Chicago archdiocese, Cardinal Bernardin has earned a national reputation as the leader of the liberal wing of American Catholicism. He chaired the committee of bishops that wrote the pastoral letter on world peace, challenging the legitimacy of nuclear weapons and the Cold War. He has spoken out eloquently on a range of pro-life issues, linking the traditional Catholic opposition to abortion with a critique of capital punishment, nuclear war, and domestic violence. Though conventional wisdom portrays the anti-abortion cause as a conservative movement, Chicago's cardinal has emphasized that it is part of a "seamless garment" of liberal, life-enhancing issues.

All in all, outstanding leadership has instilled great pride and self-confidence in Chicago Catholics. Indeed, Catholics often feel and act as if Chicago were their kind of town. It's worth emphasizing that Catholics have never formed the numerical majority in Chicago. Yet Catholic politicians rose to power in the city's Democratic machine about the same time that Cardinal Mundelein was establishing his authority in the church, so this high standard of leadership in both church and government has given Chicago Catholics very high visibility.

Another factor which made Chicago a "Catholic city" for much of the twentieth century was the lack of an entrenched or cohesive opposition. There was no other group that was strong enough, united enough, or perhaps cared enough to oppose the dominant position of Catholics. A comparative perspective is useful in this context. In Boston, even though Irish Catholics were numerous and controlled both the Catholic church and the city government, they always felt a bit insecure because of the long-standing social dominance of the so-called Boston Brahmins, the old stock Protestants who lived on Beacon Hill and attended Harvard. A similar old stock Protestant Knickerbocker elite existed in New York City. Yet more important was the emergence of another large immigrant group, the Jews, to prominence in New York business and the professions. Though Jews do not form a numerical majority of New York's population, the Big Apple is often considered a "Jewish city" in the same metaphorical fashion that Chicago is a "Catholic city." In both cases, one prominent socioreligious group has attained high visibility through outstanding leadership and soaring self-confidence (the Jews would call it *chutzpah*).

All this talk of confidence and dominance may sound distasteful to many, and certainly Chicago Catholic confidence has its dangers for it can easily cross over into arrogance. Yet only self-confident people can enter into dialogue with others and search for solutions to difficult problems. Lack of confidence makes every disagreement seem like an attack, whereas confident people can compromise and work creatively with others. At a time when ecumenical contact with other religions and political coalition-building to address social problems are both imperative, Chicago Catholics should confidently face the future by building on their own rich, historical traditions of ethnic diversity, neighborhood roots, creative leadership, and social liberalism.

This book represents a modest sampling of historical work that has been written about Chicago Catholicism. We have included a list of suggestions for further reading at the end of the volume. However, we are acutely aware of what is not included and of how much still needs to be written. We need to know much more about each of the European immigrant groups that brought their own distinctive brands of Catholicism to Chicago, as well as the more recent immigrants from Latin America and Asia. Furthermore, a start must be made in understanding the experience of African-American Catholics. The enormous contribution made by women religious to the life of the Church still remains to be examined more fully, as well as the role of laypeople, men and women, in shaping Chicago's distinctive Catholic style. Finally, historians

should turn their attention to the relation-
ships, both cooperative and competitive, between Catholics and the members of other
religious communities in the city. We hope
the sesquicentennial of the Catholic Church
in Chicago will stimulate a renaissance of historical work that will examine these and
many other topics, thus deepening our understanding of Catholicism Chicago style.

Ellen Skerrett
Edward R. Kantowicz
Steven M. Avella

1

The Ethnic Church

by Edward R. Kantowicz

The twin spires of church steeple and factory smokestack dominated Chicago's ethnic neighborhoods. This is St. Michael's (Polish) Church in the steel mill district of South Chicago.

—Photo by Edward R. Kantowicz

"Ethnicity is the skeleton of religion in America because it provides 'the supporting framework', 'the bare outlines or main features' of American religion."

Martin E. Marty

"The church, with its use of the old language, with its conservative continuance of Old World customs, with its strictly racial [ethnic] character, was the most important of the social organizations of the immigrant."

H. Richard Niebuhr

America's religious pluralism owes much of its character to the ethnic diversity of the United States. One of the most distinctive features of religion in America, its division into a bewildering variety of denominations, is based on sociology as much as theology.[1]

It's important not to exaggerate or overemphasize this main point, for religious divisions have many roots. Geography has exercised a powerful fracturing influence on the denominations. Most of the mainline English Protestant groups broke into Northern and Southern wings over the slavery issue before the Civil War, and some of these divisions persist today. Former president Jimmy Carter, for example, is a Southern Baptist. This does not mean simply a Baptist who happens to come from the South. Rather, he is a member of the Southern Baptist Convention, one of the largest Protestant denominations in the U.S.

Social class can also distinguish one religious grouping from another. In a land of social mobility, it's not unusual for people to begin life as Baptists or Methodists, then to change their affiliation to a more "high church" body such as the Presbyterians or the Episcopalians as their wealth and social status increase.

Theological divisions also run strong and deep. Historians feel more comfortable searching out sociological explanations for events, but they should resist the temptation to reduce all theological disputes to matters of class or ethnicity. However arcane the points of theology may look to an outsider, committed believers argue passionately over them and frequently form wholly new denominations because of these disagreements.

So denominationalism has both social and theological sources. Yet the fact remains that ethnicity forms a sort of skeleton undergirding the limbs and torsoes of religious bodies in America. When the census takers took a survey of American religion in 1916, they discovered that 132 of the 200 or so denominations conducted all or part of their services in a language other than English. Forty-two languages in all were reported.[2]

Ethnic Denominations

Nationalism has tended to fragment Christianity since the Protestant Reformation. The Treaty of Westphalia in 1648 ended more than a century of religious wars in Europe by imposing a settlement based on national territory. Under the principle of *Cujus regio, ejus religio,* the prince or king of each state in Europe decided the religion of the realm, and the people were expected to fall into line. Henry VIII had already imposed his state church in England. The Lutheran faith prevailed throughout Scandinavia and in many of the German states; Reformed Calvinism in Switzerland and the Netherlands; and Catholicism in France, Spain, Italy, and the Hapsburg Empire of Austria and Hungary.

When adherents of a state church in Europe immigrated to America, they naturally tried to transplant their religious institutions. The Lutherans form a good example of this impulse. American Lutheranism was a German creation from the very beginning, first brought to the colony of Pennsylvania by immigrants from the Rhineland in the mid-eighteenth century. By the middle of the next century, however, the Lutherans had become Americanized and their church was divided into three major synods, largely along regional lines. Then in the years between the Civil War and the First World War, a new immigration transformed the Lutheran church in America.

In the second half of the nineteenth century, approximately a million and a half German Lutherans arrived in the U.S. along with a roughly equal number of Lutherans from Scandinavia. The majority of Germans affiliated with the doctrinally rigorous Missouri Synod, but many smaller German synods broke off from this group and became separate denominations. Originally all the Scandinavian Lutherans organized the Augustana Synod in 1860, but within less than a decade the Danes and Norwegians broke away to form their own synods. By the end of the nineteenth century there were sixty-six separate Lutheran synods in the United States, distinguished largely by "linguistic differences, geographical separation, and varying degrees of Americanization."[3]

Chicago followed this national pattern quite closely. German immigrants founded First St. Paul's Church on the North Side in 1843. Beginning in 1851, Rev. Henry Wunder served as pastor for the next sixty-two years; and largely through his influence other German congregations were founded and the majority of them affiliated with the Missouri Synod. The Scandinavians organized the First Norwegian Evangelical Lutheran Congregation in 1848 in the Sands district just north of the Chicago River. Swedes soon found the Norwegian dominance of this church distasteful, however, and organized the Swedish Lutheran Immanuel Congregation in 1853. By 1893 there were six different language groups of Lutherans—Germans, Norwegians, Swedes, Danes, Slovaks, and English—organized into about a dozen different synods.[4]

Similarly, the Methodist Episcopal church organized separate conferences for Germans and Swedes and a combined Dano-Norwegian conference. In these cases, an English denomination was not trying to preserve old world traditions but rather was appealing to dissidents from state churches in their home countries on the Continent.[5]

Adherents to the Reformed Calvinist tradition, with its emphasis on congregational autonomy, were not pulled apart quite so strongly by the divisive force of ethnicity as the Lutherans were. Since the individual congregation enjoyed almost complete authority, it mattered little if its members spoke a different language from those of the neighboring church. Still, the resulting mosaic could be diverse. In the 1920s, for example, Chicago's Baptists embraced congregations speaking thirteen languages other than English.

In sum, the already strong tendency for Protestant churches to divide and subdivide was greatly accelerated by immigration from a variety of European nations in the late nineteenth and early twentieth centuries. In 1923, just as mass immigration from Europe was coming to an end, a Chicago city directory listed 860 Protestant congregations gathered into 31 separate denominations. About half these denominations were identifiably ethnic, including four German, four Swedish, two Norwegian, one Danish, one Slovak, and four African-American church groupings. Many of the predominantly English denominations, such as the Methodists, Baptists, and Congreationalists, listed numerous individual congregations that employed a foreign language. Only the two high-status Protestant denominations, the Episcopalians and the Presbyterians, appeared to be overwhelmingly English-speaking.[6]

The reason why Protestant immigrants organized their own parishes and denominations is clear enough. Since Protestantism is a religion of the Word, as found in the Bible and preached from the pulpit, it is imperative that its church members be able to understand the words. The doctrines of Martin Luther or John Calvin, translated into English, were of no use to a Lutheran or Calvinist from Germany.

An ethnic parish, moreover, served many social and economic functions for newly arrived immigrants. The historian of the Norwegians in Chicago has aptly described the wide-ranging activities of Erland Carlsson, the first pastor of the Swedish Lutheran Immanuel Congregation:

> Social work, as practiced by Carlsson, extended to include many services, from meeting immigrants at the railroad station to finding them a place to live and work, helping them overcome language barriers by being an interpreter, buying money orders, and assisting in many daily affairs. The religious impulse in this manner combined with a social program to form an indispensable immigrant institution.[7]

H. Richard Niebuhr, who first analyzed the "social sources of denominationalism" in 1929, added a cultural dimension to the practical functions of the ethnic parish:

> The preacher . . . was often the only educated man in the immigrant community. To him the old culture was not merely a mass of memories but a literature and an art expressive of a national genius. He expressed for his countrymen their inarticulate loyalties and fostered their sense for these cultural values.[8]

The ethnic parish, synod, or conference, therefore, served as a way station for immigrants, nourishing them spiritually and culturally after their long voyage and providing much practical assistance as well. A phrase which one historian has applied to Swedish Lutheranism in Chicago, "The pioneer church—A firm foundation for the uprooted," applies equally well to many other Protestant churches.[9]

Jewish immigrants also followed national lines in their places of worship. Most of the Jews who emigrated in the early years of the American republic came from Germany. They quickly Americanized and tended to follow the Reform tradition in Judaism that adapted the ancient rituals of the faith to the local national customs. In the late nineteenth century, however, nearly two million Jews arrived from Eastern Europe. These newcomers spoke Yiddish, an amalgam of Hebrew, German, and Polish, and observed strictly Orthodox Jewish beliefs and rituals. So by 1900, two broad tendencies could be found in American Judaism. Those with German roots tended to be Reform or Conservative Jews, whereas the more recent immigrants from the Russian or Austro-Hungarian Empires adhered to Orthodox Judaism. In Chicago, the waves of immigrants from Eastern Europe overwhelmed the older German Jewish population. By 1930, Chicago had eighty-four Orthodox congregations, but only thirteen Reform and eight Conservative.[10]

Ethnic division proceeded even further among Jewish immigrants, however. The East European Jews came from almost totally Jewish small towns, or *shtetlach,* in the Russian Empire. Arriving in whole family groups, immigrants from the same *shtetl* settled together in American cities and formed *landsmanschaften,* or mutual aid societies, to help each other out. A *minyan* or quorum of ten adult males from one of these societies might then organize a synagogue, which would also be composed entirely of Jews from the same locality in Europe.[11]

So, for example, a group of Jews from the Crimean city of Mariampol formed a benevolent society in the Maxwell Street district of Chicago in 1870 and organized the first Orthodox synagogue in the city, Ohave Sholom Mariampol. An old legend concerning the founding of this synagogue reminds us that ethnic distinctions were not the only reasons for the division of congregations. Supposedly, a group of Jews from Mariampol who attended an older synagogue in Chicago were offended when a man recited *kaddish* while wearing a straw hat. Not only their place of birth but their stage of assimilation impelled the Mariampolers to withdraw and form their own synagogue. As greenhorns in America, they found the "swell" American dress of more assimilated Jews offensive.[12]

Overall, therefore, ethnicity has tended to fragment both Protestantism and Judaism in America. Both faith traditions place considerable emphasis on the autonomy of the individual congregation and are marked by frequent divisions into new groupings of congregations, but immigration has accentuated the centrifugal tendencies in both religions.

Ethnic Leagues in Catholicism

At first glance, the Catholic Church might seem largely immune to ethnic divisions. The Church of Rome considers itself universal in scope (the word *catholic* means "universal") and tries to impose uniformity of belief and ritual throughout the world. Indeed, before the Second Vatican Council of the 1960s, the Catholic Mass and Sacraments were performed in Latin, a language equally unintelligible to immigrants and natives.

Furthermore, Catholicism is organized geographically, with each diocese carved into territorial parishes. Unlike many Protestants, who may travel a great distance to the congregation of their choice, most Catholics worship where they live. Early in this century, Archbishop James Quigley of Chicago set forth the ideal of one Catholic parish per square mile in the city. Quigley believed that "a parish should be of such a size that the pastor can know personally every man, woman, and child in it."[13]

This ideal of a neighborhood parish for all Catholics proved unrealistic, however. As Catholic immigrants from Continental Europe flooded into American cities, they demanded separate parishes with priests of their own nationality to minister to them. The Mass may have been celebrated in Latin, but the priest preached his sermon and listened to confessions in the vernacular. Furthermore, the parish was a community center for social organizations as much as a place of worship. Therefore, American bishops often allowed immigrant groups to organize national parishes, defined by language not territory, side by side with the territorial churches.

Germans organized the first national parishes in the United States. In 1846, two years after Chicago received its first Catholic bishop, the diocese authorized two German language parishes, St. Peter's and St. Joseph's. In the years that followed, many other German parishes were erected, as well as numerous Polish, Bohemian, Lithuanian, Italian, and Slovak churches. As a result, many square-mile quadrants of Chicago had two, three, or as many as six or seven Catholic parishes.[14]

Map 1 shows the resulting geographical pattern in 1916, the year after Archbishop Quigley's death. The outer parts of the city—north of Fullerton Avenue, the whole Northwest Side, the West Side beyond Western Avenue—and most of the South Side east of State Street, where Catholics were in the minority amid black and white Protestants, fit the ideal of one parish per square mile reasonably well. The empty squares on the outskirts of the city were generally not settled yet in 1916. In the inner city, however, between State and Western, Fullerton and Fifty-fifth, each quadrant is crowded with Catholic churches. This is due not merely to density of population and a high percentage of Catholics in these neighborhoods (though these were factors) but primarily to the presence of several different Catholic ethnic groups and thus a number of national parishes beside the territorial ones.

One of Chicago's most famous neighborhoods, Bridgeport on the South Side, home to five Chicago mayors, aptly illustrates the crowding of Catholic churches in a single district. Roughly a mile and a half long by a mile wide, Bridgeport is clearly marked out by natural boundaries: the south branch of the Chicago River on the north, a short finger of the river (nicknamed Bubbly Creek) on the west, a wide swath of railroad tracks running along Stewart Avenue on the east, and the Union Stock Yards and a rail line just south of Thirty-ninth Street on the south (see map 2). For most of the twentieth century, Bridgeport counted ten Catholic parishes of five different nationalities. In 1910 the neighborhood was about 70 percent Catholic. The census listed 49,650 people in Chicago's Fourth Ward, which included most of Bridgeport, whereas the pastors of Bridgeport's Catholic parishes reported about 35,000 parishioners.[16]

The Irish had been the first to arrive in Bridgeport, imported to dig the Illinois and Michigan canal in the 1830s and 1840s; and it remained a largely Irish and German neighborhood until the end of the nineteenth century. Three territorial (though largely Irish) parishes and two German national parishes

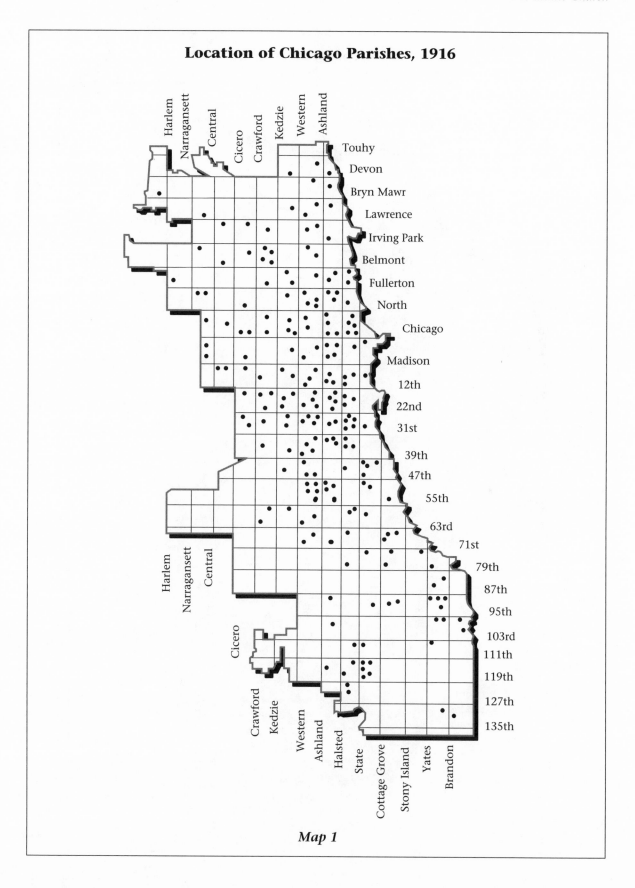

Location of Chicago Parishes, 1916

Map 1

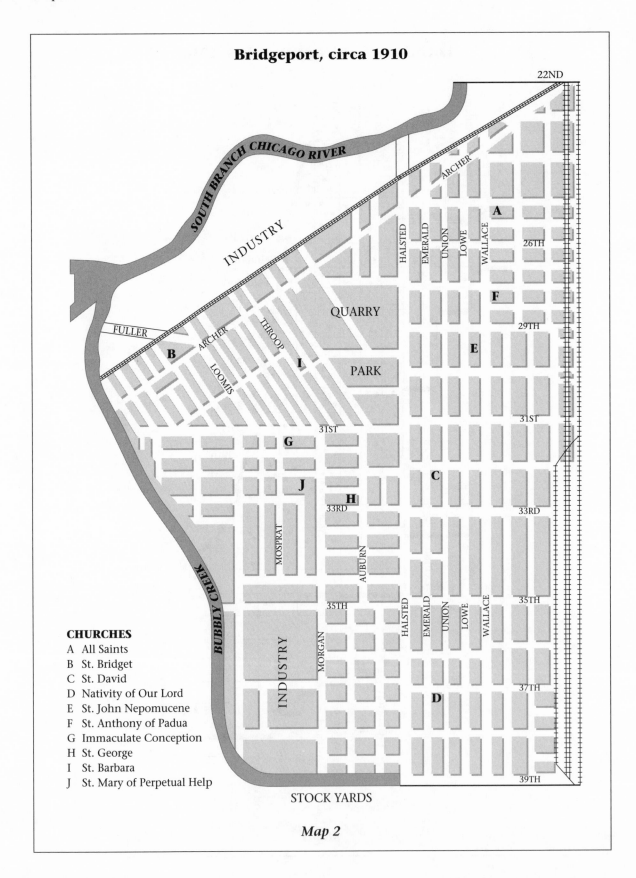

Bridgeport, circa 1910

SOUTH BRANCH CHICAGO RIVER

INDUSTRY

ARCHER

22ND

HALSTED
EMERALD
UNION
LOWE
WALLACE

A

26TH

F

29TH

QUARRY

E

PARK

FULLER

ARCHER

THROOP

B

LOOMIS

I

31ST

G

31ST

J

C

H

33RD

33RD

MOSPRAT

AUBURN

35TH

35TH

HALSTED
EMERALD
UNION
LOWE
WALLACE

INDUSTRY

MORGAN

D

37TH

BUBBLY CREEK

39TH

STOCK YARDS

CHURCHES
A All Saints
B St. Bridget
C St. David
D Nativity of Our Lord
E St. John Nepomucene
F St. Anthony of Padua
G Immaculate Conception
H St. George
I St. Barbara
J St. Mary of Perpetual Help

Map 2

were organized in the nineteenth century and a fourth territorial parish was added in 1905.[17] Just before the Chicago fire, a number of Bohemians moved down Halsted Street into the northeast sector of Bridgeport, founding the parish of St. John Nepomucene in 1870.

At the end of the nineteenth century, a much larger Slavic group, the Poles, began settling in Bridgeport, followed closely by a numerous Lithuanian immigration. St. George's was founded in 1892, the first and largest Lithuanian church in the city, often called the "mother church" of Lithuanian Chicago. A decade earlier, in 1883, the Poles had organized St. Mary of Perpetual Help parish. St. Mary's of Bridgeport did not contain the largest Polish settlement in Chicago, but the parish was large enough to be divided in 1910, when the parish of St. Barbara was erected.

Before the changes in devotional practice brought about by the Second Vatican Council, many Catholics observed a pious custom of visiting the Blessed Sacrament in nine different churches on Holy Thursday. The residents of Bridgeport could make this minipilgrimage easily on foot without leaving their own neighborhood.

Bridgeport was not unique or unusual in Catholic Chicago. Wherever immigrants clustered in multiethnic, working-class wards, each Catholic nationality organized its own parish and thrust its church steeple skyward. The laity almost always took the initiative, by forming a mutual aid society under the patronage of some national saint and petitioning the bishop for a priest who spoke their language. Though the purpose of founding an ethnic parish was to preserve the language and culture of the homeland, the very process of parish building marked a departure from Old World ways. Instead of the state erecting and supporting the parish church, individual believers adopted the American system of voluntary church support. The ethnic parish, therefore, was marked at birth as a transitional institution, simultaneously preserving immigrant customs and adapting itself to American law and practice.

Catholic parishes of each nationality were loosely federated into ethnic "leagues."[18] The individual parishes conducted elementary schools and organized a wide variety of social and charitable organizations; and they jointly financed high schools, hospitals, orphanages, and cemeteries. These leagues of the nations enjoyed no official status in Rome's canon law; they were not legally incorporated and were not recognized as separate denominations, as the Lutheran synods were. Yet, an "ethnic league" was more than a figure of speech. The Polish pastors, for example, frequently met to set policy for the Polish cemeteries and orphanages and to assess the Polish parishes for joint building projects. Individual pastors commonly made loans to pastors of new parishes within their league. For example, when St. Mary of Perpetual Help parish in Bridgeport was divided, Rev. Stanislaus Nawrocki loaned the pastor of the new St. Barbara parish, his brother Rev. Anthony Nawrocki, $28,000 from parish funds. The entire operation remained, literally and figuratively, within the family.

The ethnic leagues were very exclusive in their staffing practices. In 1916, 99 percent of the Irish clergy engaged in parish work were assigned to territorial, English-speaking parishes. Similarly, 100 percent of the Polish and Slovak priests, 92 percent of the Lithuanian priests, 86 percent of the Italian priests, and 82 percent of the Bohemian priests labored within parishes of their own ethnic league. Even the Germans, who had been assimilating rapidly in some respects, retained 90 percent of their priests in German parishes. The archbishop of Chicago generally relied on an informal "ethnic boss," either an auxiliary bishop or an influential pastor, from each nationality when making assignments to the ethnic leagues.

The priests of each league jealously guarded their constituencies, complaining frequently to the archbishop about "scavenger priests" in neighboring parishes who tried to lure Catholics of other nationalities into their churches in order to receive their Mass stipends and Sunday donations. Charity not only began, but ended, at home. Each league functioned much like a Protestant synod or conference; it formed a virtual subdiocese or quasi-denomination.

The Major Leagues

The statistics in Table 1 reveal a clear division of the Chicago Catholic archdiocese into "major leagues" and "minor leagues" at the time when mass immigration from Europe had just ceased.[19] The territorial parishes (still largely Irish in 1926), along with the German and Polish national parishes, dwarfed the rest of the archdiocese, with 79 percent of the congregations and 81 percent of the church members. The three major leagues of parishes ranked at or above the archdiocesan average on most of the measures of institutional health recorded in the table.

The territorial parishes were fairly evenly distributed throughout the city, but the largest and most impressive churches stood along the main transportation lines west and south of the Loop, where Irish Catholics predominated. These territorial parishes were in some ways just as "ethnic" as the others, for they were heavily Irish. Many bore distinctive Irish names such as St. Patrick, St. Jarlath, St. Bridget, and St. Columbkille. Their sanctuaries displayed numerous statues of Gaelic saints; and in at least one church, Holy Family, an altar carving portrayed Joseph, the foster father of Jesus, wearing a bowler hat, which must have been the height of fashion for Irish "swells" when the altar was donated. Just as the brave "Father Murphys" of Ireland had fought and died in the many rebellions against English rule, Chicago Irish pastors encouraged their parishioners to support the cause of freedom for their homeland. They permitted nationalist groups such as the Land League and the Ancient Order of Hibernians to hold meetings on an equal footing with purely religious organizations such as the St. Vincent de Paul Society or the Holy Name Society.[20]

Cross-Section of Chicago Archdiocese, by Ethnic "Leagues," 1926

League	No. of Parishes	No. of Church Members	Americanization of Clergy	Localization of Diocesan Clergy	No. of Priests per Parish	Solvency Ratio of Debt to Income	Regularization Ratio of Ordinary to Extra-ordinary Income	Per Capita Donation
Territorial (Irish)	183	367,300	79%	63%	2.1	1.5 to 1	1.95 to 1	$18.40
German	64	96,000	68%	54%	2.2	1.65 to 1	1.78 to 1	$17.28
Polish	54	258,800	53%	59%	2.4	1.88 to 1	1.85 to 1	$ 8.61
Bohemian	11	18,500	50%	27%	1.5	1.17 to 1	1.45 to 1	$12.25
Slovak	9	10,900	37%	0%	1.5	2.23 to 1	2.45 to 1	$13.53
Lithuanian	12	29,000	7%	12%	2.2	1.3 to 1	.95 to 1	$13.01
Italian	18	76,800	7%	17%	1.9	2.5 to 1	2.1 to 1	$ 3.25
Other (10 Nationalities)	29	39,000	42%	46%	1.8	2.6 to 1	1.5 to 1	$10.61
Archdiocesan Totals	380	896,300	65%	57%	2.1	1.6 to 1	1.9 to 1	$13.58

Table 1

Our first
Chicago Parish
School

:ishes were open to
within their bound-
embers of other eth-
descendants of early
increasing number of
attended them. English
nonliturgical events of
es, for the Irish immi-
their native language
erica. This fact alone set
off from other ethnic
26 a huge proportion (79
ministering in the terri-
American-born; indeed,
se priests were born in

parishes were comfortably
about two thousand "souls,"
families each) and reason-
ably supported financially. The $18.40
per capita the parishioners donated in
1926 works out to nearly two dollars a week
per family. The financial measure that I call
"regularization" in the table (the ratio of ordinary revenue to extraordinary revenue) probably loomed more important to the
Irish-Americans of the early twentieth century than it would to us today, for it mea-
sured social respectability as much as it did
financial stability. "Ordinary revenue," a term
taken from the annual reports the pastor filed
with the archbishop each year, denoted all
pew rentals and the regular Sunday, holy day,
Christmas, and Easter collections. All other
sources of revenue—including bazaars, raffles,
and bingo—were listed as extraordinary. The
Irish ratio of ordinary to extraordinary revenue nearly reached two to one in 1926, illus-
trating that these parishes followed the
normal financial procedures more closely
than others. In the eyes of the archbishop,
the Irish territorial parishes represented the
norm, and all the others were exceptions.

German parishes were also distributed
throughout the city, but the German strong-
hold lay on the North Side. The ten North
Side parishes accounted for nearly half the
church membership and financial support of
the German league. St. Michael's, just west of
Lincoln Park, and St. Alphonsus on Lincoln
Avenue, both conducted by the Redemptorist
religious order of priests, were the largest

*Holy Family Church and St. Ignatius High
School helped generations of Irish-Catholics
rise to the middle class.*
—Photo by Edward R. Kantowicz

German parishes in the city. Overall, the
German parishes were a bit smaller than the
Irish ones (about 1500 souls or 300 families
each), but on all the other measurements,
such as Americanization of the clergy and financial support, they ranked very near the
archdiocesan average. Nevertheless, the
German league was declining numerically as
more and more German Catholics became
Americanized and attended territorial parishes.
The German parishes counted fewer members
in 1926 than they had ten years earlier.

Perhaps the most distinctive feature of the German league was its orientation toward social action and charitable work. Following the tradition of German Social Catholicism that developed in the nineteenth century, Chicago's German league fostered a rich variety of organizations to serve the poor and the unfortunate. The St. Vincent de Paul Society, for example, was founded in France in 1833 and swiftly spread to other countries. Male lay volunteers raised money at parish events then distributed it personally to the needy of the parish. Less than half the parishes in Chicago supported a St. Vincent de Paul Society early in this century, but nearly all the German parishes did. Msgr. Aloysius J. Thiele, the German boss of the archdiocese, also served as spiritual director for all the St. Vincent de Paul societies.

German Catholics were also preeminent in the field of institutional child care. In 1865 a group of priests and laymen had started the Angel Guardian German Catholic Orphan Society of Chicago. Quite independent of the

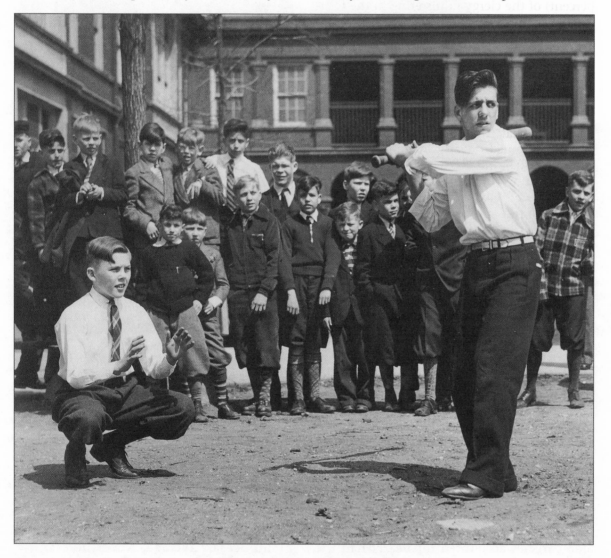

German Catholics built many institutions of social welfare, such as Angel Guardian Orphanage, whose well-dressed orphans are shown here in the 1930s.
—Chicago Tribune *photo, courtesy of the Archives of the Archdiocese of Chicago*

archdiocese, this society held title to Angel Guardian Orphanage in the Rosehill district of the North Side, at Ridge and Devon avenues, and three German Catholic cemeteries as well: St. Boniface, St. Mary, and St. Joseph. Profits from the cemeteries helped support the orphanage. The priests and nuns who cared for children at Angel Guardian pioneered a new system of child care. In 1914 and 1915 the Orphan Society built small cottages at the orphanage and assigned a sister to act as "mother" for a small group of children. The cottage system was later adopted by the official orphanage of the archdiocese, St. Mary's in Des Plaines, Illinois.

A generation later, Msgr. Reynold Hillenbrand, a German Catholic who grew up in St. Michael's parish, was appointed rector of the newly-opened St. Mary of the Lake seminary in Mundelein, Illinois. Hillenbrand had read deeply in the social teachings of the popes and had worked out a synthesis of theology and social action built around the doctrine of the Mystical Body of Christ. At the seminary he trained a generation of Chicago priests in his Catholic Action philosophy, thus earning for Chicago Catholicism a reputation for social liberalism. Hillenbrand and other German priests also experimented with a more participatory liturgy. One of his contemporaries, Fr. Bernard Laukemper, made St. Aloysius parish on the Near Northwest Side a model of liturgical revival nearly thirty years before the Second Vatican Council.[21]

The Polish league formed the largest group of nonterritorial parishes, fifty-four congregations with over a quarter million members at its height in the 1920s. Polish parishes were found in all the city's districts of heavy industry, such as Bridgeport, Back of the Yards, and the South Chicago steel district; but the greatest number concentrated on the Northwest Side, near St. Stanislaus Kostka, the mother church of Chicago's Polonia. The Northwest Side parishes, many of them administered by the Resurrectionist religious order, accounted for nearly 50 percent of all Polish church members. Polish parishes were much larger than those of other nationalities, averaging nearly five thousand members (roughly one thousand families). Several of the congrega-

tions approached twenty thousand members, the largest in the archdiocese.[22]

Polish pastors ruled their parishes in an exceptionally authoritarian manner, like feudal lords. A great number of Polish priests had emigrated with their flocks and thus the Polish league enjoyed the highest priest to parish ratio in the archdiocese. Only about half the Polish priests were American-born in the 1920s, lower than the archdiocesan average. Rather than the mixed lay-clerical orphan society that ran the German orphanages and cemeteries, a committee of Polish pastors exercised complete control over St. Hedwig's Orphanage and the three Polish cemeteries.

A Polish priest kept tabs on his constituents much like a ward boss or precinct captain. Every year during Lent, the pastor and his assistants made a door-to-door canvass of the parish, collecting an annual subscription from each family. When the family paid the minimum subscription fee (somewhere between five and ten dollars in the 1920s) the priest gave each family member a registration card and reminded him or her to perform the Easter duty, that is, go to confession and receive communion at least once during the Easter season. Family members were required to hand in their cards when they made their confession. If a family failed in this obligation two years in a row, it was "stricken from the parish registry" and thus denied the right to baptize its children or solemnize its marriages in church. This effectively cut them off from the Polish Catholic community.

Polish parishioners did not always meekly accept the priest's authoritarian direction. They rarely dared to neglect their Easter duty for the consequences were so severe, but not every adult attended Sunday Mass regularly. And even though the pastor preached the necessity for a Catholic education, many parents sent their children to the parish school for only the minimum two years required to prepare them for first communion. The spiritual life of the Polish parish, therefore, represented a delicate compromise between priestly commands and selective responses by the parishioners.[23]

St. Stanislaus Kostka was the mother church of Chicago's Polonia.

—*Photo by Edward R. Kantowicz*

The Minor Leagues

Two of the minor leagues of Eastern Europeans, the Slovaks and the Lithuanians, resembled the larger group of Poles. Their priests were largely foreign-born and the people were staunchly nationalist and Catholic. The numerically small and poor Slovak congregations carried a much higher debt load than the other ethnic leagues, and the Lithuanians relied on extraordinary fundraising methods more than any other ethnic group. Both groups concentrated in the industrial districts of the South Side and West Side, with the Lithuanian mother church, St. George, in Bridgeport and the oldest and largest Slovak parish, St. Michael the Archangel, in Back of the Yards.

The Bohemians were more concentrated geograhically than any other Catholic group in the city, with all but two of their parishes lying in a narrow belt of the West Side along Eighteenth and Twenty-second streets, and extending out into Cicero and Berwyn. More importantly, the Bohemians stood out from other Eastern Europeans by the high proportion who proved indifferent to Catholicism or any other religion. All East European ethnic groups contained a nationalist faction that was at least mildly anticlerical or secularist in attitude, but Bohemian nationalism had developed into a virtual secular religion. The Catholic Austrian Empire had ruthlessly suppressed the Protestant followers of Jan Hus in the fifteenth century, and though Bohemia remained a nominally Catholic province, its leading intellectuals were generally self-styled atheists or "freethinkers." In the United

States, the free-thought movement broadened its base and embraced a large number of Bohemian workers as well.

Freethinkers greatly outnumbered Bohemian Catholics in Chicago. Only about 17 percent of the Bohemians belonged to Bohemian Catholic parishes, whereas about 50 percent of the Slovaks and Lithuanians and a remarkable 78 percent of the Poles belonged to their own national churches. Only because of the evangelizing efforts of Benedictine priests from St. Procopius Abbey did a Bohemian league of parishes exist at all in Chicago.[24]

The remaining minor league, the Italians, also presented a missionary challenge to Catholic Church authorities. The eighteen Italian parishes, distributed fairly widely about the city and inner suburbs, but with two important centers on the Near West and Near North Sides, were quite large, averaging about fifty-five hundred members each. But unlike the Polish parishes of similar size, Italian church membership was largely nominal, based on baptismal and marriage statistics, not church attendance or a yearly canvass. Italians gave little financial support to the church. In fact, most of the Italian parishes had been founded at the initiative of Archbishop Quigley and continued only with subsidies from the archdiocese.

Italian indifference to the institutional aspects of Catholicism had deep roots in the old country. The Italian Church opposed the nationalist *risorgimento* in the nineteenth century and the Papal States long blocked Italian unification. In the case of both the Italians and the Bohemians, nationalism and Catholicism were antagonistic, conflicting forces. Thus the average Italian or Bohemian inherited a heavy weight of anticlericalism. In Poland and Ireland, however, the Catholic Church supported the opposition to occupying powers and thus the twin forces of nationalism and religion reinforced each other.

To sum up this survey of ethnic Catholicism early in the twentieth century, the leagues of ethnic parishes can be categorized as (1) assimilating groups: the Irish (who comprised the "mainstream" in territorial parishes), the Germans, and the much smaller French group; (2) staunchly Catholic and nationalist groups: the Poles, Slovaks, Lithuanians, and a smaller number of Croatian and Slovenian parishes; (3) missionary groups: the Bohemians and the Italians. The differences between groups reflected their national histories in Europe and their stage of assimilation in America. To varying degrees, all the groups relied on ethnic parishes and pastors to preserve their national identities and help them adjust to the urban environment.

The Golden Age of Chicago Catholic Architecture

The twin spires of church steeple and factory smokestack dominated the ethnic neighborhoods of Chicago. The church buildings of each nationality nearly jostled one another as they proclaimed to God and man, "Here we are!" This is too cynical and simple an explanation, however, for the massive church edifices that scraped the soot-filled sky of Chicago. Status competition certainly impelled many pastors and parishioners to build a towering church, but there were other motives. The Catholic church building, adorned with statues, murals, stained glass, and golden altar vessels, was the only place of beauty in a raw immigrant neighborhood, an oasis of quiet and harmony amidst industrial

cacophony. It was also a sacred space that elevated the minds and hearts of believers.[25]

Not every parish could afford to build a full-scale, free-standing church building, however. Of necessity, nearly every congregation began in a storefront or a makeshift wooden church. The Catholic bishops of Chicago encouraged pastors to build a school building first, wisely judging that the children would form the glue to hold the parish together. Worship services were conducted in the basement or the school hall. Only a little more than half the Chicago parishes ever raised enough money to build a full-scale church; the rest remained content with a combination church-school building.

Catholic Church Construction between 1891–1945

Ethnic League	Architectural Style					Total*
	Gothic	Romanesque	Renaissance	Other	Unknown	
Irish	31 (38%)	19 (23%)	18 (22%)	13 (16%)	0 (0%)	81 (100%)
German	17 (59%)	7 (24%)	1 (3%)	3 (10%)	1 (3%)	29 (100%)
Polish	3 (12%)	7 (27%)	13 (50%)	3 (12%)	0 (0%)	26 (100%)
Other	5 (17%)	14 (48%)	8 (28%)	1 (3%)	1 (3%)	29 (100%)
Total	56 (34%)	47 (28%)	40 (24%)	20 (12%)	2 (1%)	165 (100%)

Full-scale Catholic churches constructed in Lake and Cook counties between 1891 and 1945.
*Percentages are approximate due to rounding.

Table 2

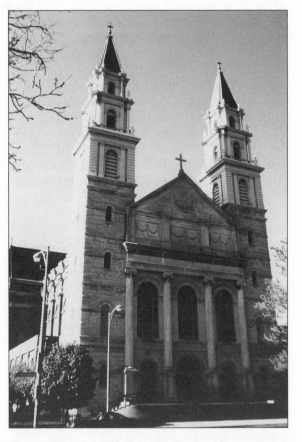

Irish churches followed the changing fashions in church architecture. Holy Name Cathedral, built right after the Chicago Fire, was designed in a Victorian Gothic style.
—*Photos by Edward R. Kantowicz*

Our Lady of Sorrows on the West Side shows the classical influence of the 1893 World's Fair.

Chicago experienced a tremendous building boom after the Chicago Fire of 1871, but Catholic immigrants were still too few in number and too poor to build many churches at that time. In the 1890s, when Catholic numbers burgeoned, many parishes began building on a large scale, thus ushering in the golden age of Catholic church architecture in Chicago.[26]

This golden age was marked by a rich variety of architectural styles. The nineteenth century was a period of tremendous eclecticism in architecture, as one historical revival followed another. Most early Chicago churches, just before and after the Fire, were built in the Gothic style, testifying to the power of the Victorian Gothic revival in England. But Henry Hobson Richardson's Trinity Episcopal Church in Boston (1877) stemmed the Gothic tide and inspired a host of Romanesque imitations in Chicago and across the country. The World's Columbian Exposition of 1893 then revived interest in Renaissance and classical designs of all kinds.

Thus by the end of the century, Catholic parishes had a large vocabulary of popular forms from which to draw.

A vanguard of local Catholic architects emerged in the 1890s to serve the ethnic leagues and manipulate the historical styles so popular at the time. In all, 40 individuals or firms built 165 full-scale churches in Lake and Cook counties between 1891 and 1945. Only two Catholic churches were built by famous, mainstream architects. Solon S. Beman, the designer of George Pullman's model town, also built Holy Rosary Catholic Church in the Roseland neighborhood bordering on Pullman; and the firm of Burnham and Root erected St. Gabriel's Church near the Chicago stock yards. Chicagoans also called in outside architects from time to time.

Most of the forty, however, were local Chicagoans, born after the Civil War, apprenticed with one of the important architectural partnerships, and making their livings largely on Catholic church work. Seven architects (or

St. Bridget's in Bridgeport reflected the Romanesque revival of the 1880s and 1890s.
—Photo by Edward R. Kantowicz

partnerships) built the lion's share (79 of 165) of Catholic churches in this period. The most noteworthy were Henry J. Schlacks, who started his practice in the German league but eventually built for all the major groups, Joseph W. McCarthy, designer of Cardinal George Mundelein's St. Mary of the Lake Seminary, and a partnership of two German Protestants, Henry W. Worthmann and John J. Steinbach, who built the largest and most magnificent of the Polish churches.

If he or she knew how to read the architectural styles, a walker in the city could learn something of the history of the Catholic ethnic groups (see table 2). Chicago's Irish churches, whose congregations represented mainstream Chicago Catholicism, employed the greatest variety of styles, reflecting the changing fashions in church architecture over the decades. Thus the earliest Irish churches built after the Fire, such as St. Anne and St. James on the South Side, St. Jarlath on the West Side, and Holy Name Cathedral were all designed in a high Victorian Gothic style. James J. Egan's design for St. Bridget's of Bridgeport, however, built in the 1890s, reflected the Romanesque revival ushered in by Richardson; and the magnificent basilica of Our Lady of Sorrows showed the classical influence of the 1893 World's Fair.

Henry J. Schlacks was the finest architect of Chicago Catholicism. This is St. Martin of Tours in Englewood, one of his earliest German Gothic designs.
—Photos by Edward R. Kantowicz

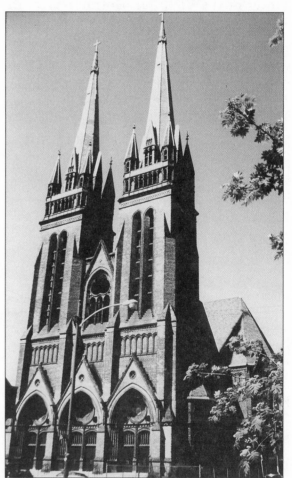

St. Paul's on the West Side, another fine example of Schlacks's German Gothic.

The single most common style among the Irish churches, however, remained the Gothic. Though the Irish would rarely admit it, this style summed up their aspirations for respectability in the eyes of Victorian Protestants. The German Catholics favored Gothic even more heavily, building nearly two-thirds of their churches in that style. Two of Henry Schlacks's designs, St. Martin of Tours on the South Side and St. Paul's on the West Side, provide handsome examples of German Gothic workmanship. Though I do not have detailed information about German Protestant churches, an unsystematic look around the Chicago area suggests that German Protestants also favored Gothic. In this way both Catholics and Protestants harkened back to the days before Martin Luther, when German Christianity was still united.

The social meaning of Gothic expressed in the previous paragraph is admittedly very speculative, but the preference of the Polish league for Renaissance and Baroque forms seems more clear-cut. The glory days of the Polish Commonwealth came in the sixteenth and seventeenth centuries when it formed the largest state in Europe, stretching from the Baltic nearly to the Black Sea, from the Oder River deep into White Russia and the Ukraine. The Polish princes imported Italian architects and artisans to build their palaces and churches in splendid Renaissance and Baroque styles.

The Polish churches in Chicago, particularly the magnificent edifices that Worthmann and Steinbach built along the Milwaukee Avenue corridor on the Northwest Side, reflected the Renaissance glory of Polish Catholicism. Fully half of the Polish churches employed classical Renaissance forms; only three Polish churches in the archdiocese were built in Gothic. St. Mary of the Angels, with a soaring dome to rival St. Peter's in Rome, is the ultimate example of the Polish Renaissance style. Fr. Francis Gordon, a leading member of the Polish Resurrectionist order, commissioned this building as a Polish cathedral, or bishop's church, for he hoped to be named auxiliary bishop for the Poles of Chicago. The episcopal call never came, but the church testifies to his daring ambition and the generos-

Most Polish churches employed classical forms of the Renaissance and the Baroque. This is St. Hyacinth's, on the Northwest Side, designed by the firm of Worthmann & Steinbach.
—Photo by Edward R. Kantowicz

ity of his parishioners. Built over an eight-and-a-half year period around World War I and costing over $400,000, St. Mary's in the Bucktown neighborhood may not be the most beautiful church in Chicago but it is certainly the most audacious. Sadly, it deteriorated over the years and was closed for a time and threatened with demolition; but heroic fundraising efforts by its past and present parishioners allowed it to reopen in 1992.[27]

Other religious denominations also adopted distinctive architectural styles that reflected their national heritages (see table 3). English Protestants often imitated the church of St. Martin-in-the-Fields, designed by Sir James Gibbs in London.[28] Greek, Russian, and Ukrainian Orthodox congregations usually built in the Byzantine style of Constantinople.

St. Mary of the Angels, inspired by Fr. Francis Gordon, C. R., and designed by Worthmann & Steinbach, epitomizes the Polish Renaissance style.

—*Photo by Edward R. Kantowicz*

Interestingly, many Jewish synagogues also adopted Byzantine forms, in order to emphasize their Middle Eastern roots and to distinguish their houses of worship from the more common Catholic and Protestant styles. Few if any Jewish synagogues were built in Gothic.

Ethnic Ecumenism

Ethnic parishes served the same basic functions that any religious institution did: worship, education, and charity. Different denominations performed these functions in varying ways. Catholics and Missouri Synod Lutherans built parochial schools alongside their churches to preserve both the religious and ethnic heritages of their people; other synods of Lutherans and most other Protestants adopted the American Sunday School as its primary means of cultural and religious education. Orthodox synagogues established *yeshivas* where young male Jews learned the intricacies of Hebraic Law.

All immigrants, however, wanted to praise God, learn more about the Word of God, and assist one another in a language they could understand. So ethnicity tended to fragment the Protestant, Catholic, and Jewish religions. Catholic bishops grudgingly conceded the right of non-English speaking ethnic groups to organize their own parishes in order to keep them from falling away from the faith. German and Scandinavian Lutherans orga-

Architectural Styles and Ethnic Groups

The nineteenth century was an era of architectural eclecticism, marked by successive waves of historical revivals. Different ethnic groups showed particular affinities for individual styles.

1. GOTHIC—This was the first style to be revived, in the 1830s and 1840s. English Victorians adopted it as peculiarly their own. Both German Catholics and German Lutherans used the style widely, harking back to the Middle Ages when German emperors vied with the Papacy for dominance in Christendom.

2. ROMANESQUE—Henry Hobson Richardson revived this style with his Trinity Episcopal Church built in Boston in 1877. No ethnic pattern developed, as all denominations and ethnic groups adopted a modest, utilitarian version of Romanesque as a sort of lowest common denominator.

3. CLASSICAL, RENAISSANCE, BAROQUE—The Chicago World's Fair of 1893 revived interest in classical forms. Italians showed a marked affinity for Renaissance styles, for obvious reasons; as did Poles, since Poland's days of greatness as a nation coincided with the Renaissance in Europe. The majority of Polish churches in Chicago are Renaissance or Baroque; only three are Gothic.

4. BYZANTINE—This was used primarily for Greek, Russian, and Ukrainian Orthodox churches, for Jewish synagogues, and for Moslem mosques. Jews adopted it in order to emphasize their Middle Eastern roots and to distinguish their houses of worship from common Christian styles. There were no Gothic synagogues.

5. COLONIAL—This traces its lineage directly to St. Martin-in-the-Fields, designed by Sir James Gibbs in London in 1726. Adopted by the New England Puritans in colonial times, it has been widely copied by Protestant denominations with English roots, particularly in small towns and suburbs. Interestingly, in the 1920s, George Cardinal Mundelein, used this style for the main chapel of his major seminary, in order to emphasize the Americanization of the Catholic Church.

Table 3

nized separate synods to preserve the beliefs and rituals of their state churches in Europe. Orthodox Jews from a *shtetl* in Eastern Europe gathered together in the same synagogue on Maxwell Street.

More than language was at stake, however. Even immigrants who spoke English, such as Irish Catholics or Scots Presbyterians, tended to worship together with people of their own nationality. An ethnic parish was a place where people felt comfortable together, where they could read between the lines when they talked to one another. It was a family, albeit a patriarchal one in most cases.

As in any family, the children grew up and moved away from their parents; so the ethnic parish was a transitional institution. Even at the high point of ethnic fragmentation early in the twentieth century, it's possible to overemphasize the divisive effects of ethnicity on religion. All the Catholic leagues remained faithful to the Pope of Rome; and, though they didn't like it, the individual ethnic parishes all conceded legal title of their property to the archbishop of Chicago in his capacity as a *corporation sole.* Though it's easy to point out churches with distinctive ethnic names, such as St. Patrick, St. Stanislaus, and St. Boniface, many more Catholic church names reflected common dogmas and popular devotions. Chicago was home to six Catholic churches named Immaculate Conception, representing four different ethnic groups; there were also six Sacred Heart churches, each one founded by a different nationality.

The Lutheran synods may have formed separate denominations but they retained a lively sense of their communion as Lutherans, and the Confession of Augsburg remained a doctrinal touchstone for them all. The German Jews resented the greenhorn Russian Jews, but their common identity as the chosen people nevertheless impelled them to much charitable work among the newcomers.

As the children of the immigrants adopted the English language and American ways, the ethnic parishes became less and less necessary. German Lutherans, for example, experienced an extended transitional process of many stages. First of all, the pastor found it necessary to perform occasional weddings or christenings in English; next he added an

extra, English-language Sunday School class. Since the children learned English quickly in public schools and on the streets, the parish soon found itself with an all English Sunday School and occasional English worship services. Eventually the English language services became a regular Sunday feature, scheduled at a more convenient time than the German services, which were attended largely by old people. At long last, the parish would be entirely English. This process, however, took a long time. Most German Lutheran parishes were only reaching the final stages when the First World War accelerated the change. Historians of Lutheranism in Chicago have concluded: "The World War, a change of pastorate, death of a prominent German member, and relocation of the church have been the most prominent in putting an end to German services. . . ."[29]

German Catholic parishes followed a similar evolution, as did Catholic parishes of other nationalities at a slightly later date. However, a Catholic parish would not change location to follow its parishioners, as a Protestant congregation often did, so it tended to remain ethnic for a longer time, a vestigial institution servicing the elderly in the inner city. The Catholic Church also experienced considerable bureaucratic inertia in making clerical assignments to ethnic parishes. As late as 1948, only 14 percent of the German diocesan priests in parochial work in Chicago were assigned to non-German parishes. St. Nicholas in Evanston, one of the most suburban and least ethnic parishes of German origin, received its first non-German pastor in 1969.

Beginning in the 1920s, then accelerating greatly after World War II, the major trend in all denominations was toward merger and consolidation, a sort of ethnic ecumenism. The sixty-six Lutheran synods existing at the turn of the century gradually combined into fewer but larger denominations until today the *Lutheran Annual* lists only ten Lutheran church bodies in the U.S. The two largest of these, the Missouri Synod and the Evangelical Lutheran Church in America, encompass fully 90 percent of the Lutheran congregations, 93 percent of all ordained ministers, and 94 percent of baptized members.[30]

Three very large events of the twentieth century have eroded particularism in the American Jewish community. First of all, Americanization and material success erased the old *shtetl* consciousness of Jews; second, the Holocaust during World War II traumatized all Jews and tended to make distinctions among them pale into insignificance; and third, the rise of Zionism and the establishment of the state of Israel has united all Jews together in defense of their homeland.

In the Catholic Church, the bishops have frowned upon ethnic parishes since World War I. The codification of canon law that Rome completed in 1918 required special permission for the erection of any new national parishes. In Chicago, George William Cardinal Mundelein tried to pursue a policy of Americanization. When he arrived in the city in 1916, he declared his dislike of hyphenism: "The people of the United States must be American or something else. They cannot serve two masters." Mundelein was a practical man, however, and he soon found he could not dismantle ethnic parishes without pushing their parishioners into schism, so he backed off and simply made it difficult to erect any new ones.[31]

Therefore, when Spanish-speaking newcomers arrived from Mexico and Puerto Rico, the Catholic Church in Chicago did not welcome them as openly as it had previous immigrants from Europe. Cardinal Mundelein showed some flexibility toward the Mexicans, however. In 1925 he invited a Spanish religious order, the Claretians, to organize the Mexican parish of Our Lady of Guadalupe in South Chicago, which became known colloquially as the "Mexican cathedral." About the same time, Mundelein also handed over

St. Nicholas in Evanston, one of the most suburban and least ethnic parishes of German origin, did not receive its first non-German pastor until 1969.

—*Photo by Edward R. Kantowicz*

St. Francis Assisi, an old German church on Roosevelt Road, to the Claretians as a second Mexican national parish. The Claretians later extended their religious work to the Mexicans living in Back of the Yards; however, their storefont church in that neighborhood was not organized as a full-scale parish, but only as a mission outpost. Immaculate Heart of Mary vicariate was a decidedly second-class facility that looked like a garage with a church facade tacked on.[32]

Though the archdiocese of Chicago officially recognized two-and-one-half Mexican national parishes, this fell far short of meeting the religious needs of the immigrant community. In some ways the existence of a few national parishes made the religious status of Mexican Catholics ambiguous. When Mexican parents found their way to the nearest Catholic church to arrange a baptism for their child, the English-speaking pastor often told them to "go to the Mexican parish," which might be miles away in a strange neighborhood. Puerto Ricans, as American citizens by birth, were not granted any national parishes at all. By the time they arrived in Chicago after World War II, the Catholic Church was expanding rapidly in the suburbs; so the last thing the Chicago bishops intended to do was build new national parishes in the city.

Mexicans and Puerto Ricans resemble in some ways the Italian Catholic immigrants who arrived earlier in the century. Like the Italians they did not bring many of their own priests with them, and they remained largely indifferent toward the institutional Church. They did not willingly support the church financially. Yet when the Italians came to Chicago, the archdiocese actively promoted the formation of national parishes and subsidized them indefinitely. It did not leave them wandering about looking for a parish community that would welcome them, as it did with the Mexicans and Puerto Ricans. Preoccupied with suburban growth, Catholic authorities after World War II forgot that the ethnic parish was a tried and true institution of immigrant adjustment and neglected to promote it among the Spanish-speaking.

In addition, by the time Latinos became numerous in Chicago, parochial school education had been priced out of their reach.

Before the Second Vatican Council, religious orders of sisters provided the teaching staff of parochial schools and the local parish subsidized most of the costs. Tuition was free in many parishes, or at most a nominal dollar or two per month. From the 1960s on, however, lay teachers replaced the teaching sisters and yearly school tuition soared to $500, then $1,000, or even more per child. Latino parents with large families and yearly incomes near or below the poverty level could not afford Catholic schools as their immigrant predecessors had.

For all their coolness toward the ethnic parishes, however, Chicago Catholic bishops did not close or consolidate many of the older ones until very recently. They preferred to let the ethnic leagues evolve and dissolve slowly on their own. However, in January 1990, Joseph Cardinal Bernardin, impelled by financial stringency, announced the wholesale closing of thirty-seven parishes and schools over the following eighteen months. Most of these were formerly national parishes in the older industrial neighborhoods of the city.[33]

In the archetypal neighborhood of Bridgeport (see map 2), two of the parishes, All Saints and St. Anthony of Padua, had already been consolidated a number of years previously. The mass closings of 1990 cut the number of parishes in half, when St. Bridget, St. John Nepomucene, Immaculate Conception, and St. George were shuttered. As a final gesture to its ethnic heritage, St. George, the oldest Lithuanian church in the city, donated all its statues and other furnishings to a parish in Lithuania. The Irish territorial parish of Nativity, home parish of both Richard J. Daley and Richard M. Daley, was not touched. Ethnicity may not have counted for much any more in the archdiocese but clout did.[34]

European immigrants believed they were building their churches for the ages; but, in fact, they were not. The edifices may have looked magnificent from a distance, but most were relatively humble constructions, fashioned from common Chicago brick, not stone or marble. In less than a hundred years, many have begun to crumble; and all of them require expensive maintenance, which was often deferred indefinitely by frugal pastors. Ethnic communities have proven even less lasting than the churches, as the children and grandchildren of immigrants attained some economic success and moved to the suburbs.

Yet it would be incorrect to conclude that the ethnic church is a vanishing institution. Chicago is still a magnet for immigrants. Some Polish Catholic churches have burgeoning congregations of recent arrivals from the *Solidarnosc* generation in Poland. Though bishops have been reluctant to create national parishes for Latinos, many formerly European ethnic churches have become thriving Mexican, Puerto Rican, or Filipino parishes simply by the weight of numbers. Another common pattern in older Catholic parishes finds one Mass on Sunday celebrated in English, another in Polish (or Lithuanian, or Bohemian), and a third in Spanish.

So long as immigrants find the city attractive, there will be a need for way stations on the journey between one country and another and between this world and the next.

2

The Irish in Chicago:
The Catholic Dimension

by Ellen Skerrett

With their annual enrollment of upwards of one thousand children, Catholic grammar schools such as St. Cajetan at 112th Street and Campbell Avenue remained a distinctive feature of Irish-American neighborhood life in the post-World War II era.

—Palomar Studios, author's collection

The Irish community in nineteenth-century Chicago was shaped by three major forces: Catholicism, politics, and nationalism. Although the Chicago Irish were deeply involved in politics and the cause of Irish freedom, Catholicism remained their primary loyalty. It was the one common bond among the mass of Irish immigrants, continuing to claim their allegiance in the New World. Whereas politics and nationalism tended to divide the Chicago Irish into warring factions, Catholicism remained a unifying force well into the twentieth century. Not only did it hold the central institutional position in the lives of Chicago's Irish Catholics but, even more important, it mirrored their changing concerns as they ceased to be an immigrant minority and entered the ranks of the middle class.

The Irish who came to Chicago were essentially rural people, and like other Catholic immigrants they brought with them a concept of a parish-centered church.[1] While parish building was an important activity for nearly all Catholic immigrant groups, it was especially meaningful for them. Unlike Germans and Poles who settled in Chicago, the Irish did not form ethnic enclaves. Although Irish neighborhoods did exist, particularly near industrial sections of the city, the majority of the Chicago Irish were not ghettoized, and their parish building resulted in Irish communities throughout the city.

As the Chicago experience makes clear, the Irish used their parishes to create cohesive communities, especially in middle-class residential neighborhoods where Catholics were a minority. Far from limiting mobility or participation in the larger society, their parishes accelerated the integration of immigrants and their children into American life. The Irish

parish in Chicago was a powerful force in transforming peasants into devout, disciplined urban dwellers. In the early years, it eased the burden of dislocation for immigrants and provided working-class Irish with models of middle-class behavior. As they improved their economic status and moved to residential neighborhoods, the parish once again provided structure, this time for an emerging Catholic middle class. As the middle-class Irish parishes became bastions of respectability, they also contributed the lion's share of financial support for Catholic secondary schools, and from the 1930s on they supplied much of the leadership for Catholic social action movements.

At its best, the parish filled important religious and social needs and became the heart of Irish-American community life. At its worst, the Irish parish turned inward and bred a fortress mentality. For generations of Chicago Irish men and women the parish reduced the awesome experience of urban life to a manageable scale. Not only did it play a large role in the development of Chicago neighborhoods, but the parish experience profoundly affected Irish attitudes about city life. Indeed, after more than a century as urban dwellers, the Chicago Irish remain a largely parochial people. To evaluate the legacy of the Chicago Irish parish experience it is necessary to view it in historical perspective.

Although the Irish controlled the hierarchy of the Church in Chicago during its formative years, the poverty of the Catholic community hampered institutional development. Chicago Catholic beginnings were inauspicious and gave little indication that Catholicism would emerge as the largest denomination in the city by the 1890s. When William J. Quarter, Chicago's first bishop, arrived in 1844 he found a single Catholic church, St. Mary's. So poor were the city's few hundred Catholics that they had been unable to complete the church's interior, much less liquidate an indebtedness of $3,000.

In many ways, Quarter was the ideal candidate to establish the new diocese of Chicago on a firm footing. Born in Kings County (Offaly), Ireland, in 1806, he emigrated at the age of sixteen in order to prepare for a career as an American priest. After ordination in 1829, he was assigned to New York City, which was in the process of becoming "the capital of American Catholicism."[2] During Quarter's tenure as a parish priest and pastor, New York's Catholic community experienced phenomenal growth as Irish and German immigrants flooded into the city. An estimated ninety thousand Catholics lived in New York in 1840 and Irish-born priests like Quarter were faced with the challenge of building churches and establishing schools, orphanages, and hospitals. The new bishop came to Chicago, then, with firsthand knowledge of urban life and an appreciation of the multiethnic character of the fledgling American Catholic Church.

The pressing need for more Catholic churches in Chicago was compounded by the problem of language. Prior to Quarter's appointment, St. Mary's on Madison Street had operated as a multilingual parish with separate services for French, Irish, and German Catholics. Chicago's first bishop was a pragmatist and in forming new parishes he arrived at a solution that satisfied each of the city's ethnic groups.

Quarter's years in the East had made him acutely aware of the diversity of the Catholic population, and he was especially sensitive to the desire of German Catholics for priests who could minister to them in their native tongue. In 1833, German Catholics in New York established the national parish of St. Nicholas, just a few blocks from St. Mary's Church on Grand Street, where Quarter began his pastorate. This was a new kind of parish based on language rather than territory, and it became "the trademark of German American Catholicism."[3] Quarter endorsed the relatively new concept of the national parish in 1846 when he designated St. Joseph's and St. Peter's as churches for Chicago's growing German Catholic population. At the same time he established the territorial parish of St. Patrick's for his own countrymen who had settled west of the Chicago River.[4]

Ethnic Identity and Parish Formation

Quarter's decision to form parishes based on language had important consequences for the structure of the Catholic Church in Chicago. First and foremost, the system of national parishes effectively separated ethnic groups from one another. Although the national parish was intended as a temporary solution to meet the needs of immigrants, it came to play a crucial role in the formation and preservation of ethnic communities. As the drive for ethnic solidarity intensified, so did the demand for national parishes, with the result that separate parishes became the norm for succeeding waves of German, Bohemian, Polish, Lithuanian, Slavic, and Italian Catholics.

German and Polish Catholics in particular created national parishes on the grand scale. In addition to building magnificent churches, both groups established schools, hospitals, orphanages, and cemeteries. For the majority of Catholic immigrants, religion and nationality were inextricably linked with the mother tongue. Understandably, national parishes as they developed in Chicago sought to preserve old-world customs and language as a way of strengthening faith and ethnic identity. Yet their success created a vacuum insofar as English-speaking parishes were concerned.

As the largest group of English-speaking Catholics in Chicago, the Irish had the most to gain from the proliferation of national parishes. Not only did the creation of national parishes isolate the Irish from other Catholic immigrants but it guaranteed Irish domination of the English-language territorial parishes. Although in theory territorial parishes were open to any English-speaking Catholic who lived within a circumscribed area, in practice virtually all English-speaking parishes established in nineteenth-century Chicago were de facto Irish. By default, the Irish gained control of English-speaking parishes throughout Chicago, and in a very real sense they dominated the Catholic Church from below as well as from above.

Like the national parishes of the Germans and Poles, the Irish territorial parishes fulfilled important religious and social needs. However the preservation of an ancestral language was not a concern of the Irish and it played no part in the formation of their parishes. Because the language question had already been decided for them before they emigrated, it did not become an issue in the New World as it did for every other Catholic ethnic group. While familiarity with English put the Irish at least a full generation ahead of other European immigrants, it also made them the most visible ethnic group. For Chicago's Irish this was a mixed blessing.

Until the Civil War, the Irish were the city's largest—and poorest—ethnic group. From a few hundred canal workers in the 1830s, the city's Irish population grew to more than six thousand by 1850, and within the next decade it tripled.[5] When construction was halted on the Illinois and Michigan Canal in 1842, Irish laborers sought employment and housing in the city and its adjoining communities, especially Bridgeport, which was the terminus of the canal. Their numbers were swelled by refugees of the Great Famine who arrived in Chicago during the late 1840s. Not only did this flood tide of newcomers overwhelm the city's small Irish community but it strained the charitable resources of the emerging metropolis.[6]

At mid-century, the presence of Irish and German immigrants was deeply felt in Chicago, where fewer than half of the city's 29,275 residents were native-born Americans. Transplanted New England Yankees decried the increasing number of foreigners in their midst, and they supported legislation aimed at restricting the right to vote, drink, and hold public office. Despite the fact that the Irish spoke English, which made them in one sense the least "foreign" of Chicago's immigrants, they bore the brunt of nativist attacks for reasons that had more to do with religion and politics than with their poverty or their regular appearance on the criminal court docket.

The Popular Image of the Chicago Irish

Unlike the Germans, who were divided along religious and political lines, the Irish were identified with the Douglas wing of the Democratic party and the Catholic Church.[7] While it is not clear what proportion of Irish immigrants were churchgoers, nativist attacks in the 1850s hammered away at the link between the Irish and the Catholic Church. Staunchly Republican, the Chicago Tribune took the lead in denouncing the increasing influence of the Irish in local politics, and its editorials warned that the Catholic Church sought political and religious supremacy in America. In 1855, it supported the mayoral campaign of Levi D. Boone, who ran as a Know Nothing candidate on a temperance ticket. In advocating temperance legislation known as the Maine Law Alliance, the *Tribune* charged that "The great majority of the members of the Roman Catholic Church in this country are Irishmen. The fact is peculiarly true in this city. . . . Who does not know that the most depraved, debased, worthless and irredeemable drunkards and sots which curse the community, are Irish Catholics? Who does not know that five-eighths of the cases brought up every day before the Mayor for drunkenness and consequent crime, are Irish Catholics?"[8]

Groups such as the Hibernian Benevolent Society were fully aware of nativist sentiment, and their St. Patrick's Day celebration in 1855 reflected the tensions that existed between Irish, Catholic, and American identities. It followed the convention of the day with speeches and musical selections. However the choice of "sentiments" and "airs" indicated a defensiveness on the part of the Irish. Except for the customary tributes to St. Patrick and Ireland, the celebration was heavily patriotic, with speeches ranging from "The Memory of Washington" to "The President of the United States" and "The Army and Navy." But for all the singing of "The Star-Spangled Banner" and "Yankee Doodle," the *Tribune* recoiled at the sentiment expressed by Rev. Bernard O'Hara of Holy Name Church that America ultimately "would be Catholic throughout its borders." The newspaper suggested that if the Catholic Church flourished in America, then the "fruits of Romanism here shall be seen in as full and abundant a harvest of beggary, degradation and want as is seen in the Catholic portions of Ireland."[9]

Throughout the 1850s and 1860s the *Tribune* portrayed Chicago's Irish Catholics as priest-ridden, and the newspaper cited the immigrant's loyalty to the Church as evidence that the Irish could never become fully American. Contrary to the *Tribune*'s opinion, at the time the Chicago Irish were not obsequious slaves of the Catholic Church or her clergy. A large segment of them were locked in disputes with bishops Anthony O'Regan and James Duggan over their arbitrary dismissal of diocesan clergy. These controversies, which pitted congregation and priests against their bishops, raised questions about the limits of episcopal authority, and they also revealed the increasing importance of the parish as a vehicle for Irish respectability.

The first crisis to galvanize Irish Catholic sentiment occurred in 1855 when Bishop O'Regan dismissed Rev. Jeremiah Kinsella and three priest-professors who served Holy Name Church and St. Mary of the Lake University. In one fell swoop the bishop fired the men who had been handpicked by Quarter to organize the first institution of higher learning in the city.

Bishop Quarter had been acutely aware of the need for an American-trained clergy, and he had established St. Mary of the Lake University to include a seminary department. Finances for such a venture were a constant problem, and in his will Quarter left all his personal property to the university rather than to his successor, Bishop James O. Van de Velde. This bequest had enabled Fr. Kinsella

to pursue an independent course. Not only was he able to keep the university running, but he hired Edward Burling, one of the city's foremost architects, to design a church for Irish Catholics who had been attending Mass in the school chapel. Kinsella's plans for Holy Name Church were ambitious. At a time when the city's Irish population worshiped in frame churches, if at all, estimates for the new Gothic structure ran as high as $100,000. To members of Holy Name parish, however, the new church was more than just a place to attend Mass. It was a powerful symbol of Irish Catholic respectability in a city where few Irish families had achieved middle-class status. As one observer recalled, "The foundations were laid as never foundations were laid in Chicago before or since. The buttresses were massive enough to have sustained an edifice the size of St. Peter's and millions of bricks were stowed away in the massive tower."[10]

That Fr. Kinsella borrowed heavily to build the new church had not bothered Holy Name parishioners but it had alarmed Bishop Van de Velde, who regarded such initiative as "Irish insubordination."[11] These conflicts remained unresolved when Van de Velde resigned his post in 1853.

Bishop Anthony O'Regan, like his predecessor, was reluctant to head the Chicago diocese, but once in Chicago he acted quickly to assert his authority. In January 1855, he dismissed Fr. Kinsella and three other well-known priests, Rev. John Breen, Rev. Lawrence Hoey, and Rev. Thomas Clowry. This action stunned Holy Name parishioners, who held a meeting to protest the bishop's decision. In a formal statement a committee of parishioners acknowledged respect and reverence for the authority of the Church and their bishop, but they disputed his reasons for removing their priests. The committee, composed of leaders of the Irish community, expressed "utmost confidence in the energy and zeal of our priests to complete our new church," and they pledged continuing financial support if O'Regan reconsidered his decision. But the bishop remained firm and the four priests had little recourse but to leave Chicago.[12] While Irish Catholics were unable to alter O'Regan's decision about their clergy, they succeeded in completing Holy Name. On November 5, 1855, the Court of Common Pleas ruled that the cornerstone blessing constituted approval of the church and awarded contractor Charles O'Connor $6,263.96 in his suit against the bishop.[13]

Priests' Rights and American Catholic Identity

The fact that the Chicago Irish paid serious attention to the issue of clerical rights indicates that they were already well on their way to thinking of themselves as American Catholics. O'Regan's arbitrary dismissal of the local clergy was an embarrassment to the city's Irish community because it gave credence to nativist charges that the Catholic Church was an institution incompatible with the American spirit of democracy. In the Protestant tradition, local congregations played an important role in forming churches and selecting ministers. Many Protestants regarded as un-American the near absolute freedom enjoyed by Catholic bishops in appointing and dismissing priests. Nor did this state of affairs go unnoticed by officials of the Congregation de Propaganda Fide, which had jurisdiction over the Catholic Church in the United States until 1908. Following an extensive tour of this country in 1853, Archbishop Gaetano Bedini filed a long report on the relationship of bishops and priests. He noted in particular that it was "difficult for a priest to work hard in his mission, to build churches and schools at great sacrifice, to obtain the good will of the parishioners and then suddenly to be transferred by the unexpected inclination of the Bishop."[14]

As the targets of nativist propaganda, the Irish were especially sensitive to claims that they could not be loyal Americans because their first allegiance was to the Church. Irish-born priests such as Quarter and Kinsella had been optimistic that the Catholic Church would thrive in Chicago, and they believed that American-trained clergymen would accelerate the process. Quarter was confident that Catholic institutions such as St. Mary of the Lake University could play an important role in the life of the city and the Church. By the 1860s the school had fulfilled this promise.

Considering the virulent anti-Catholic and xenophobic sentiments that became commonplace in the 1850s, Quarter's plans for the Church in Chicago may have appeared overly optimistic. However as far as the Irish were concerned, nativist attacks had the effect of strengthening the bond between their Irish and Catholic identities. Indeed, the Holy Name controversy underscored the prominent role accorded priests in the Chicago Irish community, and it revealed the increasing importance of church-building as a sign of Catholic power.

For many Irish immigrants, the process of forming parishes and building churches was relatively new. Although the parish system survived the Penal days, as late as 1820 there was a dearth of proper church buildings in Ireland. While Catholic "chapels" existed in Dublin and in smaller towns, the situation was much more primitive in the countryside. In parts of Connacht, for example, priests offered Mass in thatched sheds or in the open air, and they routinely performed marriages and baptisms in private homes. Although Catholic church-building increased dramatically in the early 1800s, the effect of this movement was not felt by much of the Catholic population, particularly in the west.[15]

Chicago's Irish population included large numbers of men and women from that part of Ireland, where church attendance was far from customary. Unlike later immigrants who adhered to strict religious practices, thousands of the Irish who settled in Chicago prior to the Civil War were Catholic in name only. That the Catholic Church quickly became the central institution in the lives of Chicago's Irish was due in no small part to priests such as Denis Dunne, who recognized that the real vitality and strength of the Church lay in its parishes.

Dunne was born in Timahoe, Queens County (Leix), Ireland, in 1823 but he grew up in New Brunswick, Canada, where his father and uncles found ready employment as

Old St. Patrick's at Adams and Desplaines streets, c. 1875, illustrates the growth and development of an Irish parish complex in the nineteenth century. The original frame church (1846) at the right was converted into school quarters when the present church, at the left, was completed in 1856. Despite their poverty, the Chicago Irish were enthusiastic supporters of Catholic education.

—*Courtesy of* The New World

ship carpenters. Dunne was ordained for the Chicago diocese in 1848, and his first assignment was as a professor at St. Mary of the Lake University. His rapid rise from assistant priest to vicar general of the diocese illustrated the vigor of the young Chicago Church and the opportunities available to talented Irish clergymen. After brief stints in country parishes in Galena and Ottawa, Illinois, Dunne returned to Chicago in 1854 to serve as rector of St. Patrick's Church on the city's West Side. Not long afterward, Bishop O'Regan appointed him vicar general, a post he continued to hold during the administration of Bishop James Duggan.

Dunne's years in Chicago spanned the period of heaviest Irish immigration, and he was well aware of the need for adequate churches. Not only did he lead the drive to complete the spacious brick church of St.

Patrick's, which still stands today at the corner of Adams and Desplaines streets, but he encouraged lay initiative, especially in the areas of fund-raising and charity work. Parishioners voted on contracts for the church building, and in 1859 they elected men to canvass the neighborhood for funds to liquidate the $11,700 parish debt.[16] Although it appears that the rector prepared the parish's financial reports, they were approved during meetings of the congregation.

Dunne was also instrumental in forming a chapter of the St. Vincent de Paul Society, which quickly took root in Irish parishes throughout Chicago. This group, composed of prominent men from St. Patrick's, supported free schools for Catholic children and raised money for destitute parishioners. While the St. Vincent de Paul Society remained largely parish-bound, it represented the first "Catholic" attempt to deal with social problems plaguing the Irish community in the 1860s.

Under Dunne's administration, St. Patrick's emerged as a model Irish-American parish, sensitive to newly arrived immigrants as well as to prosperous families in the congregation. Like many of the Chicago Irish, Dunne had no personal memories of Ireland, but he knew the painful history of his people and he understood the longing of Irish Catholics for acceptance by the larger society. Indeed, when the Civil War broke out he formed a regiment known as the 90th Volunteers.

Although many Chicago Irishmen were less than enthusiastic about fighting a war that promised the abolition of black slavery, others like Dunne seized the opportunity to demonstrate just how American Irish immigrants could be. At the first meeting at St. Patrick's on August 8, 1862, the organizers of the Irish Legion pledged their loyalty to the Union cause and they lashed out at fellow Irishmen "who have sought, or who are now seeking, the protection of the blood-stained felon flag of Great Britain, to escape their duty to the United States."[17] The 90th Volunteers' record of service gave new meaning to the term "Fighting Irish." Of the 980 men who left Chicago with the Irish Legion, only 221 returned in June 1865.[18] Participation of Irish Catholics in the Union Army did much to improve their image, establishing a patriotic pattern that later generations adopted in their struggle to become fully American.

More than any other Irish priest of his generation, Dunne tried to lay broad and deep foundations for the Catholic Church in Chicago. At a time when most pastors were wholly absorbed in building churches, Dunne devoted much of his energy to the cause of Catholic education, and he remained firm in his conviction that the Church must care for the young and the needy. In addition to supporting grammar schools in St. Patrick's parish, he organized an industrial school at 2928 South Archer Avenue in Bridgeport to care for "unruly and vagabond boys of [the Catholic] faith," many of whom had been left fatherless by the Civil War.[19] Although priests and laity alike recognized the need for a Catholic reformatory, Bishop Duggan withheld his support. Undaunted by the lack of official sanction, Dunne relied on the generosity of St. Patrick's parishioners and members of the St. Vincent de Paul Society to keep the institution open.

By 1865, Dunne was Chicago's most well known Irish clergyman. His work in St. Patrick's and his support of the Irish Legion and the Bridgeport Institute had won him the respect of both Catholics and Protestants. By then his duties as vicar general placed him on a first-name basis with all the city's priests. Indeed, in terms of influence, his only rival was Arnold J. Damen, who had established the Jesuit parish of Holy Family in 1857 on the prairie just west of St. Patrick's.

With priests such as Dunne in positions of authority, the future of the Catholic Church in Chicago looked promising. Then disaster struck. In 1866 Bishop Duggan abruptly closed St. Mary of the Lake University, which had only recently been reorganized by Rev. John McMullen, chancellor of the diocese. The bishop transferred McMullen to St. Paul's, a poor Irish parish on the West Side, and he turned the new university building into an orphanage. Although the seminary associated with the university survived, its precarious existence was a cause of deep concern to Rev. James J. McGovern, the president, and his professors, especially Rev. Joseph P. Roles, who also served as rector of Holy Name Church.

Not long after he closed the university, the bishop stripped Dunne of his authority as vicar general by appointing Rev. T. J. Halligan administrator of the diocese. During Duggan's extended tour of Europe in 1867, Halligan withdrew financial support for the seminary and set in motion a series of events that culminated in the removal of Bishop Duggan from office. As James P. Gaffey has shown, this little-known controversy vividly illustrated the dynamics of church authority, and it had profound consequences for the structure of the Catholic Church in the upper Mississippi Valley.[20] But it was also a watershed for Chicago's Irish Catholics.

From start to finish, the Duggan controversy was almost exclusively an Irish affair, involving priests and parishioners of Irish birth and descent who opposed the arbitrary actions of their Irish-born bishop. Yet Irish identity played no role in the conflict. On the contrary, the events of 1866–68 clearly reveal that the Chicago Irish considered themselves to be American Catholics who wished to see "the checks and balances of constitutional freedom" applied to their Church.[21] Once again, priests' rights were at the heart of the matter.

Following his return from Europe in August of 1868, Bishop Duggan closed St. Mary of the Lake Seminary and dismissed the priests who had brought charges against him, namely Dunne, McMullen, McGovern, and Roles. The response of Irish Catholics was swift. Mass meetings were held in Holy Name, St. Patrick's, and St. Paul's to endorse the actions of the clergy and to raise funds for the suspended priests. Unlike the 1855 conflict in Holy Name, which had received little public attention, the Duggan controversy was chronicled in the pages of Chicago's leading daily newspapers, the *Tribune* and the *Times*. Not only were the resolutions adopted by Irish Catholics made public, but week after week the columns of the Chicago papers were filled with articles that detailed the disagreements between Bishop Duggan and the clergy and parishioners.

As the controversy unfolded, readers discovered that the four Chicago priests had filed serious charges against their bishop ranging from excessive absence from the diocese to conversion of diocesan funds for personal use. What made their charges so compelling was the fact that Dunne, McMullen, and Roles were members of the bishop's council and hence his advisers on matters of policy. So public did the controversy become that when McMullen left Chicago for Rome to press his case against Duggan, the *Times* published his farewell letter to the bishop along with a forwarding address! Thus did Chicagoans learn on September 27, 1868, that McMullen was on his way to Rome, fortified by his conviction that "it is my sacred duty to God, religion, and my fellow-men, to do all that I can within the bounds of truth and justice, to remove [my superior] from the bishopric of Chicago."[22]

Throughout the fall of 1868, Dunne declined to comment about the Duggan contro-

versy, confident in the knowledge that "When the due time comes, my friends and I will vindicate our good names, and give evidence that we have neither *lightly nor falsely* made charges at Rome."[23] For Dunne, the vindication did not come soon enough. He died on December 23, 1868, in his brother's home on Adams Street, in the shadow of St. Patrick's. Although Bishop Duggan was present at Dunne's side, no reconciliation took place. Far from giving his blessing to the dying man, the bishop demanded a retraction. But Dunne refused to yield and thus he died "with the censure of the Bishop upon his back . . . and in such poverty that the clergy and people paid for his funeral."[24]

Reports of Dunne's death and the subsequent mental breakdown of Bishop Duggan persuaded church officials in Rome to intervene in the Chicago controversy. But nearly two years elapsed before Duggan was committed to a sanitarium in St. Louis and Bishop Thomas Foley arrived from Baltimore to administer the diocese. Foley was the first American-born bishop to head the Chicago diocese and his appointment was widely interpreted as a signal that Rome had "consulted the prevailing Catholic sentiment in [America] in favor of the elevation of natives to the highest offices of the Church."[25]

Foley's quiet, unpretentious, but effective leadership quickly brought a measure of peace to the troubled Chicago Church. Indeed the bishop maintained such a low profile during his ten years in Chicago that he never "permitted a journalist to interview him . . . never participated in popular demonstrations . . . abhorred politics, never voted . . . ."[26] His immediate vindication of McMullen, Roles, and McGovern won him the respect and admiration of the Chicago Irish, and it signaled his desire to work with the clergy. Foley was well aware of the strong ties that existed between parishioners and their clergy, and he did little to diminish the power of parish priests. But more than any of his predecessors, he realized that the parish system with its divisions along ethnic and geographic lines posed a barrier to the unity of Chicago's Catholics. Not only were the city's Catholic immigrants separated into parishes of their own, but within each ethnic group parishes were further divided along geographic lines.

That the parish system had become firmly entrenched was apparent at the time of the Chicago Fire of 1871. In announcing the formation of a citywide agency to aid victims of the disaster Foley lamented that "There has not been a sufficient union among the Catholics of the city. Dr. Whitehouse of the Episcopal Church said in a recent address that his diocese was too congregational, and I think there is something of the same kind of division among ourselves. This is due perhaps to the unfortunate geographical division of the city, but as we are all Catholics we should know no north or south or west side."[27]

While substantial numbers of the Chicago Irish thought of themselves as American Catholics, Foley's remarks indicate that they were as parochial as their German coreligionists. In 1870 the Irish controlled fifteen of the city's twenty-three parishes. Although the English-speaking parishes of the Irish were more dispersed than German parishes, they were by no means evenly distributed throughout the city. On the contrary, three distinct networks of Irish parishes had emerged, one north, one south, and one west of the Chicago River. As the number of English-speaking parishes increased during the 1870s and 1880s these sectional divisions deepened, with the result that the Irish Catholic population became even more fragmented.

In 1871 the fire destroyed St. Mary's Cathedral in the city's commercial district along with six other Catholic churches, several schools, convents, rectories, and charitable institutions. In one day Chicago's Germans lost two of their largest churches, St. Joseph's and St. Michael's, while the Irish suffered the loss of Holy Name and smaller frame churches in the parishes of St. Paul's and Immaculate Conception. Bishop Foley's decision not to rebuild St. Louis's and St. Paul's met with little opposition from Chicago's Irish Catholics because these parishes had been steadily losing members.

Irish movement away from the center of the city had accelerated in the 1850s and 1860s as housing and jobs became readily available in outlying areas. Parishes soon followed. One priest who was quick to discern the trend was Arnold Damen, S.J. In 1857 he selected a site on Twelfth Street (Roosevelt Road) just west of Halsted Street for the new parish of Holy Family, in close proximity to the lumber district and the railroad yards where Irish laborers were employed. Before long the prairie surrounding the Jesuit church became a frame-house neighborhood, and by 1871 Holy Family was the largest English-speaking parish in Chicago, with a congregation of nearly twenty thousand persons. Financed in part by the Jesuit order, the parish complex was massive, encompassing a Gothic brick church, three parochial schools, a convent-academy owned by the Madames of the Sacred Heart, and St. Ignatius College, the forerunner of Loyola University. Although few Irish parishes could rival Holy Family, church-building continued to occupy the energies of even the poorest congregation.

Catholic Church-building and Irish Neighborhoods

In the wake of the Chicago Fire, Irish pastors embarked on ambitious building campaigns aimed at replacing old frame churches with brick structures. This was no small feat as fully 75 percent of the churches in Irish parishes were built of wood. Although little is known of the ability of Chicago's Irish Catholics to provide funds for such a building campaign, the total value of parish complexes in 1873 was estimated at more than $2 million.[28]

While Chicago's newspapers routinely criticized the brick-and-mortar approach to Catholicism, the efforts of the Chicago Irish did not go unnoticed. Indeed newspapers began to comment favorably that the construction of Catholic churches "improves and helps to fill up the surrounding neighborhood and swells and enhances the value of property."[29]

The construction of a masonry church took on special meaning in Irish parishes in

Annunciation Church (1876) at the corner of Wabansia Avenue and Paulina Street symbolized the progress the North Side Irish achieved in creating community "in the waste places of the city . . . " Although overshadowed by the Polish parish of St. Mary of the Angels in 1899, Annunciation continued to serve families of diverse ethnic backgrounds until its closing and demolition in 1978.
— *Photo courtesy of* The New World

Chicago. Financed by the nickels and dimes of working men and women, the church was a powerful symbol of Irish cooperation. And its construction through voluntary contributions revealed just how American the Chicago Irish had become. While Irish churches were modest affairs in comparison with German and Polish edifices, still their existence "in the waste places of the city . . . where . . . the populace are humbly and poorly housed," was a sign that the Irish were becoming devout urban dwellers.[30]

Catholic church dedications were important events for the Chicago Irish and they turned out by the thousands to witness the ceremonies, which invariably included parades and speeches. In addition to describing the new church, contemporary newspaper accounts often commented about the changes that had taken place among Irish workers following the organization of a parish. In 1876, a *Chicago Times* reporter noted that when Rev. Thomas J. Edwards began his work among Irish immigrants from County Clare in the North Side Rolling Mill district in 1866 that

> The people were largely Catholic in name, but in name only. They paid little or no regard to the outward ordinances of religion, and cared less for its principles. To a great extent they were quarrelsome and dissolute. They were not precisely the class of people one would care to live among . . . Father Edwards saw that the people in this part of the city needed the restraining and the purifying influences of the church, and he resolved to supply this need. There was no place of worship, and there were practically no worshipers. He undertook to build the one and supply the other. In both of these attempts he has been remarkably successful.[31]

At the time the new $50,000 brick church was dedicated, Annunciation was a flourishing parish of eight hundred families. Groups such as the Total Abstinence Society and the St. Vincent de Paul Society had contributed much to parish stability, as did the parochial school that enrolled five hundred students in 1876. Women religious played a crucial role in such working-class parishes. In addition to instructing the children in the doctrines of the Catholic faith, the nuns fostered middle-class aspirations. They encouraged children to pursue their education beyond the elementary level and they recruited talented young girls for their own religious communities. The Sisters of Charity of the Blessed Virgin Mary who came to Annunciation parish in 1872 also promoted vocations to the priesthood with remarkable results: by 1916, the parish claimed ten Irish-American priests, among them Bishop Edward Dunne of Dallas, Texas.[32]

While church-building took precedence over Catholic education in most Irish parishes in Chicago, there were signs that this attitude was changing. Although all but two of the city's eighteen Irish parishes supported parochial schools in 1876, few congregations had the financial resources to maintain schools on the scale of those in St. Patrick's or Holy Family. Bishop Foley acknowledged the problem but stressed that where the parochial schools were as good as the public schools, Catholic parents had an obligation "to give their children the advantage of this Catholic education."[33]

Catholic Education in the Urban Slum

One South Side Irish pastor who materially advanced the cause of parochial schools was Rev. John Waldron of St. John's at Eighteenth and Clark streets. So great was his conviction about the necessity of Catholic education that he provided modern quarters for the children of the parish before allowing the construction of a permanent church. For more than twenty years after the parish was organized, the congregation worshipped in a plain wooden church located in the heart of a working-class slum west of State Street. Following the fire of 1871, a number of wealthy Irish families moved into the posh Prairie Avenue district at the east end of St. John's, and they were particularly anxious to see a masonry church constructed that would rival nearby Protestant houses of worship. Not only did Waldron refuse to consider their suggestion that a new church be built near the lake, but he reminded these parishioners that his duty was almost entirely to the children of the parish. He exhorted the "thrifty and prosperous" among the five hundred families in his congregation to concern themselves with the plight of poor children in St. John's who had neither books nor boots. In a stirring sermon in 1875, reprinted in newspapers across the country and in Ireland, Waldron stated his case:

> Every day last week I was out looking up the children of the parish; finding out how many do not go to school anywhere, and getting at the reasons why they stay away and run to vice and crime in the streets. In many a house I found that not one child of the family went to school. . . .

"Why don't you go, Michael?" said I to one that knew me. "Because I've got no boots," he said. He might have said, because he had no anything, for he had not enough clothes on to keep him from the chill of these cold days. You can't get children to go to either church or school without clothes and books, and that's why half the children of Chicago are not in any school. . . . What does a

The modest frame church of St. John's at Eighteenth and Clark streets served as the parish house of worship for more than twenty years after its dedication in 1859. Rev. John Waldron refused to construct a permanent edifice until modern school quarters were completed for the children of Irish immigrants.
—Photo, Diamond Jubilee of the Archdiocese

poor lad without boots care for your books? Give them the boots first, and then we can get them to the books afterwards. I told these boys that I would give them both if they would come to our schools, and you will keep my word for me.[34]

Waldron's conviction about the necessity of Catholic education was equaled only by his nationalist fervor. He proudly owned and displayed two pikes from the 1798 rebellion and during his twenty-seven years as pastor of St. John's he hosted many Irish groups, among them the Fenian Brotherhood, the Irish Rifles, the Clan na Gael Guards, and the Ancient Order of Hibernians. Although the Christian Brothers of De La Salle and the Sisters of Mercy who staffed St. John's school did not share the pastor's devotion to the cause of Irish freedom, they were in complete agreement that their students must become "intelligent, useful citizens, a credit at once to their country, their faith, and to themselves."[35] While not denying Irish identity, these religious orders did little to reinforce it, with the result that their students considered themselves Americans first and foremost.

Complex feelings about Irish identity were not unique to the members of St. John's. Although the nationalist cause engaged the passions of Chicago's Irish population in the coming decade, it did not alter support for Catholic education nor retard parish development. Far from diminishing in importance, Irish parishes remained powerful forces in Chicago's industrial slums as well as in middle-class residential districts.

Waldron was a pioneer of the American urban parish and like other Irish priests in nineteenth-century Chicago, his view of city life was intensely parochial. He spent his entire career as a priest within an area of less than two square miles, and it became for him a world unto itself. "Kerry Patch" around St. John's was a rough-and-tumble Irish neighborhood and Waldron patrolled its streets with a blackthorn stick in hand, ready to disperse "street gangs and alley loafers."[36] Contemporary accounts portrayed him as "a powerful aid to the city government in pre-

serving order and keeping peace among the riotously inclined."[37] Despite the location of St. John's in the midst of a working-class slum, Waldron waged a battle against the Rock Island in the 1860s when it appeared that the railroad would buy up property along Clark Street from Twelfth to Twenty-second streets. Although he was powerless to prevent the encroachment of other railroads, Waldron's efforts guaranteed the survival of St. John's long after the neighborhood's homes had disappeared.

By the late 1870s, Chicago's Irish had made significant gains in terms of parochial development and Catholic education. But many lay and clerical leaders were pessimistic about the future. Continued immigration, they believed, would threaten Irish communities already in existence.

In 1879, a group of civic-minded Irishmen organized the Irish Catholic Colonization Society to deal with the problem of Irish immigration. Bishop John Spalding of Peoria served as chairman of the board of directors and William J. Onahan, Chicago's most respected Irish Catholic, was elected secretary. Ironically, at the time Onahan was working to relocate Irish immigrants on farms in the Midwest, his countrymen in Chicago were no longer at the bottom of the economic ladder. Although the Irish were heavily represented among laborers and semiskilled workers, a middle class had been formed by those who had found employment in such diverse fields as politics, municipal government, education, brewing and distilling, importing, meatpacking, undertaking, theater, and sports. While much work remains to be done on the economic background and family patterns of the nineteenth-century Chicago Irish, it seems probable that their poverty has been overemphasized.[38]

Emmet Larkin has persuasively argued that the quality of Irish immigration steadily improved after the Great Famine. As a result of the development of the national school system in Ireland, the overwhelming majority of men and women who came to America in the 1860s and 1870s were literate, and many had experienced the benefits of the "Devotional Revolution."[39] Not only were these new immigrants practicing Catholics but they were accustomed to supporting parishes through voluntary contributions.

For all his work on behalf of Irish colonization, even Onahan was forced to concede that the quality of Irish immigration to Chicago improved throughout the 1880s. He noted that "these newcomers of late years are of the better class—the young, enterprising, and as a rule fairly educated," and he agreed that they would be a valuable addition to Chicago's Irish population, estimated at three hundred thousand persons.[40]

In the 1880s, then, the Chicago Irish were not wholly middle class but neither were they poverty-stricken immigrants. With nearly two full generations in the city, the Irish had become a powerful force in politics, and they had put their imprint on the Catholic Church. By 1885, the central committee of the Democratic party was overwhelmingly Irish and within the ranks of the Church, Irish clergymen were heavily represented as pastors and members of the archbishop's staff. Indeed, the highest administrative post in the diocese, that of chancellor, continued to be held only by priests of Irish birth or descent until 1971.

In the years between 1880 and 1910, Chicago's Irish Catholics continued to make important gains politically and economically. One of the significant developments during this period was the movement of Irish families away from congested neighborhoods to outlying areas of the city. In Holy Family and Annunciation parishes they were being displaced by new immigrants, Italians and Jews on the West Side, and Poles on the Near Northwest Side. In St. John's on the Near South Side, the Irish exodus began shortly after a new church was dedicated in 1881. Fr. Waldron, who had refused to build a permanent church until his congregation could afford it, now watched in sorrow as "hundreds and hundreds of his beloved poor and

William J. Onahan (1836–1919), Chicago's most well-known Irish Catholic layman in the nineteenth century, was a driving force in the movement to relocate Irish immigrants on farms in the Midwest in the 1880s. An early chronicler of the progress of Chicago Catholicism, Onahan was instrumental in the formation of the Illinois Catholic Historical Society in 1918.

—Courtesy of The New World

faithful families surrendered their humble homes to the railroads, and moved in affluence to help build up and be the first families in the many South Side parishes."[41]

Irish Parishes and Upward Mobility

While many Irish Catholics retained fond memories of life in parishes such as Holy Family, Annunciation, and St. John's, the fact remains that they left by the thousands, exchanging cold-water tenements for steam-heat "flats." Although ethnic changes played a role in the breakup of older parishes after 1880, the Irish were not so much pushed out of their old neighborhoods as they were pulled by the opportunity for better housing. Parish statistics give an idea of the magnitude of this change in Irish residential patterns. Whereas fully 75 percent of English-speaking

parishes established between 1843 and 1878 had been in the city proper, after 1880 the vast majority of parishes organized by Irish Catholics were located in outlying districts. While these new parishes clearly demonstrated mobility, they also cast light on the improving economic status of Irish Catholic families.

Prior to 1880, Irish parishes in Chicago reflected the predominantly working-class origins of their members. Although parishes such as St. Patrick's, Holy Family, Holy Name, and St. John's included some of the city's

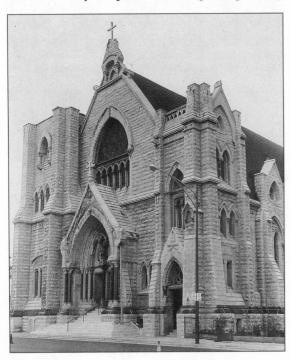

A powerful symbol of Irish Catholic respectability in a working-class slum, the French Gothic church of St. John was dedicated in impressive ceremonies in 1881. Constructed of limestone according to the plans of Irish architect James J. Egan, it served as headquarters of the Catholic Church Extension Society from 1924 to 1962 when it was razed.
—*Courtesy of* The New World

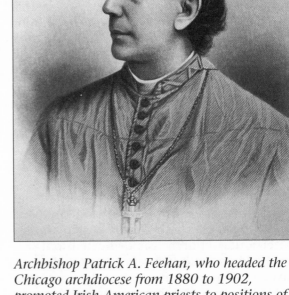

Archbishop Patrick A. Feehan, who headed the Chicago archdiocese from 1880 to 1902, promoted Irish-American priests to positions of influence in the Church and established territorial parishes in outlying districts to meet the needs of upwardly mobile Irish Catholics. He also enthusiastically supported national parishes based on language, confident that the "streams of population coming from many sources will make great people."
—*Photo by The Century Publishing and Engraving Co.,* American Irish in Chicago

wealthiest Irish families in the 1870s, by and large they drew their strength from those of limited financial means. In the 1880s, however, distinctly middle-class parishes emerged as the Irish moved to residential districts several miles from the center of the city.

Archbishop Patrick A. Feehan, who headed the Chicago archdiocese during a period of enormous growth (1880–1902), was attentive to the needs of the Irish, and he was aware that they were a highly mobile group. Because of the availability of priests of Irish birth and descent, Feehan did not hesitate to form English-speaking parishes with as few as fifty families. As a result, predominantly Irish parishes were organized throughout Chicago in both industrial areas and sparsely settled residential districts.

Of the forty-three English-speaking parishes organized between 1880 and 1902, St. Bernard's stands out as an example of the kind of parish formed by upwardly mobile Irish Catholics who moved into fashionable residential districts. In July 1887, Feehan assigned his former chancellor, Rev. Bernard P. Murray, to establish a Catholic parish in Englewood, a community located eight miles south of the downtown business district. As its name suggests, Englewood was a predominantly Protestant New England Yankee settlement.

"There goes the neighborhood" —St. Bernard's in Englewood

Fr. Murray's purchase of property on Stewart Avenue, the finest street in the area, enraged Protestant residents. A group of them offered to "repurchase the church property at a goodly advance in price," but Murray refused to sell.[42] The Protestants realized, clearly enough, that although the Irish were a minority in Englewood, the formation of a new parish would attract more Catholics to the area. Beyond anti-Catholic sentiment, however, there were other reasons to fear an Irish invasion. Already by the 1880s they held a number of appointive positions in the Town of Lake, and Protestants were well aware that Irish influence in politics would increase as the Catholic population grew. Then, too, Englewood residents firmly believed that the Irish would bring with them crime and vices associated with the city, thereby disturbing the tranquility of this suburban district.

For their part, the Irish did not view themselves as destroyers of community life. On the contrary, the founding members of St. Bernard's included prominent Catholics such as P. T. Barry, a former Illinois legislator who also served as a school trustee for the towns of Lake and Hyde Park. Fr. Murray, like other Chicago priests of Irish birth and descent, also considered himself a Catholic community builder, and during his thirty-year pastorate he was responsible for the construction of a permanent church, school, convent-academy, and hospital.

As Protestants had feared, the Catholic population of Englewood grew steadily, and by 1895 six hundred families belonged to St. Bernard's. Considering the opposition the Irish Catholics had encountered in the formation of their parish it is understandable that they wanted a magnificent church that would compare favorably with neighboring Protestant houses of worship. Murray was well aware that St. Bernard's would be a symbol of the Irish presence in Englewood, and he spared no expense in the construction of a marble edifice, said to be the only church of its kind in the Middle West.

As if to force old-line Englewood residents to acknowledge the increasing importance of his Irish Catholic community, Murray scheduled the cornerstone-laying for the same day—at the same hour—that Presbyterians were to do the same for their new church, just a stone's throw from St. Bernard's. Not only did the Catholics upstage the Presbyterians but their celebration became a demonstration of Irish religious and political power.

Contemporary accounts reveal more than five thousand Catholics from parishes all over the South Side turned out to march through

Englewood. The parade included platoons of Irish-American policemen and Irish military groups such as the Seventh Regiment and the Clan na Gael Guards. In the midst of this Catholic show of strength, members of the Cumberland Presbyterian Church began their own celebration—to the strains of "Onward, Christian Soldiers."[43]

While the Irish of St. Bernard's succeeded in establishing themselves as respectable members of the community, they were never accepted by Englewood's "old guard." In time, however, anti-Catholic sentiment declined and a number of Irish attained prominent positions in local banking, politics, and business. But in many ways the Englewood neighborhood remained divided along religious lines. Indeed, these divisions deepened as the Catholic population increased and new parishes were formed, each with its own identity.

Although it is difficult to determine precisely when the Chicago Irish began to define themselves in terms of their parishes, the experience of the Irish in Englewood suggests that anti-Catholic sentiment played a crucial

Constructed in the midst of a Protestant-dominated neighborhood in 1896–1898, St. Bernard's Church at Sixty-sixth Street and Stewart Avenue was a visible reminder that Irish Catholics were creating a place for themselves in Englewood. The Irish of St. Bernard's also contributed generously to the convent-academy and grammar school staffed by the Ladies of Loretto and a modern hospital operated by the Religious Hospitallers of St. Joseph. In a pattern repeated throughout the South and West sides of the city, St. Bernard's took on a new identity as a black parish in the 1960s.

—Photo courtesy of The New World

more Americanized with each decade but the number of its foreign born in Chicago declined steadily after 1900. Ironically, the new immigrants brought with them a stronger sense of ethnic identity than their relatives who had immigrated earlier. But they came too late and in insufficient numbers to make a noticeable difference in the Chicago Irish community.

Increasingly, groups such as the Ancient Order of Hibernians, which had flourished in the 1880s, became the province of the foreign-born Irish. Mary F. McWhorter, an indefatigable promoter of Irish history and culture, noted with dismay that children of immigrants associated the AOH with "the shanty Irish."[56] Although the Chicago Irish made significant gains economically and politically by 1910, they had little inclination to preserve their ethnicity, especially when that identity carried negative connotations.

Irish history courses taught in Chicago's English-speaking parochial schools did little to remedy the situation. Not only did the courses emphasize Catholic aspects of Irish history but their subject matter was of little interest to city children, few of whom had personal memories of Ireland. Favorite essay topics ranged from "The Educational Status of Ireland in the Fifth Century" to "The Life of St. Columbkille." While this brand of history may have filled deep psychological needs, it offered no insight into the Irish-American experience. Instead of gaining an appreciation for the sacrifices and accomplishments of the Irish in urban America, children learned how their ancestors kept the Catholic faith alive during the Penal times. In scenes reminiscent of *Studs Lonigan,* thousands of Chicago Catholic children received two diplomas on graduation night, but Irish history awards meant little to these second-and third-generation Irish who regarded themselves as fully American.

By 1920, a large segment of the Chicago Irish population had repudiated an ethnic identity in favor of a strictly Catholic identity. The Knights of Columbus, the fastest-growing Irish-American organization in Chicago after 1900, is a case in point.[57] Although there were many similarities between the Knights of Columbus and the

Mary F. McWhorter (standing) at a luncheon welcoming Irish Consul General Garth Healy to Chicago in 1942. On behalf of the Ladies' Auxiliary of the Ancient Order of Hibernians, McWhorter spearheaded the campaign for Irish history in Chicago's parochial schools after the turn of the century.

—Courtesy of The New World

Knights of Columbanus in Ireland, Irish Catholics in the United States did not look to Ireland's past for a model on which to base a new fraternal organization. Instead they selected Christopher Columbus and the Knights of the Crusades.

Between 1896 and 1918, forty-nine councils of the Knights of Columbus were established throughout Chicago, representing a membership of 25,323. While a few councils selected Irish names, the overwhelming majority preferred Catholic titles, parish names, or neighborhood designations. The KCs drew their strength from second- and third-generation Irish men who were anxious to prove just how Catholic and American they had become. The "Caseys," as they were known, pledged to support the U.S. Constitution, preserve the integrity of the ballot, promote reverence and respect for law and order, and practice their religion "openly and consistently, but without ostentation."

Of all the social, athletic, and charitable endeavors supported by the KCs, none equaled their contribution to the war effort. As had happened during the Civil War and the Spanish American War, Chicago's Irish viewed their participation in World War I as proof of their patriotism. Fully 25 percent of Chicago's KCs served in the armed forces, with a high proportion of enlistments. Chicago became the headquarters of the Knights' war activities and council members vigorously supported the Liberty Loan campaigns as investors and speakers. The KCs financed the construction of recreation centers in military training camps in America and Europe that were open to all soldiers, irrespective of creed, and they paid the salaries and expenses of Catholic chaplains, among them fifty-seven priests from the Archdiocese of Chicago.

Welfare work undertaken in World War I by the Knights of Columbus compared favorably with that of established organizations such as the Young Men's Christian Association. On a local level, virtually all councils experienced an increase in membership after 1917. The University Council, for example, held the record for the highest percentage of servicemen for any Chicago unit. Formed only in 1913, this council was caught up in the patriotic energy of World War I. Therefore, 252 of its 412 members participated in the conflict. By 1921, the University Council claimed 1,311 members. Like many other KC groups, it was affiliated with a parish—St. Ignatius in Rogers Park. It also maintained ties with nearby Loyola Academy and Loyola University. As had happened during the heyday of the nationalist movement, Chicago Irish pastors were quick to recognize the Knights as an important part of parochial life. The University Council, for instance, raised $1,000 toward the construction of a new grammar school in St. Ignatius's parish, where the number of Catholic students had doubled between 1912 and 1921.

The "steam-heat" Irish

Although Catholic schools and new Catholic organizations did little to reinforce ethnic identity, Irish parishes in Chicago did not disappear for a variety of reasons. One was Irish mobility. Unlike their German, Polish, Bohemian, and Italian coreligionists, the Irish formed few ethnic enclaves in Chicago. By the 1890s, the Irish were moving out of quasi-industrial neighborhoods such as Pilsen, Back of the Yards, and the Rolling Mill district to residential neighborhoods in outlying areas. In sharp contrast to Germans, Poles, and Lithuanians who purchased homes and businesses in the city's older neighborhoods, the Irish remained by and large renters. In 1906, for example, *The New World* apologized to its readers (75 percent of whom were Irish) for calling attention to a serious social phenomenon, namely that the Irish spurned home ownership: "They who of all others are famed for their beautiful home life are—many of them—content to live in flats, to move every May or October day, to be ever on the wing like stormy petrels."[58]

Of all immigrant groups in Chicago at the turn of the century, the Irish were the most widely dispersed. Paul Cressey has calculated that between 1898 and 1930 Irish immigrants left initial areas of concentration such as Back of the Yards for "more desirable residential districts farther from the center of the city."[59] By 1930, the median distribution for foreign-born Irish was 6.4 miles from the Loop, nearly the same as for persons of native-white parentage. Such a pattern of dispersal, Cressey argued, reflected "the more complete disintegration of their group life and a greater degree of cultural assimilation."[60]

Yet for all their mobility, the Chicago Irish were still a parochial people. While they readily moved into steam-heat flats and bungalows, they did not abandon the concept of city life as parish-centered. One need look no further than the novels of James T. Farrell for confirmation that the parish continued to be the center of neighborhood life for the steam-heat Irish well into the 1930s.

Archbishop James E. Quigley, who headed the Chicago diocese from 1903 to 1915, ensured that the city's Irish would continue to find parish-centered communities wherever they moved. He believed that "a parish should be of such a size that the pastor can know personally every man, woman, and child in it."[61] Quigley advocated the one-square-mile parish and beginning in 1904 he divided older English-speaking parishes to form new parishes that were smaller in terms of both territory and population. After consulting with local pastors, the archbishop set boundaries that would "assure a prosperous parochial community from the start."[62] As a result, each new territorial parish began with approximately three hundred families, enough to support a church and school.

In conjunction with his policy of dividing older English-speaking parishes, Quigley endorsed the concept of the combination building that contained both church and school quarters. He urged pastors to delay the construction of a permanent place of worship until the parochial school was firmly established. Although most English-speaking parishes eventually did construct separate church buildings, in the early years parish revenues were used to open grammar schools that were on a par with local public schools. While Archbishop George W. Mundelein agreed with Quigley's philosophy of parish formation, he was even more insistent that pastors provide modern school quarters before building massive churches. In addition,

Mundelein broke with tradition by refusing to form national parishes outside ethnic enclaves, in effect legitimizing the Irish-American model of parish over all others.

Quigley's and Mundelein's policies regarding parish formation met with wide acceptance among the Chicago Irish who were moving out of older congested neighborhoods. In many new apartment districts and bungalow belts, English-speaking parishes were present almost from the beginning and they provided structure for emerging middle-class Catholic communities. While a number of the sixty-three English-speaking parishes organized in Chicago between 1903 and 1939 were ethnically mixed, most still bore the unmistakable Irish imprint.

Although the relatively early dispersal of the Irish into new residential neighborhoods played a significant role in the persistence of predominantly Irish parishes, equally important was the role of the clergy. While the closing of the original St. Mary of the Lake Seminary in 1868 had slowed down the formation of an American-trained clergy, still vocations from Irish parishes in Chicago accounted for a sizeable increase in the number of English-speaking priests. Their ranks were also swelled by foreign-born Irish priests who came to Chicago at the request of Archbishop Feehan.

The Crowley Schism

Irish-born and Irish-trained priests had done much to expand the network of English-speaking parishes in Chicago during the 1880s and 1890s. In addition to serving as pastors of large territorial parishes, several foreign-born Irish priests held key positions in Feehan's administration. But the archbishop did not neglect native-born priests in favor of his own countrymen. After 1887, for example, he selected as chancellor only American-born priests of Irish descent.

Feehan's reliance on Irish-American clergymen rankled foreign-born Irish priests who felt their influence diminishing. In 1900, Rev. Thomas P. Hodnett, pastor of the prosperous West Side parish of St. Malachy's, and Rev.

Thomas Cashman, of nearby St. Jarlath's, joined forces with a country pastor, Rev. Jeremiah Crowley, to thwart the appointment of Rev. Peter J. Muldoon as auxiliary bishop. When Muldoon finally broke his silence about the controversy surrounding his appointment he declared: "The cause of the schism is that I am an American. It is the old story of the Irish priests against the American."[63] As Charles Shanabruch has detailed, the Crowley schism was a deep embarrassment to Chicago Catholics as well as to the American hierarchy.[64]

Unlike the Duggan controversy thirty-five years earlier, which centered on priests' rights and due process, the Crowley affair was basically an interclerical dispute pitting older foreign-born Irish priests against younger American-born clergymen. In a larger sense, however, it mirrored the tensions that existed within the Irish community between "greenhorns" and "narrowbacks." Although Archbishop Quigley and his successors accepted no more diocesan clergymen from Ireland into the Chicago archdiocese, they had little choice but to promote Irish-born priests to pastorates as they came of age. The result was that immigrant Irish priests continued to wield influence in Chicago parishes well into the 1950s.

In terms of structure, the English-speaking parishes formed in Chicago between 1880 and 1920 remained essentially unchanged. In contrast to German and Polish national parishes that aimed at institutional completeness, the parishes of the Irish were scaled-down parochial communities. Far from supporting a wide range of social, ethnic, cultural, and athletic activities, Irish parishes were church and school centered. By the 1920s, however, there were signs that this concept of parochial life was changing. The South Side parish of Visitation is a case in point.

Parish and Neighborhood: The Visitation Story

At the time this parish was organized in 1886, it embraced a fairly large district immediately south of the Union Stock Yard where Irish immigrants and their children found ready employment. Between 1890 and 1910 the construction of multifamily apartments along tree-lined Garfield Boulevard made the area attractive to upwardly mobile Irish Catholics, and for many Visitation became a stopping-off place on the trek from Bridgeport and Canaryville to South Shore and Beverly.

In the early days of the parish, the pastor and congregation concentrated on establishing a grammar school and building a Gothic church that dominated the boulevard at Peoria Street. By 1911, Visitation was a flourishing parish with an annual grade school enrollment of more than thirteen hundred students. And the opening of a $150,000 high school in 1915 put it in the forefront of the Catholic secondary school movement. Although the formation of new English-speaking parishes reduced Visitation's boundaries to less than one square mile by 1916, the end result was an intensification of parish identity. Moreover, the organization of the Polish parish of St. John of God at Fifty-second and Throop Street virtually guaranteed that Visitation would remain Irish.

The turning point in this parish occurred in 1924 with the arrival of Rev. T. E. O'Shea as pastor. O'Shea was a new breed of Irish priest: born in Chicago and raised in a working-class

neighborhood. He understood the aspirations of Irish parents for their children, and he was especially sensitive to the needs of the working-class youngsters who increasingly filled the parish school.

The most pressing need O'Shea addressed was that for recreation. Although the apartment buildings in Visitation parish offered a middle-class standard of living, unlike bungalow belts to the south there were few places where young children could play. In 1925, the pastor organized a parish social center with an ambitious sports program that became a model for the Catholic Youth Organization, formed five years later.[65] In 1926, O'Shea and his associate, Rev. Thomas Tormey, established a summer camp in Palos Hills that provided hundreds of working-class children with their first taste of country life. Visitation social center, with its organized activities and sports teams, did much to lessen the attraction of youth gangs, but even more important it represented a parochial solution to an urban problem.

O'Shea's concept of parish was dynamic and his focus on the needs of children made Visitation in the 1920s one of the most progressive parishes in the Chicago archdiocese. His efforts at forging links between parish and neighborhood were so successful that Irish Catholics who lived around Fifty-fifth and Halsted referred to the area as "Vis." Indeed, for more than two generations, this part of the Englewood neighborhood continued to be known by the parish name. But O'Shea's successor charted a different course and during his tenure Visitation became a bulwark against racial change.

Rev. Msgr. Daniel F. Byrnes, who headed Visitation from 1932 to 1952, was the last of a dying breed: an Irish-born and Irish-trained priest who had been incardinated into the Chicago diocese by Archbishop Feehan. Byrnes's policies were geared toward enhancing the role of Visitation as the center of neighborhood life. In addition to financing the construction of a new social center, he established the annual May crowning as the neighborhood's largest social event, involving virtually all of the four thousand families in the parish. Yet in the area of race relations Byrnes was unable or unwilling to provide leadership. In contrast to younger American-born priests of Irish descent who believed

that parishes could do much to prepare neighborhoods for peaceful integration, Byrnes's response to racial change was largely negative. As the black population of Englewood increased after World War II, the Irish pastor reminded his congregation that they lived in the "largest and greatest parish in the diocese" and at Sunday Mass he periodically read the parish boundaries.[66] His message was clear: if Irish families remained in the neighborhood, Visitation would continue to flourish.

Msgr. Byrnes's attitudes about black immigration were shared by the bulk of his parishioners, and as a result Visitation gained a reputation as "one of the most dangerous spots in the city insofar as race relations were concerned."[67] While a number of Catholic parishes did develop siege mentalities when faced with ethnic or racial change, on the whole the Irish Catholic reaction was passive. Only a small number of the Chicago Irish

The annual May Crowning on Garfield Boulevard in Visitation parish, 1947, was a remarkable display of Irish Catholic strength, involving upwards of two thousand children. Begun on Mother's Day, 1939, the celebration reinforced the strong links between parish and neighborhood.

—*Photo by* The New World, *courtesy of the Archives of the Archdiocese of Chicago*

took to the streets to defend their neighborhoods in the wake of racial succession. Like the Lonigans in James T. Farrell's trilogy, most Irish-American families reacted to black immigration by moving to other neighborhoods, even when it meant leaving behind massive parish complexes that were newly built or completely paid off. Indeed, Farrell's account of the Irish exodus from St. Patrick's (Anselm's) parish at Sixty-first and Michigan Avenue in the 1920s was still descriptive of many South and West Side parishes in the 1960s and 1970s.

Arnold Hirsch has estimated that between 1940 and 1960 more than four hundred thousand whites left Chicago.[68] Yet during the same period there was a massive movement of Catholics within the city limits, from racially changing areas such as Englewood and East Garfield Park to neighborhoods at Chicago's edge. While Irish-Americans moved to the suburbs in large numbers in the post–World War II era, a significant proportion remained in the city. Although the residency requirement for municipal workers accounted for much of this stability, the role of the Catholic Church cannot be underestimated. The existence of parishes at the city's outer fringes, coupled with a well-established system of elementary and secondary schools, ensured continuity of Catholic neighborhood life.

As early as 1915, *The New World* had admonished its readers "to sink local differences and racial antagonisms in the effort to view the Catholic Church in her entirety."[69] The newspaper also reminded its largely Irish audience that parochial boundaries were imaginary lines drawn for the sake of better ecclesiastical administration. But to no avail. Not only did the Chicago Irish continue to perceive the Church in strictly parish terms, but their concept of the city was increasingly narrow. Ironically, Catholic secondary schools, which accelerated the integration of the Irish into the middle class, played a crucial role in deepening sectional loyalties.

Although a few Catholic high schools such as St. Ignatius, St. Mary's, and Immaculata attracted students from parishes throughout Chicago, most served a distinct section of the city. Leo High School, operated by the Irish

Christian Brothers at Seventy-ninth and Peoria Street, for example, drew young men from bungalow belt parishes that developed on Chicago's South Side after World War I. Although Leo technically was a central high school, in fact it was an extension of the Irish-American parish network that had blossomed in the area bounded by Fifty-fifth Street, Ninety-fifth Street, Ashland Avenue, and Halsted Street. Not only did its students share similar ethnic and economic backgrounds but they came from the same geographical area. The result was that even as Leo students prepared for careers that would take them downtown and into the city at large, they retained an identity as South Side Catholics.

The situation was much the same for Irish-Americans who lived on the city's North and West sides. Although Catholic secondary schools organized after World War II were more diverse in terms of ethnic makeup, their very location at the edges of the city strengthened rather than weakened sectional loyalties. As far as the Irish were concerned, sectional and parish loyalties took precedence over strictly ethnic ties. As late as the 1960s, second- and third-generation Irish Catholics were far more conscious of belonging to a particular parish in a particular neighborhood than they were of their nationality.

To the generation of Chicago Catholics who came of age in the 1960s, parishes were a familiar part of neighborhood life, and they provided stability in a city that was experiencing profound ethnic and racial changes. Like the Lonigans of an earlier era, thousands of Chicago's Irish Catholics believed that the Church would halt the resegregation of their neighborhoods. On the South and West sides of the city, progressive Irish-American priests and congregations worked with community groups to prepare their neighborhoods for racial integration. St. Philip Neri parish was a driving force behind the South Shore Commission, formed in 1953, and St. Sabina's was the headquarters of the Organization of the Southwest Community, a federation of seventy-five civic, religious, and fraternal groups established in 1959. On the West Side, St. Thomas Aquinas and Resurrection supported the Organization for a Better Austin in its campaign against slum landlords, abandoned buildings, panic peddling, and "redlining," the denial of conventional mortgages by banks to families in integrated areas.

Try as they might, parish groups were powerless to solve the economic problems associated with racially changing neighborhoods. Indeed, progressive Irish-American parishes were no more able to achieve racial stability than conservative parishes that attempted to keep blacks out of their neighborhoods altogether. The end result was a massive movement of middle-class white families from Chicago's bungalow belts and lakefront neighborhoods.

Constructed between 1910 and 1924, the parish complex of St. Thomas Aquinas on Washington Boulevard near Laramie Avenue assured the continuity of Catholic neighborhood life for Irish families who moved into steam-heat "flats" in the Austin district. In the 1960s and 1970s, St. Thomas Aquinas parish waged a spirited campaign against unscrupulous real estate dealers who engaged in blockbusting tactics designed to accelerate racial change.

—Author's collection

The Irish Parish Model

Irish-American families who left Chicago in the 1960s and 1970s swelled the Catholic population of such suburbs as Wilmette, River Forest, La Grange, Mount Prospect, Arlington Heights, Oak Lawn, and Orland Park. As Andrew Greeley has observed, many Irish Catholics who moved to the suburbs built "parish neighborhoods."[70] Oak Lawn, for example, with its five Catholic parishes, is in many ways simply an extension of Chicago's South Side neighborhoods. Although the existence of a Catholic parish eased the transition from city to suburbs for many families, others regarded suburban parishes as different from the cohesive communities they left behind. Moveover, the lack of parochial schools in new suburban areas meant that Catholics had no alternatives but

Altar boys at Holy Family Church, 1962. Chicago's largest Irish parish in the nineteenth century, Holy Family served wave after wave of immigrants on the Near West Side. Although ethnic and racial tensions in the surrounding neighborhood were often difficult, Irish, Italian, African-American, and Mexican parishioners each claimed the church as their own.

—Archives, Holy Family Parish

to send their children to local public schools, thus accelerating the process of structural assimilation.[71]

Demographic studies indicate that the future growth of the Archdiocese of Chicago will occur outside the city proper, in suburban Cook and Lake counties. For Irish-Americans who choose to remain in Chicago, parishes provide continuity and structure in an increasingly black and Hispanic city. Although parochial schools on the city's far Northwest and Southwest Sides no longer enroll as many students as they did in the 1950s and 1960s, they persist as important components of Catholic ethnic neighborhood life. And in older city neighborhoods that once were Catholic strongholds, parochial schools now serve minority populations. In 1982, for example, black and Hispanic students accounted for 40 percent of the city's Catholic school enrollment.[72]

But the dissolution of Chicago's Irish-American parishes does not necessarily mean the death knell for Irish identity. Lawrence J.

St. Benedict the African Church, dedicated in 1990, represents the merger of eight Catholic parishes in the Englewood neighborhood. Built on the site of the original St. Bernard Church—which was razed in 1967—St. Benedict's marks a new beginning for the African-American Catholic community in Englewood. The modern structure, with its twenty-four foot immersion baptismal font, incorporates bells from the old German Gothic church of St. Martin at Fifty-nineth Street and Princeton Avenue.

—Courtesy of St. Benedict the African parish

McCaffrey has argued persuasively that residents of urban Irish neighborhoods were religiously and emotionally—but not culturally—Irish.[73] He contends that the vast majority of the American Irish have been severed from their historical roots by Catholic education. Not only did Irish-American Catholic educators ignore the Irish dimension of their heritage but they emphasized a Catholic culture that was devoid of ethnic identity. As the Chicago experience makes clear, the English-speaking parish system pioneered by the Irish did little to reinforce ethnic identity, Irish or otherwise.

Still, it comes as a surprise that the resurgence of interest in Irish identity places such little emphasis on Catholicism. Considering that the vast majority of Irish communities in urban America were parish-based, it is nothing short of remarkable that Irish identity has so quickly shed most of its Catholic moorings. Indeed, the generation of Irish-American Catholics who came of age in the 1960s led the way in embracing an ethnicity that has little connection with the Catholic Church and its urban working-class past.[74] Whereas the old identity was almost wholly Catholic-centered, the new one seeks its roots in Irish history, literature, music, and art. While the rekindling of Irish identity is a cause for celebration, the new version may prove to be as narrow and brief as the old.

Of all the forces that shaped the Irish community in Chicago, the Catholic Church exerted the most powerful influence. And the Irish in turn put their unmistakable imprint on it. Unlike other European immigrants who sought to recreate Old World peasant parish structures, the Irish in Chicago formed parishes and schools that met their special needs as American Catholics. Far from limiting mobility or assimilation, the parochial institutions created by the Irish hastened their integration into the larger society. Although Chicago's Irish-American parishes have all but disappeared, their parish model continues today, providing structure for emerging black and Hispanic Catholic communities.

3

Cardinal Mundelein of Chicago and the Shaping of Twentieth-Century American Catholicism

by Edward R. Kantowicz

George William Cardinal Mundelein. This portrait, taken around 1924 by Mundelein's personal photographer, was reputedly the cardinal's favorite.

—Photo by John Laveccha, courtesy of the Archives of the Archdiocese of Chicago

The interior of the Feehan Library is modeled on the Barberini Palace in Rome.
—Photo by The New World, *courtesy of the Archives of the Archdiocese of Chicago*

When George Cardinal Mundelein of Chicago built his massive major seminary of St. Mary of the Lake in the 1920s, he designed its facades on early American, neoclassic lines, but he molded the seminary rules from Roman models. The exterior of the seminary library resembled Thomas Jefferson's University of Virginia, but the interior was an exact replica of the Barberini Palace in Rome. American on the outside, but Roman to the core—this had been the goal of the American Catholic Church from the days of John Carroll's conse-

cration as first bishop in 1789. The leaders of the Catholic minority tried to forge a community that was different in values from the American norm, but not too foreign, a community separate but equal.[1]

Remaining separate was not difficult for a church composed largely of immigrants. Builder bishops and brick-and-mortar priests raised enough churches and parochial schools in the nineteenth century to ensure a separate institutional base for Catholics. Doctrinal intransigence and puritanical morals also kept Catholics distinctive in a Protestant but increasingly secular nation. Yet until well into the twentieth century, American Catholics did not feel equal to other Americans or even to other Catholics elsewhere in the world.

Though the Catholic community was the largest American religious denomination as early as 1850, it lacked status and respect, both in Rome and in America. Rome considered the United States a mission territory as late as 1908, and in its mediation of various Church disputes in the nineteenth century, the Roman Congregation of the Propaganda, which administered the Church in mission lands, consistently misunderstood events in America. American Protestants, for their part, feared and mistrusted the Catholic Church as an un-American invader of the Republic.[2]

Just before the turn of the century, a number of "Americanist" bishops, notably John Ireland and James Cardinal Gibbons, attempted to upgrade the American Catholic image. They labored to explain American conditions to the cardinals of the Propaganda, and they established connections with political leaders in Washington, all the while trumpeting in sermons the Church's compatibility with American ideals. But in 1899 Pope Leo XIII condemned a vague set of doctrines that he called "Americanism." Though no individual was directly censured, American Catholic leaders felt confused and dispirited, and American Protestants believed that their misgivings about the Church had been confirmed. American Catholics remained too Roman for the native Protestants and too American for Rome.[3] It fell, then, to the leaders of twentieth-century American Catholicism to make the separate Catholic community feel equal, fully Catholic, and fully American.

In the years surrounding World War I, a generation of American-born but Roman-

trained bishops came to power in the largest urban dioceses of the United States. These men—such as Cardinal Mundelein in Chicago, William Cardinal O'Connell in Boston, Denis Cardinal Dougherty in Philadelphia, John Cardinal Glennon in St. Louis, and, at a somewhat later date, Francis Cardinal Spellman in New York—were "consolidating bishops" who, like their counterparts in American business and government, saw the need for more order and efficiency in their bailiwicks.[4] Despite its hierarchical structure and theological dogmatism, the Catholic Church in the United States

The exterior of the Feehan Memorial Library at St. Mary of the Lake Seminary shows an early American, neoclassic facade.

—*Photo by* The New World, *courtesy of the Archives of the Archdiocese of Chicago*

had been decentralized and disorganized. The consolidating bishops of the first half of the twentieth century centralized and tightened the administrative structure of the Church in the largest dioceses and tied American Catholicism more closely to headquarters in Rome. They also gained new respect for the American Catholic Church, both in Rome, where their financial support became the mainstay of the "prisoner in the Vatican," and in the United States, where their business ability and political influence bolstered the self-image of their American subcommunity.[5]

To become fully American, yet remain distinctive, required confidence and a sense of security. The American Catholic Church, with its dual nature, had always presented a paradox in this respect. Supremely confident ideologically, the Church knew that it was right and everyone else was wrong. Yet, as a Church of immigrant outsiders, it showed an acute lack of confidence socially. The goal of Cardinal Mundelein and his colleagues was to overcome this lack of social confidence and, in the homely expression of many Church leaders, to "put the Church on the map." By their actions, the consolidating bishops gave the American Catholic Church self-confidence and clout at home and at the Vatican.[6]

Mundelein can serve as a case study of these episcopal leaders who shaped the twentieth-century Catholic experience in America.[7] His life reads like an American success story. Born in 1872 and raised in the oldest German parish in New York City, he turned down a bid to the Naval Academy in 1889 and entered instead upon priestly studies for the Brooklyn diocese. Ordained in 1895, he became chancellor of the diocese two years later, a monsignor at age thirty-four, and an auxiliary bishop at thirty-seven. In 1915, when Rome appointed him to head the Chicago archdiocese, one of the three largest in the country, he became the youngest archbishop in America. Mundelein administered the Catholic Church in Chicago from 1916 until his death in 1939, becoming a cardinal in 1924. Clergy and laypeople alike esteemed him primarily for his business acumen. One of his secular admirers flattered him: "There was a great mistake in making you a Bishop instead of a financier, for in the latter case Mr. Morgan would not be without a rival in Wall Street."[8]

Yet he was also a thoroughgoing Romanist. He studied theology in Rome for four years at the Urban College of the Propaganda and was ordained in the Eternal City. He wrote a treatise defending Pope Pius X's condemnation of Modernism, earning admission to one of the ancient Roman scholarly academies. As archbishop of Chicago he carefully organized and promoted the annual Peter's Pence collection for the support of the pope, regularly producing more revenue for this cause than any other diocese in the world.

Though a striking individual, Mundelein shared many characteristics with his episcopal contemporaries in the heavily Catholic cities of the Northeast and the Midwest. In 1920, eleven of the twelve bishops in the dozen largest dioceses of the United States were American-born, and seven of the twelve had received a significant portion of their seminary training in Rome. Counting only the six largest sees, five of the six bishops were Roman-trained. Mundelein was younger than his colleagues, and he was not Irish, as all of the others in the largest dioceses were, but his tenure of twenty-three years in Chicago came close to the average of twenty-five-and-one-half years for all twelve bishops. These bishops, then, were American-born, Irish (except for Mundelein), Roman-trained, and long-tenured as leaders of the most Catholic cities in America. Their twelve dioceses (all except New Orleans were in the northeast quarter of the United States) contained 46 percent of the nation's Catholics.[9]

The leaders of big-city Catholicism set the tone for the American church. In rural areas and in large parts of the South and West (what Catholics called "no-priest land"), Catholics remained either invisible or apologetic, but in the large cities of the Northeast and Midwest, Catholic leaders visibly threw their weight around in an attempt to instill self-confidence in their flocks. The activities of big city bishops to gain prestige and raise Catholic self-esteem can be considered under five headings: giantism, "going first class," businesslike administration, Americanism, and advising presidents and politicos.

Giantism

Like any insecure class of outsiders, the Catholic bishops began with the assumption that bigger is better. Building on a massive scale proclaimed Catholic importance. This impulse had been present in the American Church for a long time, as St. Patrick's Cathedral, built on Fifth Avenue in New York in the nineteenth century, illustrates. In the twentieth century, both the National Shrine of the Immaculate Conception in Washington, D.C., and Cardinal Glennon's new cathedral in St. Louis were designed in the eclectic style that can best be described as Babbitt Byzantine or simply Catholic Big. In Chicago, Mundelein showed better architectural taste; he attempted to restrain individual pastors who wanted to memorialize themselves with massive piles of masonry.[10] Yet he was not immune to the virus of giantism. An instinctive adherent to the Chicago philosophy of Daniel

Quigley Preparatory Seminary was Cardinal Mundelein's first building project in Chicago.
—*Photo by* The New World, *courtesy of the Archives of the Archdiocese of Chicago*

Burnham—"Make no little plans"—Mundelein showed his giantism most clearly in the building of Chicago's seminaries.

The archdiocese of Chicago, despite its size, had no major seminary for training diocesan priests when Mundelein arrived in 1916. Even the high school minor seminary, begun by his predecessor Archbishop James Quigley, was still crowded into temporary quarters. Three months after assuming his post in Chicago, Mundelein announced that he would build a large Gothic structure to house the minor seminary and dedicate it as a memorial to his predecessor. When the new Quigley Preparatory Seminary opened its doors two years later, Mundelein could not resist boasting: "This will unquestionably be the most beautiful building here in Chicago, not excluding the various buildings of the University of Chicago."[11]

Though pleased with Quigley Seminary, Mundelein viewed it essentially as a completion of his predecessor's work. He planned his own monument, the major seminary of St. Mary of the Lake, on a grander scale. In 1918 the archdiocese purchased a faltering correspondence school along with several hundred acres of land surrounding a swampy lake about forty miles northwest of the city center. Over the next few years, additional purchases of small parcels in the area rounded out the property at 950 acres. Mundelein was planning for more than a seminary. He envisioned a Catholic University of the West to rival and perhaps surpass the struggling Catholic institution in Washington, D.C. The country property he had bought would house the divinity school and a central administration for the university. Individual religious orders, such as the Jesuits and the Dominicans, would be invited to locate their own houses of divinity studies around St. Mary's Lake, making this institution the most high-powered theological center outside of Rome. The secular subjects would be taught at the preexisting Catholic colleges of Loyola and DePaul in the city, but all would be combined and coordinated under the one umbrella of the University and Seminary of St. Mary of the Lake.[12]

St. Mary of the Lake Seminary, Mundelein, Illinois, planned originally as a full-scale Catholic university, turned out to be the most lavish major seminary in the country.
—*Photo by* The New World, *courtesy of the Archives of the Archdiocese of Chicago*

Mundelein himself recognized the audacity of this project. He wrote privately, before any plans had been announced: "It will take millions to complete it, and I doubt whether I will live long enough to do it, though I will plan it and perhaps begin it."[13] He was able to begin in 1920 when Edward Hines, founder of a large lumber company in Chicago, donated $500,000 toward the divinity wing of the university in honor of his son who had died in France during the war.

This donation was not completely unexpected, nor, for that matter, gratis. A few months previously, Mundelein had done Hines a favor when his first attempt to erect a monument to his son had turned into a nightmare. Hines had built a large hospital building on the grounds of an old speedway that he owned, intending to sell it at cost to the government for the care of war wounded. However, amid charges of graft and profiteering,

Congress held up appropriations for the purchase of Speedway Hospital for nearly a year and a half. Though the government finally took over the hospital on March 13, 1920, and no wrongdoing was ever proven on the part of Hines or anyone else, the unfavorable publicity had induced the directors of the Continental Bank, Chicago's largest banking institution, to drop Hines from his position on their board. Mundelein intervened, using his personal influence to have Hines retained on the bank board. After first satisfying himself by inquiries in Washington that Hines was blameless in the Speedway Hospital affair, Mundelein wrote directly and candidly to J. Ogden Armour, one of the principal directors of the bank: "I have reason to expect that Mr. Hines will be very liberal in support of some of my undertakings . . . and I will confess that independent of the merits of the case, I shall consider as a personal favor to me whatever assistance you can lend."[14]

Armed with the $500,000 donation, Mundelein announced his plans at the end of April 1920, giving Hines full publicity for his generosity. Blueprints had been prepared previously by a young Catholic architect, Joseph W. McCarthy, who had apprenticed in the firm of Burnham and attracted the bishop's attention with some church-building he had done in Chicago. The plans envisioned nine major buildings for the divinity school aligned along the arms of a Latin cross, with the main chapel, a monumental plaza, and a ceremonial dock and boathouse forming the upright of the cross. A large mausoleum for Edward Hines, Jr., was included in the plans. All the buildings were to be in red brick, early-American, neoclassic design, with the main chapel an enlarged copy of a Congregational meetinghouse in Old Lyme, Connecticut. Mundelein had, on a previous occasion, pro-claimed his fondness for this architectural style, calling it "symbolical of the twin devotions of your heart, love of God and love of country."[15]

The university portion of Mundelein's scheme quickly fell through. The individual religious orders were not eager to merge their independent institutions or to relocate their houses of divinity. The Catholic University in Washington, D.C., viewed the Chicago plan as a direct threat and lobbied against it in Rome. But Mundelein pushed ahead with his seminary, which opened in the fall of 1921 with the first buildings still incomplete. Substantially finished by 1926, when the first class was ordained, St. Mary of the Lake Seminary was finally completed with the dedication of its auditorium in 1934. By considerable arm-twisting at the Vatican, Cardinal Mundelein obtained from Rome the status of

First Congregational Church of Old Lyme, Connecticut, Cardinal Mundelein's model for the main chapel at St. Mary of the Lake Seminary.
—*Photo by* The New World, *courtesy of the Archives of the Archdiocese of Chicago*

The main chapel, St. Mary of the Lake Seminary.
—*Photo by* The New World, *courtesy of the Archives of the Archdiocese of Chicago*

pontifical university for St. Mary of the Lake in 1929, an honor that permitted the conferring of doctoral degrees in theology.[16]

Though Mundelein's dream for St. Mary of the Lake was not completely fulfilled, the seminary and its extensive campus gave him a showcase. Visiting cardinals or other dignitaries were inevitably driven the forty miles out into the country for a grand tour or, in the early days, a cornerstone laying. Lake County, where the seminary was located, was heavily Protestant, and the archdiocese even had to fight off a local court challenge to St. Mary's tax-exempt status. Nevertheless, the citizens of the nearby town of Area, like good boosters everywhere, recognized the importance of their institutional neighbor. In 1925 they voted to rename their town Mundelein. Local real estate developers advertised that their tracts stood near an "Athens of America."[17]

The secluded acres of Mundelein, Illinois, formed a backdrop for the most spectacular example of giantism during the cardinal's regime, the Twenty-eighth International Eucharistic Congress of 1926. First held in France in 1881, the biannual Eucharistic Congress had become a massive pilgrimage of priests, prelates, and laypeople. This devotional gathering had come to the New World only once, to Montreal in 1910, and never to the United States. Since the gathering always climaxed with a street procession, fear of anti-Catholic demonstrations usually kept the congress out of Protestant lands. At the congress in London in 1908, the British government banned the procession altogether. But Mundelein's thou-

sand-acre seminary provided a solution to this problem. Though most of the events of the 1926 congress were conducted in Chicago churches or in the lakefront Soldier Field, some eight hundred thousand pilgrims went by auto or by interurban rail to St. Mary of the Lake for the final day's procession. Such a massive demonstration was hardly private, but since it took place on private property, no one could protest. The Chicago Catholic weekly newspaper, *The New World,* cautioned its readers: "Let there be no mistaking the fact that the Eucharistic Congress is no endeavor to demonstrate strength. There is no thought behind it of a flaunting of vast numbers before non-Catholics. . . . It is distinctly a religious manifestation."[18]

Nevertheless, a "flaunting of vast numbers before non-Catholics" is precisely what the Eucharistic Congress was, a once-in-a-lifetime media event for the Catholic church in Chicago. And it was sucesssful in those terms. Protestant ministers in the Bible Belt may have been scandalized by this Romish display; one New York Methodist clergyman remarked that "the pomp of services, the exaltation of ecclesiastics may remove the thoughts of men from the humble Nazarene." But in Chicago boosterism and civic pride overcame any non-Catholic fears. The *Chicago Tribune*'s welcoming editorial summed up the local attitude: "Chicago was chosen for the congress partly because the city is centrally located. . . but even more because the city is typically American. The tribute to the city is one which Chicagoans have not been slow to appreciate."[19]

Going First Class

Giantism and a flaunting of numbers were basic parts of the Church's drive for status in the twentieth century. A more subtle form of the same impulse could be described as "going first class" whenever possible. Mundelein's seminary again illustrates the point. At a time when nearly all Catholic seminaries comprised a single building with spartan dormitory accommodations for the students, St. Mary's was a sprawling, multibuilding complex. Each seminarian had a private room and bath, a luxury

that scandalized many older priests and one that many of the immigrant-bred students certainly did not enjoy at home. Eighty acres of the grounds were laid out as a golf course for the seminarians and for the priests of the archdiocese. On major holidays, the cardinal tried to devise unique surprises for the seminarians. He once flew in fresh lobsters for the entire student body, but most of the Midwestern boys had never seen such a strange meal before and returned it to the kitchen untouched.[20]

"Going first class" was the rule in other areas besides seminary training. The legal work of the archdiocese had traditionally been handled on an ad hoc basis by individual Irish Catholic lawyers and partnerships. In 1923, when the county court of Lake County struck down the tax exemption for a major part of the seminary property, Mundelein feared that the small law firm handling the case might be inadequate to secure a reversal on appeal. One of his closest lay advisers, a State Street clothing store executive, suggested that the law firm of Patterson, Kirkland, McCormick, and Fleming be called in. The McCormick was *Chicago Tribune* publisher, Colonel Robert R. McCormick, who founded the firm in 1908. Since then the firm had become Chicago's most prestigious, handling the *Tribune*'s business and many other major accounts. After senior partner Perry Patterson successfully completed the appeal of the seminary tax case, he proposed to Mundelein that the archdiocese abandon ad hoc arrangements and retain his firm on a yearly basis for all legal work. Mundelein readily agreed, writing Patterson: "I have followed your good advice and have placed Patterson, Kirkland, McCormick, and Fleming under contract to act as the watchdogs of my treasury and the defenders of my rights, always on the principle of the Fathers of our Republic, 'millions for defense but not a penny for tribute.'"[21]

The imperial tone in Mundelein's response to Patterson was thoroughly in character. As a cardinal prince of the Church, Mundelein affected the style of a Renaissance prince in public. He clearly loved ceremony both for its own sake and for the reflected glory it shone on his Church. He was an inveterate collector of old manuscripts, famous autographs, rare stamps and coins, and a connoisseur of old wines. He bought large numbers of paintings—not Old Masters, which were too costly, but large canvases "from the school of" Rubens, Titian, or some other well-known painter—to line the walls of the seminary buildings. In 1930, McCarthy, by then Mundelein's personal architect, completed a villa for the cardinal across the lake from the major seminary buildings. This house, a close copy of George Washington's Mount Vernon, became Mundelein's principal residence, even though the archdiocese already owned a handsome episcopal mansion in the city just off Lincoln Park.[22]

"Going first class" as a prince of the Church was a calculated risk for Mundelein. It could, and perhaps did, evoke Protestant fears of the Church's foreign and antirepublican connections. On the other hand, Americans love a show, and they frequently fawn over royalty with all its ceremony. Mundelein shrewdly gambled that a magnificent display of Catholic power and self-confidence would do more good than harm to the American Catholic image, and he carefully included American trappings, such as the Mount Vernon model for his villa, in the display.

The Business of America Is Business

In the 1920s, the "business of America was business," so going first class meant, above all, cultivating a businesslike image. The cardinal formed close friendships with the local financiers on La Salle Street, such as Walter Cummings and William Reynolds of the Continental Bank and Harold L. Stuart of the Halsey-Stuart brokerage firm, upon whom he often called for short-term loans. He also retained enough connections in New York circles so that he could occasionally do an end run around the local banks and obtain more favorable rates on Wall Street. Probably his most talked about business friendship was with the utilities magnate, Samuel Insull, but this relationship has been much exaggerated. The two had met through their broker, Stuart, and apparently admired each other's abilities; but they had few, if any, mutual business dealings. When Insull's utilities empire came crashing down in the early 1930s, Mundelein appeared as a character witness at the Insull mail fraud trial in November 1934. He was not testifying for Insull, however, but for one of the codefendants, Stuart, who was probably the cardinal's closest financial adviser.[23]

Mundelein's own reputation as a fund-raiser was well merited. During the 1920s, Chicago Catholics contributed annually, on the average, about $120,000 to Peter's Pence, over $200,000 to the work of the missions, and almost $750,000 for local Catholic charity work. The Chicago cardinal employed numerous publicity gimmicks in the course of fund-raising. One year he sponsored a contest among parishes for the greatest support of the missions, figured on a per capita basis, and rewarded the three winning parishes with sacred relics and church vessels blessed by the pope. When soliciting from business establishments, Mundelein employed what he called "the methods of our Jewish friends" by pointing out the advertising value of the diocese's lists of contributors.[24]

When persuasion and publicity failed, he resorted to obligatory assessments or taxes on each parish. Such assessments had been used in the past in emergency situations, but they became a regular part of diocesan finance under Mundelein. For example, in 1924 a quota was imposed on each parish to help defray the mounting costs of seminary construction. If a pastor could not raise the amount of his quota in a special collection, he had to make up the difference from ordinary parish revenues. One million dollars was raised in this particular levy; and despite the compulsory nature of the assessment, the money was presented to Mundelein publicly as a freewill offering in honor of his selection as a cardinal. The Eucharistic Congress was financed by a similar assessment.[25]

Mundelein was even more successful at administering money than at raising it. Church finance and administration had been exceedingly decentralized in American dioceses. Local pastors generally made the major decisions about building loans, contractors, architects, and insurance with only loose supervision by the board of consultors (a kind of senate made up of important pastors) or the chancery office (the central administrative bureaucracy). As a result, some pastors built outrageously expensive churches as personal monuments, whereas other parishes had to struggle along in temporary quarters for lack of funds. Mundelein took all crucial brick-and-mortar decisions away from the individual pastors. Before a pastor could build, he had to go through a nine-step process that included the bishop's approval of the architect, a full discussion of the parish finances by the board of consultors, and the constant supervision of the project by a two-man subcommittee of consultors. Pastors were encouraged to consolidate short-term loans into mortgages, and the chancery office helped find lenders at reasonable rates.[26]

In order to shift capital internally within the archdiocese, Mundelein used his corporate bonding power to create a central banking mechanism. Legally constituted as a corporation sole, the Catholic Bishop of Chicago had the power to issue bonds. Mundelein's predecessors had occasionally used this power to sell Catholic Bishop of Chicago (CBC) bonds on the open market. Mundelein continued the practice, but he also required parishes that showed a surplus in any given year to invest the money only in CBC bonds. In effect, the wealthier parishes loaned money to the poorer parishes with the bishop and the chancery office as intermediaries. In 1926, for example, nearly $2 million was shifted in this manner. Later Mundelein refined the system, upon the advice of Stuart, by supplementing the CBC bonds with a several million dollar line of credit at the major downtown banks. Together the two forms of centralized credit allowed for rational planning and management of diocesan growth. Cardinal Spellman of New York is sometimes credited with devising the first central bank in a Catholic diocese, but Mundelein's system predates Spellman's by twenty years.[27]

Both in fund-raising and administration Mundelein applied modern American business techniques to an archaic institution. Money management was at the heart of the American Catholic drive for status, as Rome became increasingly dependent on American largesse. At the turn of the century, the whole American church donated about $80,000 to the pope in Peter's Pence offerings. In 1920, Chicago alone sent $120,000 to the pope. When Mundelein was in Rome to become a cardinal, he noted the impact American financial largesse had made: "I had not been in Rome for fifteen years. Then we were looked upon as a nation of dollar-makers and dollar-seekers. Now the attitude was changed. We had shown that when it was a question of human lives . . . we threw our dollars away for this purpose even quicker than we made them. The attitude was now one of respect."[28] It was Mundelein's conviction that the American church had taken the place of France as the "eldest daughter of the Church." As France in the nineteenth century had defended the Papal States militarily and protected the Catholic missions in colonial lands, American Catholics now sustained both the Vatican and its worldwide missions with money.

Businesslike management earned the respect of American business as well. The Archdiocese of Chicago never had any problems marketing its CBC bonds; even during the depression of the 1930s these bonds rarely dropped below par. Ordinarily the archbishop was able to borrow from the banks at a percentage point below the market rate of interest. There was an oft-repeated comment, variously attributed to Julius Rosenwald of Sears and Roebuck, Frederick Eckert of Metropolitan Life, or to other business leaders, that Mundelein missed his calling by going into religion rather than business.[29]

100 Percent Americanism

Mundelein and his colleagues also strove to earn respect and approval in the non-Catholic community by a policy of vigorous, 100 percent American patriotism. But, while doing this, they had to be careful not to stir up a new "Americanism" controversy in Rome. Pope Leo XIII's 1899 letter, *Testem Benevolentiae*, which condemned "Americanism," had been veiled in ambiguity. Basically, the condemnation formed part of the Vatican's long-standing feud with doctrinal modernism; it manifested a deep fear of any attempt at the development of doctrine. Thus, what the pope condemned as "Americanism" included the notion that Catholic doctrine ought to be watered down or soft-pedaled in the modern world as well as the idea that active virtues and individual effort were superior to contemplative prayer and obedient submission to authority. But the pope carefully pointed out that he was not censuring the "characteristic qualities which reflect honor on the people of America" nor "the laws and customs which prevail [in the United States]." In short, if American individualism and pragmatism were raised to the level of theological doctrine, the pope condemned them. But if they were only practiced by American Catholics, he would look the other way. This byzantine line of reasoning gave Mundelein's generation of American Catholic leaders their opportunity to solve the Americanism puzzle. They avoided theological and philosophical reason-

ing altogether, and constantly reiterated their rigid adherence to Roman doctrine, thus making their anti-intellectualism into a virtue. They then plunged headfirst into symbolic and emotional bursts of American patriotism on issues they knew would not irritate Rome.[30]

Mundelein, for example, aligned himself with the "100 percent" attitude toward ethnic assimilation in America. In his first interview after being appointed to the Chicago archdiocese, he stated firmly that he did not believe in hyphens: "The people of the United States must be Americans or something else. They cannot serve two masters." He believed that the transitional phase of immigrant accommodation in ethnic parishes had lasted long enough and that new immigrant groups should be nudged toward full assimilation. In the very first months of his administration in Chicago, Mundelein appointed a new central school board that decreed that all instruction in Catholic schools be carried on in English, with the exception of some classes in catechism and reading that might be presented in an immigrant language. The "English only" order earned widespread praise outside the Church, though it was resented by immigrant Catholics. Mundelein's action anticipated and partially deflected the widespread movement by nativist politicians in the 1920s to legislate against foreign languages in the schools.[31]

World War I elicited an even greater outpouring of American patriotism from Catholic leaders. Within days of the United States declaration of war in 1917, the American archbishops hurriedly assembled and pledged unequivocal Church support to the president and the war effort. Back in Chicago, Mundelein reiterated this support: "The moment the President of the United States affixed his signature to the resolutions of Congress, all differences of opinion ceased. We stand seriously, solidly and loyally behind them. They have perhaps information that is hidden from us; they may know that danger threatens this nation from more than the one quarter towards which we are looking." He also took the occasion to taunt the Catholic Church's detractors: "We would ask whether the individuals or organizations, few though they may be, who have harassed us in the courts or maligned us in their scurrilous sheets in these later years, will now give some evidence of the love of country so loudly professed at a time when the country did not need them."[32]

Mundelein backed up his words with action, suspending temporarily some of his own ambitious fund-raising and building plans. When the first liberty loan was solicited in June 1917, the Chicago archbishop announced his personal purchase of $10,000 worth of bonds. He instructed every pastor to invest at least $100 of parish funds in the liberty loan, even if they had to borrow the money to do so. Mundelein appointed one of his most trusted pastors, the editor of the local Catholic newspaper, as head of a committee to coordinate Catholic cooperation with all subsequent liberty loan, Red Cross, and other war drives. Bonds of the third liberty loan were even sold in church vestibules.[33]

This outpouring of wartime partiotism, as well as the efforts toward ethnic assimilation, showed clearly the deep longing for social acceptance on the part of American Catholic leaders. The hasty and unqualified support for the war effort also manifested a justifiable fear of criticism and repression. Such Americanism, however, sincerely reflected the attitudes of Mundelein and other church leaders. Mundelein prided himself on his third-generation Americanism and frequently alluded publicly to his grandfather who had died in the Civil War. His choice of early American architecture for the seminary was a deeply felt symbolic statement, and the Congregational church after which he modeled his main chapel was one he had visited as a boy on a New England vacation. Shortly after announcing his parochial school reorganization, Mundelein wrote to Theodore Roosevelt: "I need not tell you of course . . . that there is hardly any other institution here in the country that does so much to bring about a sure, safe and sane Americanization of the children of immigrant people as do our parochial schools. My endeavor always will be to keep them up to the highest standard possible, so that they may be my monument rather than costly churches after I have gone, and the children that come from them be every bit as good American citizens as they are Catholics."[34]

Political Influence

A final factor that raised the Catholic Church's self-image in America was the role of Mundelein and other leading bishops in advising presidents and politicos. Political influence was a necessity for the leaders of an extensive institution like the Catholic Church. The Church had many interests—a separate school system, tax privileges, the welfare of its largely immigrant membership—to protect from political assaults. Naturally, political ties were closest with the Irish-dominated local Democratic party. In the early years of Mundelein's administration, the bishop's personal representative in the state legislature was the Speaker of the House, an Irish Democrat named David Shanahan, who buried many bills threatening Catholic schools. In the 1930s Mundelein built a close friendship with Edward Joseph Kelly, boss of the Chicago machine. When Kelly moved to a Gold Coast apartment upon his wife's death, he donated his house to the archdiocese for use as the residence of the diocesan mission band. Though Republican politicians were not as solicitous of

*President Franklin D. Roosevelt and Cardinal Mundelein at the cardinal's
residence in Chicago, October 5, 1937.*
  —*Photo by* The New World, *courtesy of the Archives of the Archdiocese of Chicago*

Catholic needs, some Republicans, such as Mayor William Hale Thompson, cleared Catholic patronage appointments with the Catholic archbishop.[35]

Mundelein played a very minor role in national politics until the Great Depression. Then, during the New Deal years, he became widely known as the most liberal Catholic bishop in America and Franklin Roosevelt's staunchest Catholic supporter. The two men had met each other casually sometime around 1910, when both were rising stars in their respective fields in New York, but a close friendship did not develop until Roosevelt was president. Roosevelt initiated the relationship for purely political reasons. A priest at Catholic University in Washington suggested through an intermediary that Mundelein was sympathetic to the New Deal and that, since the cardinal was an avid collector, a presidential autograph might flatter him. Roosevelt sent Mundelein a jaunty letter and an autograph for his saint's day, April 23, 1933. The cardinal immediately wrote back and arranged a courtesy visit to the White House in May.[36]

Mundelein and Franklin Roosevelt established an immediate rapport and a genuine friendship. The fact that both were devoted collectors gave them an initial point of contact, and both came to respect the other's abilities. In their dozen or so meetings after 1933, they called each other by their first names. In between meetings, they kept up frequent communication through intermediaries. From 1935 until Mundelein's death in 1939, Thomas Corcoran, the president's assistant, and William Campbell, the cardinal's lawyer, were the principal couriers between the two men. By chance, Corcoran was at Mundelein's villa on presidential business the night the cardinal died.[37]

The Mundelein-Roosevelt relationship was a useful one for both parties. The president needed prominent Catholic support, particularly in the late 1930s when Alfred E. Smith, Charles E. Coughlin, and other Catholics began to attack the New Deal as communistic and when many Church leaders suspected the administration of sympathy for Spanish loyalists and Mexican anticlericals. Mundelein provided such support enthusiastically. He introduced Franklin Roosevelt for an honorary degree at Notre Dame in December 1935 at the time of Fr. Coughlin's break with the administration; he deflected Catholic criticism of Hugo Black's appointment to the Supreme Court, and he adopted a judicious, even-handed stance of neutrality on the Spanish Civil War. The cardinal, for his part, wanted reassurance that federal welfare funds would be equitably distributed to the unemployed, great numbers of whom were Catholic, and also wanted to ensure some institutional role for the Church in making the distribution. In 1935, Mundelein's personal lawyer, Campbell, was appointed National Youth Administration (NYA) director in Chicago. He closely coordinated the NYA work with that of the Catholic Youth Organization in the city. The cardinal could not be unaware, either, of the prestige that a close relationship with the president would bring to his church. Certainly Chicago Catholics swelled with pride when Franklin Roosevelt lunched at the cardinal's residence after delivering his "quarantine address" in Chicago on October 5, 1937.[38]

In the last two years of his life Mundelein served the president in the additional role of unofficial diplomat. After trips to Rome in 1938 and 1939, the cardinal reported to the president whatever news from troubled Europe he had obtained at the neutral listening post of the Vatican. On these trips, too, he was negotiating the president's plan to send a personal emissary to the Vatican and establish quasi-official relations. Shortly after Mundelein's death, the newly appointed Archbishop Spellman of New York, who was also in contact with Franklin Roosevelt through Corcoran, completed these diplomatic arrangements, and Roosevelt announced the appointment of Myron Taylor as his representative to the Vatican.[39]

Mundelein's true importance to the Franklin Roosevelt administration should not be exaggerated. He was in no sense a policy adviser, and the New Deal would not have been different without him. Nevertheless, a German bishop from the conservative, isolationist Midwest supporting both the foreign and domestic policies of the administration was a genuine asset to the president.

More importantly, Franklin Roosevelt's friendship was a spectacular asset to the Catholic Church in America. Ideologically, the New Deal permitted Catholic leaders to exercise the prophetic role of social critics without appearing disloyal. The turn-of-the-century Americanist bishops, such as John Ireland, had been spread-eagle Fourth of July patriots and social conservatives, fearful that even a hint of social criticism would mar their image of Americanism. During World War I, the whole Catholic hierarchy, including Mundelein, hastened to support the war effort lest the Church appear disloyal. But when the president himself flailed at "economic royalists" during the Depression, Catholic leaders could exercise a more critical role without appearing un-American. Mundelein did not hesitate to attack the power of concentrated wealth on a number of occasions in the 1930s, and his auxiliary bishop, Bernard J. Sheil, was an outspoken supporter of John L. Lewis and the Congress of Industrial Organizations.[40]

More concretely, Franklin Roosevelt gave extensive patronage recognition to Catholics. Two members named to the original cabinet and about one-quarter of all judicial appointments were Catholics, while the president was himself surrounded by Catholics in his personal entourage—Corcoran, Grace Tully, and Marguerite ("Missy") Le Hand. The personal connections of Mundelein and Spellman with the president completed the image of importance that Catholics enjoyed during the New Deal.[41]

In November 1938, when Mundelein sailed to Rome for the beatification of Mother Cabrini, it was an open secret that he also had presidential business to conduct with the pope. Franklin Roosevelt, with Mundelein's foreknowledge, stage-managed a triumphal entry into Europe for the cardinal in order to impress both Mussolini and Pius with the importance he attached to Mundelein's mission. The battle cruiser *Omaha*, United States flagship in the Mediterranean, escorted Mundelein's steamship into Naples on November 5, and both Rear Admiral Henry E. Lackey and American ambassador to Italy William Phillips greeted the cardinal at a luncheon aboard the cruiser. Ambassador Phillips and a papal undersecretary of state then escorted Mundelein to Rome by special train. Such red-carpet treatment of an American cardinal, both by the papacy and by the American government, was indeed satisfying to American Catholics. It signaled the achievement of a status long strived for—fully American and fully Catholic.[42]

In his career as archbishop of Chicago, Cardinal Mundelein had manifested the thoroughly American belief that the best way to win respect was to buy it, whether with financial support for the pope or political support for the president. He exploited also the American weakness for royalty and display and understood that humility, though a virtue, was no way to gain attention. The other leading bishops of the early twentieth century shared many of Mundelein's characteristics. Most of them either built or expanded seminaries in their dioceses, reorganized their central administrations, collected large sums for the pope, the Propagation of the Faith, and local charitable works, and exercised political influence both publicly and privately. Cardinal O'Connell of Boston even pursued a brick-and-mortar dream as grandiose as Mundelein's seminary. With a multimillion-dollar bequest left him by a theater magnate, O'Connell bought up hilltop sites for a "Little Rome" in Brighton, Massachusetts. A monastery, a hospital, a retreat house, the Jesuits' Boston College, and the cardinal's mansion itself dotted the hills of Brighton as part of O'Connell's program for "getting the Catholic Church in Boston out of the catacombs." In New York, at mid-century Cardinal Spellman refined the administrative work of his predecessors into an efficient, centralized system of diocesan banking, purchasing, and insurance. In his additional role of bishop ordinary of the armed forces, he rivaled Bob Hope in the publicity accorded his whirlwind troop tours.[43]

The careers of O'Connell, Mundelein, and Spellman spanned the entire period from the turn of the century to Vatican II. Their leadership and that of similar bishops in other cities, plus the growing numbers and wealth of American Catholics, achieved separate but equal status for the Catholic Church in the United States. Inheriting a strong institutional base and a morally intransigent faith, the twentieth-century bishops "put the Church on the map" and "got it out of the catacombs" by providing highly visible leadership and instilling pride and confidence in American Catholics. Winthrop Hudson has pointed out in his popular history of American Protestantism that by the 1950s it was impossible to imagine that the death of any national Protestant leader could command the attention that accompanied the death of an American cardinal.[44] With money, morals, and masonry, Cardinal Mundelein and his contemporaries raised the status of the American Catholic Church so that it could command such attention.

4

Reynold Hillenbrand and Chicago Catholicism

by Steven M. Avella

Reynold Hillenbrand at the time of his ordination to the priesthood,
September 1929.

—*Photo by* The New World, *courtesy of*
the Archives of the Archdiocese of Chicago

"Jack," the older priest said with tears in his eyes, "some people say I wasted my life on small groups and formation." It was a poignant moment because the older man had been the younger man's teacher, patron, model, and guide. The older priest was Msgr. Reynold Hillenbrand—father of specialized Catholic Action in the Archdiocese of Chicago, co-founder of the Christian Family Movement, prominent liturgical reformer and champion of the lay apostolate—the younger man to whom he made this painful confession was Msgr. John Egan, guiding light of the Cana Movement, self-taught expert in urban affairs, and one of the Chicago clergy's most forceful proponents of racial justice. The question Hillenbrand asked was the deeper one any priest asks after a long life of ministerial service: did it do any good? Egan consoled his mentor and assured him that his life and labors had not been in vain. "Vatican II was different because of you," Egan assured him. "The Church is different—and better."[1] Egan was not fabricating soothing words to comfort a troubled old man. Reynold Hillenbrand's fifty-year priestly career was one that had a significant impact on Chicago Catholicism and the American Catholic experience.

Historians of American Catholicism have often turned to Chicago as an important window on the American Catholic experience. Chicago Catholicism has been a laboratory to study powerful ethnic groups like the Poles, the triumph of the organizational revolution, the Americanization of immigrants.[2] Most significantly, those looking for a clearer understanding of the effects of Vatican II on American Catholicism have cited Chicago Catholicism's pioneering efforts in the social, liturgical, and ministerial reforms and resurgence of lay activism that characterized the postconciliar period. Looming over these preconciliar movements was the dynamic character and ministry of Reynold H. Hillenbrand (1904–1979) commonly acknowledged as godfather, organizer, and the leading inspirational figure of social and liturgical reform in Chicago Catholic life.

Hillenbrand had the good fortune to have his contemporaries acknowledge his contributions to liturgical reform and social action. His name was well known among the small group of social activists in Chicago as well as among the liturgical reformers of the 1930s, 1940s, and 1950s. The first national recognition of his work came in an article in *Jubilee* magazine by Charles Harbutt, which cited Hillenbrand and his associates as making Chicago "the center of an amazing rebirth of the Christian spirit."[3] In 1963, co-worker Dennis Geaney on the pages of the newly born journal *Chicago Studies* wrote a piece entitled "The Chicago Story" that lauded the "scholarly and dynamic direction of . . . Monsignor Reynold Hillenbrand."[4] The first scholarly treatment of Hillenbrand's role in the lay apostolate was in Dennis Robb's 1972 doctoral dissertation, "Specialized Catholic Action in the United States," which drew heavily on Hillenbrand's own papers and interviews with him.[5] Jeffrey Burns's work on the Christian Family Movement contributed a substantial amount of information about Hillenbrand's role in that flourishing family movement of the 1940s, 1950s, and 1960s.[6] In 1989 Chicago priest Robert L. Tuzik gained access to the Hillenbrand Papers at the University of Notre Dame and completed the first doctoral dissertation on Hillenbrand's contribution to the liturgical movement in the United States.[7] Other general studies and specialized papers have dealt with Hillenbrand as well.[8] The general thrust of these early works on Hillenbrand is probably best captured in Fr. Andrew Greeley's book *The Catholic Experience*. "There can be no doubt," Greeley wrote in 1967, "that in the 1930s and 1940s Hillenbrand was a giant who exercised tremendous influence on the seminarians, the young priests, and the laity of Chicago."[9]

Formation for a Life of Action

Reynold Henry Hillenbrand was born in Chicago July 19, 1904, the second of George and Eleanor Schmitt Hillenbrand's nine children. Reynold's father was a dentist in Chicago and the family lived a contented middle-class life on the Near North Side of Chicago near Lincoln Park and the huge red-brick St. Michael's Church. The parish church was run by German Redemptorists, and the Hillenbrand children attended the excellent grade school run by the School Sisters of Notre Dame and the commercial high school staffed by the Brothers of Mary.

There were priests on both sides of the Hillenbrand family and two Hillenbrand boys, Frederick and Reynold, determined to enter the seminary upon completion of their commercial studies at St. Michael's. Reynold entered Quigley Preparatory Seminary in 1920 just two years after his brother Frederick and spent four years at Archbishop Mundelein's splendid seminary complex on the corner of Rush and Chestnut Streets. There he developed a lifelong love for English literature and served as editor of the seminary newspaper and the seminary annual. In 1924 he moved on to the newly-built seminary at Area, Illinois (later renamed Mundelein) and began his final years of preparation for the priesthood.

St. Mary of the Lake Seminary was a world unto itself. Archbishop Mundelein saw it as the jewel of his diocesan crown and lavished attention and money on the institution. Every seminarian had his own room, and Mundelein himself lived on the grounds and came to know each of the young men personally. The discipline of the seminary was adapted from the North American College in Rome as the zimarra-attired students walked the beautiful grounds in their respective *cameratas* (or designated groups). The teachers were the Jesuits of the Missouri Province and the classes were conducted in Latin. The Jesuits at this time were in the full swing of the neoscholastic revival that had been gathering steam in the universal church since the late nineteenth century. The clarity, precision, and rationality of neoscholasticism was drilled into the seminarians at St. Mary of the Lake through a systematic coverage of Christian Pesch's four-volume manual of dogma. Hillenbrand loved the Jesuits and wrote to his parents in 1924: "As has always been repeated in the past, the Jesuits are THE teachers. There is not a single one whom not everybody liked at first and continued to do so."[10] This world of revealed truths, logically deduced positions, and ideological clarity was an essential component of Hillenbrand's "thought-world."[11]

Hillenbrand's spiritual formation blended with the rigorous intellectual training of the dogma classes. Nightly, according to Jesuit practice, Hillenbrand made points of meditation to be considered the next day. His preserved notes reveal an introspective and earnest seminarian, highly idealistic, who was capable of intense concentration on any issue. "I can be disillusioned," he wrote in his diary, "I can become suspicious, become cynical, can let these things work on my morale so I cannot see the hundred good qualities and possibilities." He urged himself: "Be overlooking, be understanding, sympathetic, kindly, gentle and so teach and lead [youth] to higher things." Above all, in the seminary he developed a deep personal attachment to the papacy and papal teaching that would be the leitmotif of his life. In one paean of devotion to Pope Pius XI he wrote:

> Thank God for our Holy Father and for the blessings He has given Him. He is a great man in many ways: Pope of the Missions; he has settled the Roman Question which vexed the Church until

now. He depends on the prayers of the faith [sic]. My Catholic sense has been blunted and my Catholic growth stunted if I do not pray for him everyday and for his many projects, especially for the missions. He needs God's grace and blessing.[12]

His attachment to the papacy was more than a passing phase of a youthful and romantic seminarian. The words of the Holy Father were always for him "the living voice of Christ" in the present time. Robert McClory later described this "literal cleaving to papal documents as the unquestionable word" as the chief characteristic of Hillenbrand's career.[13]

Hillenbrand excelled at his studies and by the end of his second year was selected for graduate work at the seminary. He was ordained a year early in September 1929 and remained at the seminary to complete his doctorate writing a thesis on the indwelling of the Holy Spirit.[14] Years before the encyclical *Mystici Corporis Christi* was written, theologians were expanding their notions of the activity of grace in the human soul.[15] The theology of grace was understood more and more as a dynamic force rather than a static possession. (Indeed Hillenbrand had eschewed the classic term "sanctifying grace" in favor of the richer notion of "divine life.") The renewed emphasis on the immanence of God and the power of God's activity in the heart of the believer would be an important backdrop for Hillenbrand's later work in liturgical and social reform and his encouragement of lay activism.[16]

But his seminary formation only gave a theological and spiritual framework for his future career. In June 1931, Hillenbrand completed his doctoral studies, and Cardinal Mundelein sent him and his classmates on a one-year jaunt to Rome. This was not a formal study opportunity (although they did have classes in Latin) but a more leisurely program of sight-seeing and general cultural broadening.[17] Hillenbrand resided in the damp buildings in the French Canadian college and took maximum advantage of the one-year sabbatical. He toured France, Switzerland, and northern Italy and even visited the controversial stigmatic Theresa Neumann. But even more, he used his time and money to observe the unfolding of the liturgical movement in some of the great Benedictine abbeys of Europe. Moreover, he was in Rome just as Pius XI issued his encyclical *Quadragesimo Anno* and used the occasion to discuss social issues with the French-speaking priests of the house who told him about the efforts of Canon Joseph Cardijn to do what the pope was asking in the encyclical: rechristianize the social order.

Hillenbrand returned home in 1932 to take up an assignment as a teacher of English at Quigley. Although his tenure was brief, his love for literature and his ability to entice some of the tough kids from Chicago's South Side to read Byron, Keats, and Shelley was warmly appreciated by them years later.[18] But returning to Chicago in 1932 was anything but pleasant. Walking back and forth to Quigley or strolling in the downtown, Hillenbrand came face to face with the effects of the Great Depression that had descended on the once-thriving metropolis like a shroud. Chicago was hit particularly hard by the economic slump as its once booming economy ground to a standstill.[19] Thousands were thrown out of work and thousands more transients simply "ended up" in Chicago because it was the termination of the rail line. By 1930 a Hooverville had appeared on Randolph Street at the edge of the Loop, and by May 1932 Chicago's unemployment rolls included 700,000 persons or 40 percent of its work force. Unpaid public school teachers fainted in their classrooms for lack of food, and private charities buckled under the tremendous demands for assistance. Hillenbrand read these statistics and saw the ravages himself in the poor souls who came to the rectory door for handouts, or from his parents who told him hard-luck stories about patients who could not pay their bills.

Of all the places to live in the city of Chicago, Hillenbrand's residence at the cathedral rectory was the best for someone who was developing an active social conscience. The rector of the cathedral, the wide-girthed Msgr. Joseph Morrison, was one of the outstanding pastors of the city. An energetic and volatile man, he served Mundelein as master of ceremonies and developed a deep interest

Reynold Hillenbrand after being named
a monsignor.
        —Photo compliments of LaVeccha Studio

in the liturgy. (Morrison's own interest in the liturgy had been encouraged by his role in the Eucharistic Congress that met in Chicago in 1926 in which Hillenbrand was also a participant.) As shepherd of a large urban flock he watched with alarm as more and more of his parishioners descended into poverty.

Morrison was not an intellectual but had the practical pastoral sense that *something* had to be done to alleviate the terrible human suffering. He was especially sensitive to the fact that the cathedral had just built a new, spacious rectory before the depression and worried how this would look to the rising numbers of poor living in Hoovervilles a few blocks away.[20] Morrison opened the doors of the cathedral rectory to groups of social activists and others who were attempting to apply Catholic social teaching to these difficult circumstances. Hillenbrand was deeply impressed by Morrison's interest in liturgical and social issues but above all by his commitment to do more than talk about the issues. Action was the key to effective pastoral min-

istry, and Hillenbrand emerged from the cathedral rectory with an energetic commitment to the implementation of the social teachings of the Church especially as they were articulated in the papal encyclicals. At no other time and place in history did papal calls for social reconstruction seem more apt than in a city literally breaking down because of the excesses of liberal capitalism. With *Rerum Novarum, Quadragesimo Anno,* and other lesser papal statements as his guides, Hillenbrand dedicated himself to the task of social regeneration. Again and again he would call for a more corporate, organic social system—one that saw the rugged individualism of American life give way to a more cooperative and integrated social order.

One additional event served as a catalyst to Hillenbrand's important work of social reconstruction: his appointment to the Mission Band. In 1933, Mundelein proclaimed a celebration of the famous "double jubilee"—the ninetieth anniversary of the establishment of the diocese and the twenty-fifth of his own consecration as bishop. To commemorate this, a mission band of diocesan priests was established and Hillenbrand was appointed as its head. For the next three years, Hillenbrand traversed the diocese giving missions to virtually every parish, and what he saw goaded him to action. He continued to observe firsthand the depression-induced sufferings of Chicagoans, but he also saw an indifference among many priests to the plight of the poor among them—an indifference born of their own comfortable life-style and of a lack of vision. He spoke of this in his first address to seminarians when he urged the young men to

see[s] beyond their comfortable parishes and beyond their own comfortable lives—to see the suffering in the world, to have a heart for the unemployed, not to shy away from misery, but to feel the injustice of inadequate wages . . . to have some of the vision that [Dorothy] Day and [Peter] Maurin and priests who are coping with social problems have.[21]

Even before his appointment to the leadership of St. Mary of the Lake Seminary, Hillenbrand found an outlet for his social-reform zeal. In 1935 he began giving instructions to the young Catholic women preparing for street-preaching with the Catholic Evidence Guild at Rosary College.[22] His appointment to one of the most influential posts in the archdiocese, the leadership of the seminary, came the following year.

Clearly Mundelein's favor rested on the Hillenbrand brothers. Mundelein's niece, Rita Eppig, and later the cardinal himself, became dental patients of the elder Dr. Hillenbrand, and younger brother Harold Hillenbrand became the traveling dentist to the remote major seminary. Older brother Frederick had become the librarian at St. Mary of the Lake and was later selected to establish a Chicago-clergy residence in Rome. In addition to this personal acquaintance with the family, Mundelein was impressed by Reynold's academic achievements and his youthful drive. Academic dean of the major seminary, Fr. John "Pop" Furay, S.J., was also a strong supporter of Hillenbrand for a leadership post at the major seminary. When Msgr. J. Gerald Kealy resigned as rector to take a pastorate in 1936, Mundelein appointed the thirty-one-year old Hillenbrand to replace him. In introducing him to the students, Mundelein is reported to have said: "I know the seminary can be a dull place, so I've given you a man with imagination."[23] The eight years Hillenbrand spent as rector of the major seminary (1936–1944) were perhaps the most innovative period of that institution's history. Hillenbrand's keen interest and enthusiasm for social and liturgical issues was felt in seminary life and captured the imagination of the students. Although his position as rector of St. Mary of the Lake did not involve direct control over the academic program of the graduate school of theology (this was in the hands of the Jesuits), he was able to affect the lives of the seminarians by reshaping the seminary's liturgical life, inviting prominent outside speakers, and altering the college curriculum. By the time he was dismissed from his post in 1944, more than five hundred seminarians of the Archdiocese of Chicago had some exposure to the charismatic rector who called them by their first names.

The Heyday: Seminary Rector

At the very core of Hillenbrand's vision was the goal of social reconstruction according to the corporatist or organized vision of society adumbrated in the social encyclicals. Clearly this version of society was at the heart of his liturgical and social reform interests. At St. Mary of the Lake, Hillenbrand vigorously urged liturgical reform in order to impress the seminarians with the proper vision of society that they would carry out in their work. The community or corporate spirit built up at the Eucharist was to be the model for other social relations. The purpose of the Mass, he would say later

> is to restore the corporate sense and the corporate action . . . to learn our oneness at the altar and to bring that oneness to the other relations of life. This oneness must be brought to our homes . . . to our political life . . . to our social life . . . to our economic life . . . into working life . . . to our international life.[24]

Liturgy, however, was not only a means to an end, but because it was an occasion when God's own life flowed into his people, it provided a supernatural impetus for the work of "restoration of all things in Christ" (a quote from Hillenbrand's favorite pontiff, Pope Pius X). Hillenbrand was not himself a liturgical scholar or theorist, but he drew heavily from, and popularized the work of, the liturgical movement that had its American headquarters at St. John's Abbey in Collegeville, Minnesota. In the late 1920s, Hillenbrand had begun reading *Orate Fratres*, the periodical of the movement, and became closely associated with the work and teaching of Dom Virgil Michel, O.S.B., the American father of the movement. Hillenbrand lived by the often quoted syllogism of the liturgical movement:

> Pius X tells us that the liturgy is the indispensable source of the true Christian spirit. Pius XI says that the true

Christian spirit is indispensable for social regeneration. Hence the conclusion: The liturgy is the indispensable basis of Christian social regeneration.[25]

After consultation with Michel, Hillenbrand began making significant changes in the liturgical life at St. Mary of the Lake. Since a goal of liturgical reformers was the breakdown of individualism that crimped and truncated authentic worship, Hillenbrand pressed for additional communal participation in the Mass by the seminarians. He introduced the practice known as *Missa Recitata,* into the seminary schedule on Sundays and feast days, whereby all the seminarians joined in the responses at Mass. He insisted as well that major celebrations be held in the seminary chapel rather than the dormitory chapels where daily Mass was usually read. Hillenbrand himself often presided at these celebrations, which included communal chanting and group responses, and preached a homily based on the scripture readings of the day. As time went on, Hillenbrand refashioned the daily prayer schedule by introducing group chanting of prime and compline to replace the manual of morning and evening prayers, and altered Holy Week ceremonies by eliminating the traditional Good Friday *Tre Ore* and replacing it with the ancient liturgical rite of the Mass of the Presanctified. The first Mass of Easter was transferred to a sunrise service on Easter Sunday morning in order to "bring[s] out the joyousness of Christ's victory and bring us closer to the spirit of the first Easter Morning."[26] Outside speakers such as Maurice Lavanoux of the Liturgical Arts Society, Gerald Ellard, S.J., and Martin Hellreigel as well as Virgil Michel himself shared their research and insights into the history and development of liturgy. Hillenbrand amplified many of the ideas of the liturgical movement by his own Saturday evening classes with the deacons. In these lectures he distilled some of the best scholarship on liturgical history and theology and presented them to the students, while at the same time encouraging them to continue independent studies in these matters by introducing them to the publications of the Collegeville's Liturgical Press.[27] A little closer to home, he also urged his fellow faculty members to curtail the practice of celebrating daily Requiem Masses (which were shorter) and urged them instead to celebrate the memorial of the day (the Ferial Day Mass as it was then called.)[28] The effects of this liturgical instruction on Chicago's presbyterate was evident already in 1939 when Ellard reported in a glowing article in *Orate Fratres* that 65 of 250 city parishes in Chicago had the dialogue Mass. Moreover, institutions of higher education such as DePaul University and Rosary College reported regular usage of the *Missa Recitata* as did seventeen of sixty-six Catholic high schools.[29]

At the same time Hillenbrand moved decisively into the leadership of the national liturgical movement when he promoted the convocation of the first National Liturgical Week at Holy Name Cathedral in the fall of 1940. The theme of this first gathering, "The Living Parish," was selected by Hillenbrand himself. He gave the keynote address at the gathering and materially assisted the formation of the National Liturgical Conference that emerged from the National Benedictine Liturgical Conference.[30] Hillenbrand held office in the former conference for many years and spoke often to the gatherings, insisting vigorously on the unity of liturgy and social action. To keep the embers of liturgical reform alive, Hillenbrand organized a Summer School of Liturgy at Mundelein in July 1941 and another in the fall of 1943.[31] After the Liturgical Week in Denver in 1946, Hillenbrand, Morrison, and several others cooperated in the formation of the St. Jerome Society, later known as the American Vernacular Society.[32]

There is one other quality of Hillenbrand's liturgical reforms that must be discussed and that was his insistence that the liturgy be aesthetically beautiful. Hillenbrand himself was a cultured man and believed that worship should uplift the community. He was struck by the powerful simplicity of Gregorian chant, and monastic worship in particular provided an important model for the proper performance of liturgy. It was this insistence on liturgical beauty and decorum that later caused him to distance himself from some of the more casual liturgies and folk music of the postconciliar period.

Nonetheless as a seminary rector, as a popular speaker, and as an occasional writer and contributor to *Orate Fratres* (later renamed *Worship*), Hillenbrand's effect on liturgical reform in both the Chicago church and the American Catholic community was significant. The importance of liturgy as the drive shaft of social reform was central to Hillenbrand's vision.

The Social Reformer

The social question was the other feature of Hillenbrand's work in the shaping of Chicago Catholicism. Clearly, to Hillenbrand and others at the time, the corrosive effects of liberal individualism had very nearly destroyed society. He would come back to this theme again and again but never so forcefully as in an address to the National Liturgical Week in 1945:

> People the world over are sick of individualism, of being sundered from others, of the tragic loss which comes from thinking and acting alone. They are sick of individualistic, subjective piety because it lacks depth and vision. They are sick of the individualism that has undone so many homes . . . People are sick of the individualism that had made of political life an unspeakably sordid thing: sick of the stinking individualism in our economic life that has denied to the worker his rightful place in industrial life; sick, above all, of the individualism in international life that has left the world a shambles. . . . [33]

The theology of the Mystical Body of Christ provided the ultimate paradigm of how society was to be reordered. Like his insistence on liturgical reform, Hillenbrand saw to it that seminarians began to hear more and more about the Church's social teachings and see the vital connection between worship and life. During his years as rector, a steady stream of important Catholic figures associated with social issues came to speak to the cloistered seminarians at Mundelein. In February 1938, Dorothy Day made her way to the seminary to describe the work of her Houses of Hospitality, including one she had opened on Blue Island Avenue in Chicago. The seminarian-chronicler recorded the event with a kind of awe:

> Tonight the seminarians were treated to something different. For the first time in the history of the seminary, they heard an address in the auditorium by a woman. She was none other than the well-known leader of the Catholic Workers movement which has spread from New York through the United States, Miss Dorothy Day. She impressed the seminarians with what she said and in how she said it, particularly when they were told she had left a sick bed to speak to them. [34]

Hillenbrand had encouraged former seminarians like Edward Marciniak and John Cogley to volunteer time to the House. Although put off by Peter Maurin's radical rejection of society and urban life, Hillenbrand was a life-long supporter of the House of Hospitality. Other speakers in the 1936–44 period included Fr. John Gilliard, S.S.J., who spoke of his work among blacks, Baroness Catherine de Hueck (whom Hillenbrand considered eccentric), Australian lecturer Paul McGuire, Edward Skillin of *Commonweal*, Hispanic advocate Bishop Robert Lucey of Amarillo, interracial activist Fr. John LaFarge, S.J., and labor mediator Msgr. Francis Haas. To Haas he wrote gratefully: "They [the seminarians] know so little of the social action of the Church that anything you tell them would be of great interest and profit." [35]

Social education was accomplished not only by the outside speakers but also by an alteration in the seminary curriculum. Mundelein's seminary structure called for five years of study at the minor seminary and six at the major seminary. As a result of reforms recommended by an Apostolic Visitation (conducted by then Milwaukee Archbishop Samuel Stritch and St. Francis Seminary

Reynold Hillenbrand was an important inspiration for men such as Msgr. John Egan, pictured here testifying before the city council opposing the expansion plans of the University of Chicago in the Hyde Park-Kenwood neighborhood. Prior to his activism in urban affairs, Egan had been one of the mainstays of the popular Cana Conference of Chicago.

—Photo by The New World, *courtesy of the Archives of the Archdiocese of Chicago*

Rector Albert G. Meyer) the fifth year was clipped off the Quigley curriculum and an additional year was added to the major seminary course work. Hillenbrand used this expansion to add additional courses in religion to the seminary curriculum that included systematic study of Catholic social teaching. Moreover, he urged the newly arrived Archbishop Stritch to send away bright young men for graduate work in order to fill slots created by the new seminary program. Stritch acceded to this (although he initially thought these young priests would be school visitors) and sent men to the Catholic University of America in Washington, D.C., (long forbidden to Chicago priests during the Mundelein era) and brought them back to the seminary. The circle of priests who drew close to Hillenbrand, including those he sent away for higher studies and those who worked with

him in Chicago, had distinguished pastoral careers and often cited "Hilly's" influence as one of the most important in their lives. A partial list includes Social Action Department director and syndicated columnist George Higgins, labor and civil rights activist Daniel Cantwell, catechetical authors James Killgallon and Gerard Weber, Cana pioneer and urban reformer John Egan, Bishops Aloysius Wycislo and William McManus, William Rooney, the founder of the Catholic Commission on Intellectual and Cultural Affairs, and Catholic Actionists William Quinn, James Voss, and Charles Marhoefer.[36]

Hillenbrand's passion for social reconstruction, like his liturgical efforts, went beyond the hallowed halls of the major seminary. The 1930s were a propitious time for priests interested in social issues, especially those that related to labor organization. It was the heyday of CIO organizing in Chicago, especially among steelworkers and meatpackers.[37] Hillenbrand's support for the rights of workers to organize came directly from his reading of the social encyclicals but also from his exposure to the writings of social theorist John A. Ryan. Hillenbrand had certainly read Ryan's articles in the pages of *America* and *Commonweal,* but he had actually heard Ryan speak at a Summer School of Catholic Action for Priests held at St. Francis Seminary in Milwaukee in July 1937. The summer school was a catalyst for important efforts on behalf of social justice. The next year Hillenbrand and his associates, Frs. William Boyd and John Hayes, conducted a Lenten series at the cathedral entitled "A Catholic Slant on Economics."[38] Following up, the three priests also launched a series of labor schools in the industralized areas of the archdiocese.[39] At these schools Hillenbrand, Hayes, Boyd, and others held informational sessions for workers. They reassured those who may have been unsure that unionization was consonant with Catholic doctrine and even imparted practical skills in parliamentary procedure and a knowledge of labor history to help the workers take control of the unionization process— if for no other reason than to edge communist agitators out. By the beginning of the 1940s there were twelve labor schools scattered at strategic sites along the archdiocese. Hillenbrand himself regularly instructed Slovenian steelworkers in nearby Waukegan at Mother of God parish. The labor schools eventually moved under the auspices of the Sheil School of Social Studies and continued into the late 1940s. Out of the labor schools, as well, developed the Catholic Labor Alliance. The Alliance (which eventually changed its name to the Catholic Council on Working Life) continued the labor schools, sponsored popular forums, and issued a hard-hitting publication called WORK edited by a Hillenbrand associate, Edward Marciniak. Another Hillenbrand disciple, Daniel Cantwell, served as chaplain to the Alliance.

In the summer of 1938, Mundelein approved the convocation of a Summer School of Catholic Action for priests on the seminary campus, and Hillenbrand took a major hand in organizing the conference. He was looking for a more effective way of implementing the papal call for social reform. Action, he had learned from Morrison and others, was more important than words. Plans and programs existed aplenty to translate papal teaching into reality. These included the mobilization of older devotional groups such as the Holy Name Society or of fraternal organizations such as the Knights of Columbus and industrial conferences sponsored by the Social Action Department of the National Catholic Welfare Conference (NCWC) (in which Hillenbrand had been a participant). Bishop Edwin Vincent O'Hara had pressed for the development of study clubs of priests and laypersons. But Hillenbrand was dissatisfied

Reynold Hillenbrand's ideas and vision were carried on by a number of Chicago clergy and laity. In this photograph, one of Hillenbrand's closest allies, Msgr. Daniel Cantwell (center) is flanked by Sen. Eugene McCarthy, CFM lay leader Patrick Crowley, and John Nuveen.
—Photo by The New World, *courtesy of the Archives of the Archdiocese of Chicago*

with these approaches. They seemed in his estimation to be dominated by the clergy and, even worse, detached from the action of the Mass, which channeled divine life into human existence. It was during the summer school of 1938 that the appropriate methodology became evident to him. The insight came during a speech delivered by Fr. Donald Kanaly of Oklahoma on the work of Canon Joseph Cardijn of Belgium. Kanaly had been a student at Louvain and had observed firsthand the work of Cardijn in using small groups of workers and students to reclaim industry and urban life for Christianity. Cardijn's principles, Kanaly explained, were nothing more than a distillation of St. Thomas Aquinas's teachings on the virtue of prudence. To adequately practice this virtue one had to first observe a situation carefully, make a judgment about it based on proper ethical principles, and then act on those principles. This was especially effective with people in similar circumstances ministered to others in like circumstances (like-to-like). Kanaly urged the formation of "cells" or small groups of workers "not composed of boys or girls of the goodie type . . . [but] composed of typical workers."

Kanaly's speech electrified Hillenbrand. He was not unfamiliar with the Cardijn methodology (also known as Jocism—short for *Jeunesse Ouvriere Chretienne*) but he had never understood it as clearly as Kanaly explained it. The small like-to-like characteristics of the Jocists seemed to Hillenbrand a much better and more thorough way to change the hearts and minds of people than the more diffused Catholic Action study groups or the industrial conferences that focused heavily on the dissemination of information and clerical direction. For the remainder of his life, Hillenbrand would immerse himself in the work of founding small cell groups that would be motivated to re-Christianize the social order by an intensive program of education, prayer, and action. Soon after the conference he began to share the Cardijn methodology with his students and later began a cell at Chicago's Senn High School. The lay character of these cells was to be maintained at all cost. Even though each cell had a chaplain, Hillenbrand wanted

to make sure that the priest did not become the dominating figure. As he explained the role of the chaplain in a speech to the National Liturgical Week:

> Each cell has a priest as chaplain, but Pius XI wisely called him the "ecclesiastical assistant." His work with Catholic Action is indispensable, yet he is only an outsider in this lay movement. His chief task is the spiritual formation of these apostles. His chief practical chore is helping the head of the cell with the preparation of the weekly meeting. He takes no part in the actual meeting, though it is a useful thing for him to listen to it.[40]

Additional access to the "layperson market" was made possible for Hillenbrand by Paul McGuire, an Australian layman who was on a lecture tour in the United States sponsored by the Knights of Columbus. McGuire's key topic was on the evils of communism as manifested in the Spanish Civil War, but he had also witnessed the activities of the Jocists in France and recognized in this movement a potent Catholic response to the organizational skills of the communists. In May 1939 McGuire spoke at the Basilica of Our Lady of Sorrows, a popular gathering spot for many young Chicago Catholics and succeeded in forming twenty Catholic Action cells (as these groups would be known until the late 1940s) among the people of the parish. The beginnings of the cell movement at the Basilica were the stimulus for Hillenbrand's organizing activity. In the next year he met and began collaboration with Fr. Louis Putz, CSC, who had been a chaplain to the Jocist movements during an assignment in Europe. That year, Hillenbrand held a meeting of priests associated with cell work in Chicago and formed an informal federation of Catholic Action Cells directed by a board of seven priests. By June of 1941 one of the first Summer Schools of Specialized Catholic Action was held at Holy Name Cathedral. Scores of young people from the Catholic Interstudent Catholic Action organization (CISCA) were ready participants in the grow-

Reynold Hillenbrand's entire life was spent forming small groups of Catholics in the techniques of Specialized Catholic Action. This photograph shows him with a CFM group in Chicago.

        —*Photo by* The New World, *courtesy of the Archives of the Archdiocese of Chicago*

ing cell movement as well. At the Sheil School of Social Studies, philosopher George Drury devised a core course in Christian formation designed to accommodate the needs of young apostles. Cells developed among Catholic high school and college youth, working women, and even among the few males who were left in the city during the war years. As the groups grew, the association with international Jocism became more desirable, and after 1947 the groups formally identified themselves (at least in Chicago) as Young Christian Workers and Young Christian Students. Over all this prolific growth, Hillenbrand hovered, providing study guides, directing instruction, urging cell members to maintain ideological cohesion by preserving the impact of like-to-like action. By 1946, the growth of these cells required direction and coordination, and Cardinal Stritch appointed one of Hillenbrand's associates, Fr. William Quinn, to serve as archdiocesan director of the Catholic Action Federations.

The Beginning of the End

Hillenbrand's style of activist leadership depended first, last and always on the beneficence of his ecclesiastical patron, Cardinal Mundelein. As Mundelein's designate, he had virtual carte blanche at the seminary. When Samuel Stritch succeeded Mundelein in 1940 this was destined to change.

On the surface it semed that Stritch would be easier to work with than Mundelein. He was far less a hands-on administrator than his predecessor and inclined to give free rein to most clerical initiatives as long as they did not embarrass him. Moreover, ideologically Stritch and Hillenbrand shared the same neoscholastic ideology and the same conception of the proper social order.[41] But Stritch did not share Hillenbrand's dynamic theology of grace (grace was a gift from God, it did not grow or develop) nor did he look with favor on any "innovations" in the liturgy. Indeed Stritch did permit the Liturgical Week to be held under his auspices in 1940 and even delivered a fairly positive closing address. But the liturgical movement would forever remain a mystery to him and slightly suspect in his mind. In one of the few active disciplinary interventions of his eighteen-year episcopate Stritch forbade certain liturgical practices such as an offertory procession at the Doddridge Farm location of the Ladies of the Grail in his diocese. When pressed that this innocuous practice "went back to history" and was practiced in Benedictine monasteries in Europe, Stritch retorted: "Things which are local customs in monasteries and cloisters and approved or tolerated for these places may not be made general practice."[42] Moreover when Benedictine Michael Ducey tried to organize the foundation of a Benedictine abbey dedicated to the study of liturgy at Wilton Center, Illinois, Stritch encouraged the project and then withdrew his support at the last minute.[43] Stritch was regularly informed by disgruntled faculty members at Mundelein about liturgical practices at the seminary and at one point made some indirect comments at the opening of the school year regarding liturgical irregularities. But perhaps the most maddening thing (from the orderly Hillenbrand's

perspective) was Stritch's inability to ever come down decisively on an issue. Much of this stemmed from the archbishop's own gentle personality and the bouts of depression that debilitated him during his episcopal career. Stritch was loath to offend and could never bring himself to be decisive enough to send the clear and unambiguous signals on his liturgical preferences that Hillenbrand could easily discern. Given this ambiguity, Hillenbrand proceeded despite the complaints that mounted from baronial Chicago pastors who were confronted by their newly ordained assistants and also by the Jesuits.

The Jesuits found Hillenbrand difficult. His policy of increasing numbers of diocesan priests on the faculty gave the Sons of Loyola some rivalry for the hearts and minds of the students. This was especially evident in 1944 when Stritch had to order the seminarians to take the Jesuits as spiritual directors. Moreover, Hillenbrand did not work well with the academic dean of St. Mary of the Lake, Fr. John Clifford, S.J. who was Stritch's personal theological adviser and a golf companion of the powerful Msgr. George Casey, vicar general of the archdiocese. Clifford did not appreciate Hillenbrand's frequent absences from the campus and, even more probable, disagreed with the rector's "liberal" understanding of the work of grace in the human person.[44]

But, ironically, Hillenbrand and Stritch would especially differ over the proper approach to social questions. This is truly ironic because Stritch shared Hillenbrand's distaste for large concentrations of wealth and very deeply felt that his native South had been economically pillaged by greedy northern capitalists. However, Stritch, like many American bishops of the Coughlin era, was intensely nervous about clerical activism in social issues and equally worried that excessive zeal might sow the seeds of class hatred. After many years of work as a labor mediator[45] and a proponent of labor organization, Hillenbrand took a dim view of many employers and in particular the conservative Illinois Manufacturers Organization (that included some prominent Catholic businessmen), which he once accused of being inheritors of "an evil tradition."[46] This attitude had earlier aroused some members of Chicago's business community who complained to Stritch about the anti-business attitudes of the rector and reminded him that St. Mary of the Lake had itself been built "largely through the gifts of businessmen."[47] Stritch strongly reprimanded Hillenbrand but, as in the case of the liturgy, never sent a clear signal that further social activism would be banned. Hillenbrand later recalled that when he went to see Stritch about the matter, the archbishop brushed it off and seemed embarrassed that he had come down so hard on the seminary rector.[48] In 1944, Hillenbrand involved himself in the organizing efforts of retail workers at Montgomery Ward. The case was controversial because it involved a strike during the war and also the activities of Sewell Avery, the president of Ward's, who refused to comply with the Labor Department's orders to negotiate with his workers. In solidarity with the workers, Hillenbrand joined a picket line in front of the Montgomery Ward's offices. This time Stritch acted. The picket line appearance coupled with the mounting complaints led to Hillenbrand's "promotion" to Sacred Heart Parish in Hubbard Woods, a prestigious but conservative North Shore suburb. Hillenbrand's successor at Mundelein was Msgr. Malachy Foley, a mathematics professor aptly characterized by historian Edward Kantowicz as "a pious fool of an Irishman."[49] Foley dismantled many of Hillenbrand's seminary programs and purged the faculty of "Hilly's Men." By 1946, St. Mary of the Lake was indistinguishable from most American seminaries.

Many believed that it was Hillenbrand's lack of political skill that got him into trouble.[50] If he had "stroked" the right people in the chancery and participated in clerical socializing at Forty Hours devotions and other clergy events he might have deflected the criticism that did him in. This is probably true. My own amplification of this would be to add that his ejection from the seminary was only because he was an unbending ideologue. Like many strong-minded individuals he was ill suited for jobs that required compromise and a certain catering to less-than-sympathetic superiors. This he would not or

could not do. He did not "learn his lesson" with the seminary dismissal nor would he be able to adapt to subsequent developments in the Specialized Catholic Action Movements, the CFM and in his parish.

His life after 1944 continued to be busy and demanding. Stritch gave him ample leeway to follow his interests. He made the best of his new parish assignment by introducing liturgical reforms such as communal singing, the restored Easter Vigil, and an innovative interior renovation of Sacred Heart Church in 1957 that highlighted the artistic work of Ivan Mestrovic. He promoted the specialized Catholic Action Movements with unflagging ardor, pointing out in an address on the role of the priest at the 1951 session of the Liturgical Conference that the priest's task was spiritual formation: "This is most readily done in the specialized movements of the apostolate—the Christian Family Movement, the Young Christian Workers, the Young Christian Students, and the rural counterpart, still unstarted."[51] In the late 1940s his interests turned to the formation of the Christian Family Movement (CFM), a natural outgrowth of the men's and women's cells that had developed in Chicago during and after World War II. Working closely with lawyer Patrick Crowley and his wife Patty, Hillenbrand directed the development and instructional programs of the CFM and exercised a firm hand over the burgeoning organization. He continued to lecture and organize liturgical and family-life events and found many of his liturgical ideas vindicated by Vatican II.

But time had made Hillenbrand increasingly stubborn, authoritarian, and jealous of his prerogatives. The effects of a nearly fatal accident in Oklahoma in 1949 left him crippled and even more prone to numbing migraine headaches. He spent nearly a year recuperating in Oklahoma and upon his return became an increasingly difficult person with whom to live and work. His continued insistence on papal documents as the foundation for all meaningful Catholic activity gradually began to seem fossilized and maladapted to new advances in scripture studies and the advent of historical theology—many of these developments pressed by the very people whose intellectual curiosity he had stimulated, encouraged, and "turned loose" on the Chicago Catholic community.[52] Even his strong suit—liturgical reform—began to show wear in the early 1960s when his theological understanding of the sacrificial nature of the Mass clashed with younger scholars on the newly formed Archdiocesan Liturgical Commission.[53] By the postconciliar period, Hillenbrand had become a remote figure, distant even from his former admirers and clerical friends.

Trouble began in the CFM when Hillenbrand refused to allow the program of instructions to "deviate" toward internal family issues and rigidly insisted on a social agenda. He eventually broke with the Crowleys, who served on the papal commission studying the contraception question, when the couple expressed their support for a change in the Church's ban of artificial contraception. For Hillenbrand, this was tantamount to treason.

In the liturgical life of Sacred Heart Parish his insistence on all the school children attending Mass every day at 10:10 A.M. (right in the middle of the morning school sessions) created tensions with faculty, parents, and children that tacitly challenged Hillenbrand's insistence on the role of the Mass as a tool for teaching the children. Finally in 1973 John Cardinal Cody resolved the increasingly tense situation at Sacred Heart by imposing an administrator upon Hillenbrand. A year later, a few months shy of Hillenbrand's seventieth birthday, Cody insisted on Hillenbrand's complete retirement. This broke his spirit and he retired to a reclusive existence ministered to by his family and a few friends until his death in 1979.

In summarizing what had happened to Hillenbrand, a long-time admirer and confidant, Dennis Geaney, wrote:

Vatican II theology pulled the rug from under his hierarchical theology of the laity, social action, and liturgy. . . . Reiny's genius lay in his insight that lay formation, social action, and liturgy were integrative elements of a new church, but the intuition could not flourish under his authoritarian thumb in an American Church that had a new awareness of the democratic spirit.[54]

Like so many influential people, Hillenbrand's greatest strengths also were his greatest weaknesses. Hillenbrand was a strong-willed, highly principled man. The force of his character and the power of his ideas bore much good fruit in liturgical renewal, family-life issues, and race relations and made a mighty contribution to the long neglected role of the laity. Few could match him or his contemporaries in the good they accomplished. But his strong-mindedness came to be viewed as a tyrannical, unbending authoritarianism, maladapted to the constituencies of middle-class American Catholics whom he served. The ultimate irony of Hillenbrand's life was that as much as he strove to build community and to restore a sense of corporate solidarity among people, he ended up isolated and alone largely because he was so highly individualistic.

5

The Rise and Fall of Bernard Sheil

by Steven M. Avella

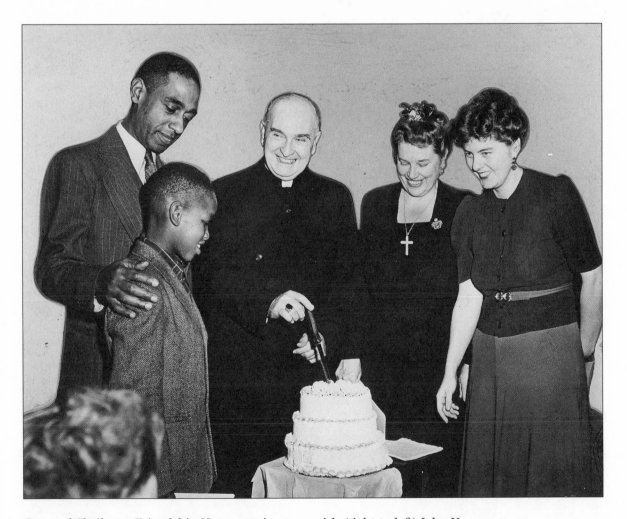

Bernard Sheil at a Friendship House anniversary with (right to left) John Yancey, Catherine DeHueck Doherty, and Ann Harrigan. The little boy is unknown.
—Photo by The New World, *courtesy of the Archives of the Archdiocese of Chicago*

On the morning of September 2, 1954, Msgr. Edward Burke, chancellor of the Archdiocese of Chicago, received a startling phone call from Stanley Pieza, religion editor for the *Chicago American*. Pieza was calling for comments on reports that Bishop Bernard Sheil planned to resign the leadership of Chicago's Catholic Youth Organization (CYO) that day at a noon press conference. Burke was taken aback by the report and hurried to the offices of Samuel Cardinal Stritch and called the prelate out of a meeting with his consultors. Stritch was equally stunned by the news and abruptly dismissed the consultors while he huddled with Burke and Vicar General Msgr. George Casey. For years, the relations between the "senior auxiliary" and the chancery had been strained. As far as Stritch, Burke, and Casey were concerned, Bishop Sheil was a loose cannon—capable of doing and saying anything. Determined to head off a public relations fiasco, the trio piled into the archiepiscopal limousine and motored to Sheil's CYO offices at Thirty-one E. Congress. They were met there by the director of Chicago's Holy Name Societies, Msgr. Edward Kelly, and ushered into Sheil's presence. One can only surmise what was said and promised at this hastily called meeting, but when the time came to meet the press, Stritch was firmly in command and told the reporters that he had "reluctantly" accepted Sheil's resignation and

that he was appointing Kelly to take over the CYO.[1] With that, Sheil moved off the stage of history, leaving the Chicago press and his numerous friends and enemies to speculate on the reasons for his sudden departure. The man who had once controlled what one historian called a "veritable social-service empire," the friend of Franklin D. Roosevelt and Harry Truman, the "People's Bishop," watched from the sidelines as Kelly dismantled the once proud and energetic organization.

What had happened to Sheil? Only the year before he had been feted lavishly on the occasion of his twenty-fifth anniversary of episcopal consecration at a gala event in the Palmer House. Numerous dignitaries gave speeches that went on past midnight, lauding Sheil's devotion to youth, organized labor, civil rights, and adult education. There wasn't a need or an issue of modern society that Bernard J. Sheil's Catholic Youth Organization didn't have a plan or program to deal with. In the end, Sheil had more ideas than he had money to pay for them or interest to sustain them. Sheil's multifaceted activities began as a combination of idealism and a way to win the necessary support to push him a notch higher in his ecclesiastical career (a diocese or archdiocese of his own) but degenerated into a concatenation of programs that had no focus or basis other than Sheil's will.

The Beginnings

Sheil was born in Chicago, February 18, 1886.[2] Although he often claimed he was born poor, his parents were solid middle-class types, who apparently did quite well in the coal business. He attended St. Columbkille school on the Northwest Side and St. Viator College in Bourbonnais where he demonstrated above average skills as a debater and a varsity pitcher. Despite offers from the Chicago White Sox, he became a priest in 1910 and served his first years of priestly ministry at St. Mel's Parish on the West Side. At the outbreak of World War I, he was transferred to Great Lakes Naval Training Center for a year and after the war went to Holy Name Cathedral, with additional duties at the old Cook County Jail on Illinois Street. "Benny," as he was known, was garrulous and friendly, gifted with a natural eloquence and a wide, flashing smile that endeared him to people instantly. He won the attention of Archbishop George Mundelein, who appointed him to a number of administrative positions in Chicago's curia and consecrated him an auxiliary bishop in 1928. Two years later, in 1930 Sheil gathered together the disparate elements of existing youth and fundraising programs under the umbrella of a new organization called the Catholic Youth Organization. The CYO was the launching pad of what promised to be a rewarding ecclesiastical career.

The CYO: The Early Years

Bernard Sheil created the Catholic Youth Organization with the blessings and financial help of his chief ecclesiastical patron, George Cardinal Mundelein. Here he presents the cardinal with one of the boxing awards given by the organization.

—*Photo by* The New World, *courtesy of the Archives of the Archdiocese of Chicago*

The first years of the CYO were devoted to reclaiming Chicago youth caught in the grinding urban poverty of the depression era and highly susceptible to juvenile delinquency and communist agitation. Sheil's answer was athletics, especially boxing tournaments which attracted thousands of every race, religion, and ethnic group. If not everyone was comfortable with a Catholic bishop pushing the morally dubious sport of boxing, Sheil snapped back that he would run checkers tournaments if someone could prove to him that this would appeal to crime-prone urban youth. Until then, boxing worked, he maintained, and he would continue to use it. The CYO blossomed in the 1930s, and Sheil added new programs to the athletic core, including the addition of a flying school at Holy Name Technical Institute in Lockport, Illinois, and a Seeing-Eye-dog service for the blind.

Organized Labor and Democratic Politics

But by the late 1930s, Sheil was plainly bored with athletics. Newer issues crowded the horizon such as labor organization, foreign policy, and community organizing. His mentor, Cardinal Mundelein, was already known as one of the favorite American Catholic bishops of the Roosevelt administration. With the encouragement of Mundelein and a close friend, William Campbell (later a federal judge), Sheil began to speak out for liberal causes. His greatest moment came in July 1939 when he appeared in the Chicago Coliseum in support of the efforts of the packinghouse workers to organize under the auspices of the CIO. Sheil's public embrace of the rights of organized labor and of its leader, John L. Lewis, was highly instrumental in the ultimate victory of the packinghouse workers' cause.

Aligned with his support of the packinghouse workers was the critical support he gave community organizer Saul D. Alinsky in organizing the tough Back of the Yards neighborhood. Sheil served on the board of Alinsky's Industrial Areas Foundation and introduced the organizer to wealthy philanthropists like Marshall Field and Eugene Meyer.

Even before the packinghouse workers appearance, Sheil's fine public speaking voice

Bernard Sheil was bitterly disappointed when he was not chosen to succeed Mundelein in 1940. Instead the nod went to Archbishop Samuel A. Stritch of Milwaukee. Here Sheil escorts the new prelate to his Chicago home accompanied by Auxiliary Bishop William O'Brien.

—*Photo courtesy of* Chicago Herald-American

had been deployed against the Catholic media star of the 1930s, Fr. Charles Coughlin. When Sheil delivered a blast against the radio priest in a December 1938 broadcast, White House staffer Tommy Corcoran (who had helped write it) reported to his superiors, "Bishop Bernard J. Sheil is Auxiliary Bishop of Chicago; he is the individual who publicly raked Coughlin over the coals . . . this information ought to leak out to the press so that they will know who Sheil is."[3] Sheil further endeared himself to the Roosevelt White House on the day after Mundelein died in 1939, when he took to the airwaves to deliver an address he had planned to deliver at a CYO convention in Cincinnati, supporting alterations in neutrality legislation called for by FDR. Roosevelt himself was grateful for the speech and wrote to Chicagoan Frank Knox,

"Bishop Sheil's speech on Monday night was grand."[4] Sen. Scott Lucas of Illinois had the entire text entered into the *Congressional Record*.

FDR and his entourage saw Sheil as an asset and expended some effort to have him named Mundelein's successor or assigned to the soon-to-be-created Archdiocese of Washington, D.C. But the Vatican was not interested and appointed Samuel Stritch, the Nashville-born Archbishop of Milwaukee, to the Chicago post and former Catholic Relief coordinator Patrick O'Boyle to Washington. Secretary of the Interior Harold Ickes said of the Stritch appointment, "We suffered a blow today."[5] The one who really suffered was Bernard Sheil. The day he welcomed Stritch to Chicago, in an elaborately staged demonstration at Union Station, Sheil's days of influence and power were over.

The CYO Chapel furnishings were designed by artist Ann Grill who also taught for the Sheil School. This is a photograph of the baldachino and crucifix in the chapel.

—*Photo courtesy of Peter Fish Studios*

Relations with Stritch

Stritch was a kindly and gentle man, but he knew a rival when he saw one. He had been suspicious of Sheil for years, especially when the Chicago auxiliary tried to centralize the youth-work efforts of the National Catholic Welfare Conference under his CYO umbrella. He had heard rumors of Sheil's fiscal profligacy and felt his open intervention in CIO organizing activities to be unbecoming for a Catholic bishop. But, above all, Stritch did not need Sheil as Mundelein did. The old cardinal was a shy and forbidding man who needed the glad-handing, backslapping Sheil to put a human face on his episcopate. Stritch was his own public relations man—charming, affable, easygoing, and thoroughly at home with public life. When Stritch refused to reappoint Sheil to the post of vicar general, the auxiliary knew he was being consigned to the outer darkness. He could accept the role of the dutiful and humble auxiliary, confirming children, consecrating altars, and receiving nuns' vows, or he could strike out and create his own ecclesiastical empire and hope his efforts would win support for a diocese of his own. Given his already swollen ego and his close links with high government officials and the wealthy, he chose the latter course.

Education for Democracy: Creating a New CYO Empire

The "new look" for the CYO began in 1938 when Sheil reorganized the CYO bureaucracy. In that year he created a social service department that undertook social welfare operations such as child guidance clinics and community centers. Two years later he created the centerpiece of his new CYO, an education department. This department functioned in a manner reminiscent of FDR's brain trust by assembling scholars and writers who provided the fodder for the bishop's steadily increasing public speaking engagements. Of the "new and revised" CYO, public relations man Ralph Leo wrote:

> The infant days of the CYO were at an end; the days that lay before would be days of adult achievement, or robust action, of major responsibilities, of democratic vistas. . . . For the first time . . . the traditional notion that the CYO was a boxing organization began to give way before the rediscovery of the CYO as a symbol of youth work and youth achievement and as an expression of the democratic idealism that Bishop Sheil's generous humanitarianism and boundless social vision gave it.[6]

After the war began, Sheil selected Fr. James V. Shannon, a brilliant, if somewhat erratic, priest-teacher from the Chicago seminary system, to serve as his chief theoretician and speech writer. Shannon's speech writing brought life to the bishop's new role as a spokesman for social justice. Shannon helped Bishop Sheil discover what Catholic thinkers of the early twentieth century called "the social question." A product of Catholic intellectual life of the late nineteenth century and papal encyclicals like *Rerum Novarum* (1891) and *Quadragesimo Anno* (1931), Catholic social thinking rejected liberal, laissez-faire capitalism and atheistic communism or socialism. It urged instead a return to a more "natural" organic social order, encouraged the formation of vocational groups such as labor organizations, and relied heavily on natural law as the basis of human rights. Sheil found this message easy to promote in depression and wartime America and became a major spokesman on every major problem confronting America: race relations, labor organization, postwar reconstruction, adult education, and the changing face of urban life.

Implementing the bishop's desire to be a leading Catholic spokesman for social issues meant more than speech writing. Various social activists like Baroness Catherine DeHueck and the young persons of the Catholic Interstudent Catholic Action (CISCA) groups

A class at the Sheil School of Social Studies probably on racial matters. Notice the large number of women in the photo as well as the interracial mixing.

—*Photo courtesy of Peter Fish Studios*

had pressed for additional programs in "social education." Sheil and Shannon agreed that more had to be done to amplify and build on what the bishop had said. This gave birth to the idea of a school or forum for adults that would be an adjunct to the work of Sheil's public addresses. Shannon brought on board a former seminarian from St. Mary of the Lake Seminary, George Drury, and the two of them opened the Sheil School of Social Studies in February 1943 at CYO headquarters. The goal of the school was articulated by Drury in handsome flyers designed by CYO artist Jerry Keefe: "To give to people to all people, an even fuller knowledge of the truths of reason and revelation to enable them to build a better world." Since it charged no tuition and it had the name of the popular CYO bishop attached to it, the school got off to a strong start. It offered an array of courses from George Drury's highly theoretical program called "The Basic Course" (a systematic introduction to the truths of

Christian revelation), to popular courses in languages, history, creative writing, drama, and vocational arts. Every Friday night the Sheil School Forum would be held, attracting prominent Catholic scholars or government officials who came at their own expense and spoke for no stipend. The Sheil School Forum also "adopted" other programs that were floundering on their own. For example, the labor schools begun in the diocese by Msgr. Reynold Hillenbrand and Fr. John Hayes were given rooms for their classes at Sheil School. Moreover, Sara Benedicta O'Neill's St. Benet's Book Store (one of the few places where Chicago Catholics could purchase copies of *Commonweal* and quality Catholic literature) was attached to the Sheil School. Enthusiastic young persons like Nina Polcyn, Betty Schneider, and Robert Burns came to work for the Sheil School, accepting pitiful wages and virtually no job security. But what working for Sheil lacked by way of financial remuneration, it made up for in excitement. A medley of interesting characters moved in and out of the school, recruited by Sheil, including Harlem poet Claude McKay, former Polish Consul General Karol Ripa, and former Undersecretary of State G. Howland Shaw. CYO workers found themselves entertaining well-known scholars and media celebrities whom Sheil had invited for talks or benefits. Writer James O'Gara summarized the popularity of the Sheil School by calling it a "Catholic Times Square." "Stay there long enough," he wrote, "and you can meet almost anybody."[7]

Public Speaking

While the school lifted off, Sheil took to the hustings, delivering speeches with a flair and an apparent sincerity that impressed audiences and won favorable public attention. He was a fixture at CIO conventions and spoke to garment workers, retail grocers, bartenders, foremen, building service employees, stage-hands, and motion picture operators. He addressed conferences on welfare needs, recreation, industrial problems, and juvenile delinquency. He testified occasionally before congressional committees and commented publicly on such issues as minimum wage, race relations, fair employment practices, the

Another of Sheil's numerous enterprises was Friendship House, a program designed to encourage friendly communication between the races. Here Betty Schneider, long-time staffer at the house, discusses Catholic teaching on racial justice.

—Photo courtesy of Peter Fish Studios

Taft-Hartley Act, and universal military training. Before the 1940s were over, Sheil was lauded as "The People's Bishop."

His best speeches were given during the war on the meaning of democracy and race relations. Sheil added his voice to those who ideologically mobilized the American people during World War II by making democracy a "fighting faith." Using texts drafted by Shannon, Drury, and Edward Joyce, a later recruit to the CYO, Sheil probed the meaning of democracy, its roots in the human freedom granted by God, and the necessity of extending democracy's benefits to those who did not share its fullest blessings in American society. This brought him to some of his boldest and most courageous statements on behalf of racial justice, years ahead of many leaders in the American Catholic community. "It is the most dangerous kind of hypocrisy," he wrote, "to wage a war for democracy and at the same time deny the basic benefits of democracy to any group of citizens." But he was not content to indict American society alone. The Church was also party to the hypocrisy of racism. "The church in this country at this moment is face to face with this problem. It must be met by a reaffirmation in action of the great Christian virtues of justice and charity. Jim Crowism in the Mystical Body of Christ is a disgraceful anomaly."[8] Sheil hired black persons, like social worker Dora Somerville, for important jobs in the CYO, decried the "hideous question of restrictive covenants" that denied blacks access to all-white neighborhoods, and encouraged black pride in a 1941 article in *Negro Digest* entitled "If I Were a Negro."

When he took on Fr. Coughlin in 1938, Sheil also vigorously attacked anti-Semitism. This endeared him to Chicago's Jewish community, who took up a large collection for Pope Pius XI in 1939 and handed it to Sheil to personally deliver to the pontiff. Sheil was one of the few American bishops to speak out against the destruction of European Jewry during the war. Afterward, he was a strong supporter of the State of Israel and lent his name to the sale of State of Israel bonds. He became the first non-Jewish recipient of the B'nai B'rith award in 1951, and his friend Judge Campbell recommended him for a diplomatic mission to Israel.

If sheer activism could have assured Sheil elevation in the ranks of the Catholic hierarchy, his peripatetic style and the extent of his activities would have qualified him to become pope. However, as the decade of the 1940s unfolded, it became evident that these efforts were not enough to overcome the suspicion and ill will of his colleagues in the episcopate and priesthood. He may have been loved by the union worker, the civil rights activist, or the New Dealers, but he was not so kindly regarded by the king makers of the American hierarchy or even by those who worked closest with him.

Holding the Empire Together

Following World War II, normal relations between the Vatican and the American Church resumed. Soon after the hostilities ceased there was a spate of episcopal appointments and diocesan reorganizations in the United States that had been stalled by poor communications. This would have been Sheil's time to receive his reward but, despite the fact that rumors of his impending appointment to some major American diocese still abounded (*Newsweek* predicted in 1946 that Sheil would succeed Cardinal Glennon in St. Louis), nothing came.[9] After 1946, it dawned on Sheil that his chances for advancement were diminishing. Restless and bored by the social action initiatives of the early 1940s, Sheil once again reorganized the CYO. The occasion for the change was his growing dissatisfaction with Drury and the complaints of other CYO staffers that the "Basic Course" was too Catholic and intellectual for the average devotee of the Sheil School. Moreover, the "Basic Course" imperiled crucial Community Chest support because it was so sectarian in nature. Drury's exit came in 1946 when he, Margaret Blaser, and Nina Polcyn attempted attorney, William O. Burns, violently rejected the idea, and Drury found himself out of a job by the summer of 1946 (Shannon was already out of the picture). The school carried on well enough as a general adult education program under the leadership of Viatorian scholar Edward Cardinal and public relations chief Charles Carroll Smith, but by the late 1940s another reorganization occurred that replaced virtually all the existing staff. One of the new faces that loomed large in Sheil's new inner circle was a war widow named Irene Wiltgen. Mrs. Wiltgen had come to know the bishop through her association with Sheil House, a campus ministry center at Northwestern University founded by Sheil and directed by Fr. Cornelius McGillicuddy. Sheil had given substantial money for the handsome home on Sheridan Road that was a chaplain's residence and a gathering spot for Catholic students at the university. Mrs. Wiltgen became Sheil's personal secretary and "protected" Sheil from "unnecessary intrusions." By the account of CYO workers, she exercised a great deal of influence over Sheil, who grew increasingly isolated and remote.

The staff shakeups were only symptomatic of serious internal problems in the CYO. The quashing of plans for an employees' union dealt a blow to the idealism and morale of the organization. But the biggest problem was money. The CYO had always had a precarious financial existence and had to rely on a variety of fund-raising techniques. Sheil had orig-

Bureau. While he was alive, Cardina[l] delein was generous with the organ[...] not only transferring archdiocesan f[...] critical moments but also assigning p[...] work with Sheil and allowing the au[...] assign the parishes blocks of ticket[...] athletic events that had to be so[...] diocesan transfers to CYO enterpr[...] have reached a high-water mark wh[...] administered the archdiocese after tl[...] of Mundelein. Sheil also tapped int[...] funds such as the Community Chest[...] ceived substantial help when the C[...] designated an agency of the New[...] National Youth Administration. (It helped that William Campbell was the Illinois state director.) Elaborate benefits such as a Knights of Columbus-sponsored barbecue, which featured popular entertainers Jimmy Durante and Frank Sinatra (the CYO could never get Catholic crooner Bing Crosby) made lots of money. Annually on Sheil's birthday, *Chicago Tribune* sportswriter Arch Ward (whose daughter Sheil had buried) organized a corned beef and cabbage dinner that provided another source of revenue. Sheil was well connected with wealthy sorts like transportation magnate Jack Keeshin, philanthropist Frank J. Lewis, department store and newspaper mogul Marshall Field, and Blackstone Hotel owner Fred Morelli. His long-time friend, Judge William Campbell, kept him in touch with influential politicians and moneyed people.

Financial Problems

But the income never kept up with the expenditures. Sheil seemed incapable of saying no to anyone who proposed a worthy project for his sponsorship. Typical was the creation in 1949 of WFJL, an FM radio station. (The FJL stood for Frank J. Lewis who bankrolled the project.) Although a pioneer in Catholic religious broadcasting, the station reached few Catholic homes since FM radio was still a perk

of the rich and famous, and it constituted an enormous drain on the slender finances. At one point, CYO public relations man Robert Burns commented that Sheil could reach more people by simply shouting out the window. The bishop was not amused. Sheil's unpaid bills to restaurants, construction firms, record companies, and printers mounted. Whenever anyone suggested retrenchment or indicative of his relations with other bishops was his attitude toward the National Catholic Welfare Conference, the chief coordinating body of the American bishops. He showed his contempt for the organization by rarely attending meetings and when he did, absented himself to have lunch at the White House or gather with his own select group of Washington cronies.[11]

But because he traveled so much on his speaking tours, Sheil occasionally angered a local bishop by his statements and the causes he espoused. Sheil rarely paid attention to the canons of episcopal protocol that required the visiting bishop to at least inform the local ordinary if he were going to participate in a public event. Some bishops did not care much. Others could be quite jealous of their turf. One unfortunate and undiplomatic quarrel occurred when Sheil appeared as a guest at a New York dinner honoring Methodist bishop Francis J. McConnell, well known for his support of organized labor. This drew the ire of auxiliary bishop James F. McIntyre of New York (later cardinal archbishop of Los Angeles and a protege of Francis Cardinal Spellman) who wrote to Stritch urging that Sheil be restrained from attending. McIntyre also blamed Sheil for the fact that Frank Sinatra, "the idol of the bobbysoxers," played the role of a priest in the movie *The Miracle of the Bells*.[12] Sheil, he complained, had pushed for Sinatra's selection because the singer had promised to donate his salary to the CYO. All of this, to be sure, found its way back to Cardinal Spellman who took a dim view of Sheil and resented his visits into his bailiwick. Antagonizing Spellman in those days was like stirring up a cobra. You knew he would strike back. If Sheil had any support in Rome (unlikely despite a favorable review of his CYO in *L'Osservatore Romano*), Spellman's pull with Pius XII would have neutralized it.

Attack on Joseph McCarthy and Resignation

By 1953, Sheil knew he was through. Debts continued to mount, and recurrent bouts with respiratory ailments sapped his strength. Coincidental with the decline in his fortunes was the climax of Sen. Joseph McCarthy's Red Scare. Sheil had often been the target of the epithet "communist" but had steadfastly rejected Red-baiting throughout his career. "I have always believed," he once wrote to a fellow bishop, "that Communism is no danger in a society where justice and charity prevail."[13] The answer to communism was social reform, not repression. Although he did temporarily retreat from this position in the early

1950s when he lashed out at "liberals" in the State Department, by 1954 he had returned to his original feelings about Red-baiting. The fact that Spellman supported "McCarty" (as Sheil called him) was probably enough for Sheil to change his mind. In March 1954, McCarthy had boldly marched into Chicago to speak at a St. Patrick's Day celebration. A month later, Sheil took on the Republican senator from Wisconsin at the annual convention of the CIO, held that year at the Chicago Opera House. Using a speech drafted for him by *Commonweal* editor, John Cogley, Sheil blasted McCarthy:

> Are we any safer . . . because General [George] Marshal was branded a traitor? No we aren't. But we are a little less honorable. . . . Are we any safer because nonconformity has been practically identified with treason? I think not. . . . Are we any more to be feared by the Communists because of all the hundreds of headlines the Senator from Wisconsin has piled up? I don't believe so. This kind of ridiculous goings-on is seriously described as anti-Communism. If you will pardon a very lowbrow comment, I say "Phooey!"[14]

Later, Sheil underscored his disdain for McCarthy in an interview with television journalist Edward R. Murrow.

Because of its proximity to his attacks on McCarthy, the resignation of Sheil was linked with these events. Stritch was the recipient of numerous angry letters from enraged Sheil supporters, who accused him of "firing" the good bishop. There is simply no evidence in existing documents or among the principal figures still living today who had access to Stritch to substantiate this claim. Although Stritch did not like clerics "meddling" in partisan politics, he himself had no use for McCarthy or his Red-baiting tactics and would hardly have fired Sheil for speaking out. Sheil resigned because he was out of money, isolated from many of his once close associates, ill, and without hope for advancement. His great hope to be the American Catholic voice for democracy and social reform could not sustain itself without the resources or the prestige of a significant diocese and predictable, expanding financial support.

Stritch turned the CYO over to Msgr. Kelly, who ascertained its indebtedness at about half-a-million dollars (which the archdiocese graciously paid off with its own funds) and then proceeded to dismantle its various programs. Some, like the dental clinic, the CYO band, and a polo farm in Lake County, were abolished altogether. Catholic Charities absorbed some of the old programs such as the Sheil School, which was reincarnated as the Adult Education Centers, as well as the Sheil Guidance Service and Sheil Reading Clinic. The Confraternity of Christian Doctrine took over the Vacation Schools, and the Lewis (Holy Name) School of Aeronautics was transferred to the Diocese of Joliet to become the nucleus of today's Lewis University. The CYO athletic programs remained intact but became more parish-oriented and less centrally directed from CYO headquarters.

Slipping into Obscurity

Sheil resumed pastoral activity at St. Andrew's parish, a position he had held since the 1930s, but long neglected by his years of CYO service. In the early 1960s he managed to wangle himself an honorary archbishop's title and a seat on one of the conciliar commissions. But Sheil did not attend Vatican II and in 1966 was compelled to resign his pastorate by John Cardinal Cody. At the age of eighty, Sheil retired to a comfortable house in Tucson, Arizona, with his secretary, Irene Wiltgen, and lived in virtual obscurity until his death in 1969.

Sheil's name continues to evoke warm memories for many Chicago Catholics. They remember the athletic competitions that put excitement into an otherwise drab and boring urban existence, the famous flashing smile, the powerful voice, the bishop's raw courage to take stands in defense of labor and black

Americans while many American bishops were wishing that both would just go away.

Yet for those who knew him intimately, the recollections are more tinged with disillusionment and even bitterness in a manner reminiscent of the memoirs of Ronald Reagan's former aides. In 1955, Beth Carroll, a former CYO employee, wrote a candid piece in *Harper's* magazine entitled "Bishop Sheil, Prophet Without Honor." She blamed Church officials for not recognizing Sheil's gifts and abilities and contributing to his downfall.[15] But, in the last analysis, she placed the blame for Sheil's sorry end squarely on the shoulders of the bishop himself. This critique was echoed nearly thirty years later by the man Sheil fired in 1946, George Drury.[16]

Drury, who had long observed Sheil from the time of the 1926 Eucharistic Congress through the experience of the Sheil School, highlighted the importance of Sheil's athletic past. Like an athlete or an actor, Sheil was a restless soul, living only for the moment he was "on" and always striving for better and better roles. Sheil's restless temperament allowed him to generate many good programs to which he devoted the fullest measure of his talents, skills, and expertise. But this same characteristic also meant he easily tired of people and projects. Once the lights dimmed and the crowds went away, Sheil's attention waned and he moved on to newer things. Needless to say, the lofty task of social reconstruction, of reclaiming people from lives of helplessness and hopelessness, needed more than a blast of publicity or a well-delivered speech. In the last analysis, Sheil lacked the depth of character necessary to sustain the work he had begun. This, more than finances, health problems, or clashes with fellow bishops, contributed to his decline and fall.

6

Cardinal Meyer and the Era of Confidence

by Steven M. Avella

Cardinal Meyer was never known for his gregariousness or his ability to make small talk. This photograph shows a happy and jovial Meyer, a side rarely seen in public.
—Photo by The New World, *courtesy of the Archives of the Archdiocese of Chicago*

A spirit of uneasiness hung over the Council *aula* on that morning of November 19, 1964.[1] The third session of Vatican II was scheduled to end soon, and the council fathers were waiting anxiously for a preliminary vote on a schema concerning the controversial topic of religious liberty. The debate over the document had been intense, and it had already weathered repeated attempts by the Council's conservative block to sidetrack its passage. Despite all this, it appeared certain that an overwhelming number of bishops would approve the preliminary draft, thus propelling it to ultimate passage. If nothing else, the watching world would soon know that Roman Catholicism had at least embraced the principle of religious freedom.

Abruptly, the president of the twelve-member council of presidents, Eugene Cardinal Tisserant, rose from his chair and announced that the planned vote on the schema would be delayed until the next session. "Several Fathers are of the opinion," Tisserant reported, "that not enough time has been allowed for an examination of the text on Religious Liberty, which appears to be an essentially new document."[2] A mild applause greeted the announcement, but within moments an audible rumble of disbelief and anger swept through St. Peter's Basilica. At the end of the presidential table, the normally placid and dignified cardinal archbishop of Chicago, Albert Gregory Meyer, looked up in stunned incredulity. Since Tisserant had made the declaration on behalf of the council presidents, Meyer wondered if he had been missed in the poll. He hurriedly consulted the cardinals seated near him and inquired if they had been asked. Neither had been. Realizing still another attempt was underway to derail the vote and stung by his apparent duplicity, Meyer stalked from his place to the front of the presidential table and began to remonstrate with the French cardinal. Tisserant brusquely informed him that the decision had been made and that there would be no retraction. "This is a perfect travesty," Meyer is alleged to have retorted.[3]

Meyer walked away from the presidential table and joined a group of ideological allies that included Paul Emile Cardinal Leger of Montreal, Joseph Cardinal Ritter of St. Louis, and Bernard Cardinal Alfrink of Utrecht. Meanwhile, pandemonium was erupting on the council floor as angry bishops spilled out of their chairs and gathered in knots to vent their unhappiness with Tisserant's decision. As the dissatisfaction mounted, Bishop Francis Reh of the North American College hastily drafted a petition beseeching Pope Paul VI to intervene personally and permit the vote. The petitions multiplied, almost magically, and in a short time gathered over six hundred signatures. Buoyed by the rising tide of anger, Meyer agreed to bear them to the pope in company with Cardinals Leger and Ritter. At the conclusion of the morning session the three prelates presented the requests of the council fathers to the pope. Paul VI, who had been watching the unfolding drama on closed-circuit television, had already consulted council parliamentarian Francesco Cardinal Roberti and calmly told the trio that he would not overrule Cardinal Tisserant. But, he assured the crestfallen cardinals, the issue of religious liberty would be at the top of the agenda for the next session of the Council. Not until December 8, 1965, did Pope Paul VI solemnly promulgate the revised Decree on Religious Liberty, *Dignitatis Humanae*. Eight months earlier, Albert Cardinal Meyer, who had assumed a major role in the struggle for its passage, had been laid to rest in the cemetery of St. Mary of the Lake Seminary in Mundelein, Illinois. So much had Albert Gregory Meyer become the acknowledged intellectual leader of the American hierarchy of Vatican II that, at the time of his death, he was tearfully eulogized by theologian Yves Congar as "the *peritus* of the bishops."[4]

Meyer's role in this historic confrontation has not gone unnoticed. The intellectual metamorphosis of this conservative and utterly conventional Midwestern prelate had been one of the truly remarkable stories of the council. His occasional council interventions brought bishops scurrying back to their seats from the coffee bar, and one group of French bishops took their lead from him in determining how they would vote on various issues.[5] However, Meyer, the angered advocate of religious liberty, had not always been so bold. This same Meyer, who had burst virtually unannounced into the papal apartments, had been known for his complete docility to his ecclesiastical superiors, and especially for his lengthy speeches that were heavily larded with excerpts from papal allocutions. Not only was it difficult for anyone who knew him to accept the exaggerated press reports of this episode, but it was hard to imagine that he would even be remotely connected with it at all. Clearly Meyer had changed at the Council. In hindsight, the events of that November morning in 1964 were symbolic of the momentous changes that had already occurred among American Catholic bishops and a harbinger of changes to come among their flocks.

Historians seeking to understand the reasons for the seismic changes in American Catholic life after Vatican II have often understood them as a logical development in the wake of important changes that had occurred in the postwar-preconciliar era, a period already dubbed "the transitional church." Indeed this so-called Indian summer of American Catholic life is replete with examples of important and far-reaching changes that would contribute to the phenomenon of post-Vatican II Catholicism. As the postwar baby boom significantly increased the numbers of Catholics in the United States, Catholics were finally making their move to the American middle class, leaving behind the old blue-collar ethnic neighborhoods and buying homes in mushrooming suburbs. Pressures to expand the existing parochial school systems intensified in almost every diocese, necessitating massive building campaigns and fund-raising drives. Personnel to staff these burgeoning institutions came from overflowing convents and seminaries, which provided priests and sisters in abundance. Underneath these highly visible signs of Catholic mobilization were even more profound indications of significant change. Catholics were becoming better educated as more and more of their numbers availed themselves of government sponsored opportunities for higher education. Significant reforms percolated throughout the Catholic educational network. Catholic sisters, the bulwark of the teaching force in the elementary and secondary schools, were better prepared and educated, while Catholic higher education struggled to improve its quality at the urging of Msgr. John Tracy Ellis and others. American society itself seemed to be shaking off its traditional prejudices against Catholicism by finally electing a Roman Catholic president in 1960.[6] Referring to the changes described above, Jay P. Dolan has written: "These undercurrents of reform pointed out [that] . . . a new age and a new people demanded a new Catholicism."[7] From the vantage point of the postconciliar era, there seemed an inevitability to the changes eventually mandated by the Council.

But the fact is that no one expected the changes that occurred in Catholicism to be quite as dramatic as they were. The large numbers of priests and sisters who resigned their ministries, the contraction of the once flourishing Catholic school system, and the decline in church attendance caught everyone off guard. Commentators on the postconciliar period refer to it as a "maelstrom" or a "revolutionary moment."[8] Changes did indeed occur, but it is hard to maintain, given the booming conditions of preconciliar American Catholicism and the generally conservative ideologies of preconciliar "reformers," that changes came in response to liberalizing pressures in Church and American society. Rather, the key motivating force behind the transformation of American Catholicism was the strong ideological certainty that was part and parcel of the dominant neo-scholastic philosophy of the Church at that time.[9] The leadership elite that opened the floodgates of change at Vatican II responded to the changing social, economic, and political conditions of the world not by departing from the immutable truths of the Catholic faith, but by a burst of confidence, inspired by the example and words of Pope John XXIII that these truths could be applied with salutary effect to modern issues.

Changes occurred in American Catholic life not because of a more progressive American experience, but as a definite stage in the development of conservative American Catholics who had acquired confidence to expose the Church to new external forces. Meyer (to borrow the words of Robert Bellah and his associates) was a "concentrated image"[10] of this confidence at work. He consented to and embraced important changes in Church life by means of the same principles of certainty and clarity that had characterized the mind of the Church throughout his life. American Catholics like Meyer were buoyed to a new phase of their existence by the tides of confidence that broke down the defensive walls of the ghetto to a wider sphere of Catholic influence. An examination of Meyer's career bears this out.

Early Life and Career

Albert Gregory Meyer, the youngest of five children of a Milwaukee grocer and his wife, was born March 9, 1903, in Milwaukee. The Meyers were natives of a small German farming community in Racine County, and Albert grew up with one foot in the world of a fading German ethnicity and the other in a wholly American milieu. A tall, scholarly, solemn young man, Meyer entered St. Francis Seminary in Milwaukee in the fall of 1917 at the age of fourteen.

St. Francis had been opened in 1855 as a seminary for German ethnics, but like many other German institutions in Milwaukee, its character had been decisively altered.[11] Since 1903, the Archdiocese of Milwaukee had been governed by Archbishop Sebastian Messmer. Although he was a German-speaking Swiss and partial to his own, Messmer was above all a strong and effective centralizing bishop, determined to undercut the strong ethnic loyalties that often polarized Milwaukee Catholics (especially the Poles).[12] In particular, he exercised a strong control over the seminary, tightening its rules, weeding out its weaker faculty and administrators, while making provisions for a corps of specially selected priests with Roman degrees to teach there.

At the conclusion of his classics course, Meyer was one of the students selected by Messmer to complete his theological studies in Rome as a student at the Urban College of the Propaganda and the North American College. He was ordained to the priesthood in the summer of 1926 and selected later that year to remain in Rome to take advanced studies at the Pontifical Biblical Institute. The Biblicum, as it was called, had yet to see the advent of historical-critical methodology (in fact it had its origins in opposition to that approach), and Meyer's classes there, even under Fr. Augustine Bea, S.J. (later ghost writer of *Divino Afflante Spiritu*) were basically extensions of his dogmatic training.[13] However, he did pick up valuable instruction in ancient and foreign languages (something that would stand him in good stead at Vatican II) as well as the opportunity to take an extended study trip to the Holy Land. Meyer's priestly and intellectual formation took place in a year when Roman authority and neoscholasticism were the twin poles of the Catholic universe. Despite the conformism that Roman ideology encouraged, it also had a dimension of intellectual self-confidence. Truth was real, objective, knowable, and, once understood, was to be acted upon. Neoscholasticism was not just an abstract theological approach, but a true ideology, a set of ideas and principles that were the guiding stars of his life and the lives of many of his contemporaries. Meyer was an example of the best that the era of consolidation, centralization, and "Romanita" could produce.

He returned to Milwaukee in 1930 and served briefly as a curate in a Waukesha,

Wisconsin, parish. In 1931, Archbishop Samuel Stritch appointed him to the seminary faculty. His hopes of teaching scripture were dashed, however, by the continued presence of Fr. Andrew Breen, a noted scripture scholar, whom Messmer had rescued in 1920 from clerical exile in his home diocese of Rochester, New York. Instead, Meyer was assigned to the chair of dogmatic theology together with courses for the collegiate and high school students who attended St. Francis Seminary. He won the favor of the two archdiocesan ordinaries under whom he served, Samuel A. Stritch and Moses E. Kiley.

Stritch, an amiable and easygoing man, had not gotten along with the brusque and efficient Msgr. Aloisius Muench, who had been in the rector's chair when he arrived. When Muench was appointed to the Diocese of Fargo, North Dakota, in 1935, Stritch replaced him with sociologist Fr. Francis Haas.

But Haas was so consumed with labor relations and other government work that he was virtually an absentee rector.[14] In 1937, Stritch appointed Meyer rector, recognizing in him a humble and docile man with a penchant for order and a reputation for administrative capability. Moses E. Kiley, who became archbishop in 1940, put Meyer's docility to the test. Kiley had been a spiritual director at the North American when Meyer was a student priest, and the two had become close friends. But as an ecclesiastical superior, Kiley could be a harsh, puritanical autocrat, who made life difficult for those who worked under him, including Meyer. He regularly interfered with even the minutiae of seminary life and administration and ran roughshod over anyone who dared oppose or question him.[15] Nonetheless, Meyer remained in the archbishop's favor. A restructuring of the dioceses of Wisconsin occurred after World War II, creat-

Albert G. Meyer as a young boy growing up in Milwaukee.

—Photo courtesy of the Meyer family

Meyer as rector of St. Francis Seminary in Milwaukee.

—Photo courtesy of the Archives of St. Francis Seminary, Milwaukee

Meyer, seated on the extreme left, is pictured here with Fr. Peter Schnitzler, his grade school Latin teacher, and the boys who were destined for the seminary.

—Photo courtesy of the Meyer family

ing a new see in the state capital at Madison. Bishop William Patrick O'Connor of Superior, Wisconsin, was selected to head the new dio-cese, and Meyer was chosen to succeed O'Connor in Superior. He was consecrated a bishop by Kiley on April 11, 1946.

Bishop of Superior

Meyer was loath to leave St. Francis, but he dutifully threw himself into the task of governing the sixteen-county Diocese of Superior, described by one of its priests as "a diocese of forests and farms, with the forests in quite secure possession of most of the territory."[16] The years in Superior (1946–1953) were a period of episcopal novitiate. Despite limited finances and widely separated centers of Catholic life, Meyer attempted to consolidate and unify the missionary diocese and establish some control over the "medley of clerical characters" who occupied the parishes and far-flung missions of the rural see. The pro-tracted winters in Superior also enabled him to keep up on some of his scholarly interests by writing a series of sermon guides that were disseminated all over Wisconsin and beyond. But the relatively slow pace of life in Superior was atypical of the general American Catholic experience in the large urban dioceses of the Midwest and East. The postwar boom in American Catholic life had already begun and would only reach Superior in the late 1950s. Meyer would meet the forces of transition head-on, for upon the death of Moses Kiley in 1953, Meyer was called back to Milwaukee to become its seventh archbishop.

Milwaukee: Burgeoning Growth

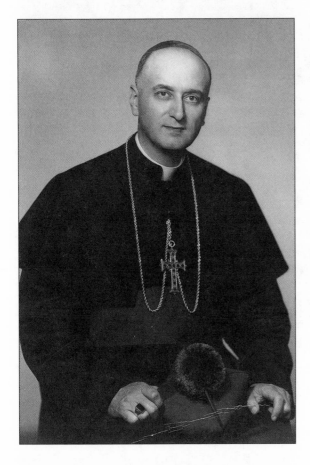

Meyer as Archbishop of Milwaukee.
—Photo compliments of the Archives of the
Archdiocese of Milwaukee

He departed the placid shores of Lake Superior for the bustling shores of Lake Michigan where the pace of growth and the demands on his leadership were greater. The Archdiocese of Milwaukee was indeed growing and booming, but its transitional years had been somewhat forestalled by the policies of Archbishop Kiley. The old prelate had been chronically ill since 1951 and stubbornly refused to delegate one iota of his episcopal authority to any of his subordinates. This created a huge backlog of neglected building and expansion projects that were crying for attention. Institutional expansion became the centerpiece of Meyer's five-year episcopate as he set to work, immediately responding to the

challenges of the expanding Church. He reinvigorated the board of consultors (Kiley rarely consulted it) to approve property purchases for new parishes, borrow money, and deliberate on the architectural prodigies of ambitious pastors.[17] Significant growth in Catholic numbers was occurring in the major urban centers of the see, Racine, Waukesha, Kenosha, Sheboygan, and Fond du Lac, but the axis of archdiocesan life continued to be the city and county of Milwaukee where over 80 percent of the see's nearly five hundred thousand faithful lived and worshiped. The city of Milwaukee had gone on a binge of annexation adding eight suburbs to the urban domains between 1950 and 1957. The extension of city services (especially the expressway system) to these newly added areas encouraged droves of people to abandon urban neighborhoods and businesses and relocate.[18] Keeping the Church current with this growth was the special task of the Chancellor, Fr. Leo Brust, who regularly pored over utility and telephone company surveys to determine the best sites for new parishes and then rushed out to inspect and purchase thousands of dollars worth of prime land. Meyer wrote to a Milwaukee priest stationed in Rome: "It seems that every other week practically we are consummating some new property deal to keep up with the expansion."[19] Schools too were bursting at the seams, and new buildings and additions were going up everywhere. Moreover, the Archdiocesan Office of Education under Msgr. Edmund "Buck" Goebel was constantly pressing religious communities to open new high schools to accommodate the growing numbers of Catholic teens. Religious life and seminary enrollments skyrocketed, necessitating the single largest building program at the archdiocesan seminary since Archbishop John Martin Henni had put up the handsome main building in 1855. Moreover, the devotional life of the people was in the pink of health. Huge Holy Name rallies, block rosaries, Marian Year devotions, and the activities of a coordinated Sodality movement regularly made the pages of the archdiocesan newspaper, the *Catholic*

Herald-Citizen.[20] Altogether, Meyer oversaw the establishment of twenty-two new parishes, the construction of thirty-four new churches, seventy-four new grade schools, three central high schools, and sanctioned a $3 million addition to the major seminary.[21]

Underneath this frenetic pace of planning and building were other changes that were altering the landscape of Milwaukee Catholicism. The black population of the city of Milwaukee nearly trebled during the 1950s, jumping from twenty-three thousand to over sixty thousand. As Milwaukee's black community pushed outside the imposed boundaries of their district just north and west of the city's business district, changing neighborhoods affected the old urban churches and schools that had once been the strongholds of Milwaukee's German community. Because the job market for blacks was relatively good in the prosperous years of the 1950s and the Socialist city government of Mayor Frank Zeidler was perceived as favorable to black citizens, the Milwaukee community and the Church were spared the effects of serious racial unrest.[22] Meyer's concern for blacks extended primarily to the minority of black Catholics who were tended to by the Capuchins, the Racine Dominican Sisters, and the School Sisters of Notre Dame. But questions of racial justice, integration (especially on the largely Polish South Side), and housing were not long in coming. Among the few Milwaukee Catholics who were seriously discussing the implications of racial matters were a core group of articulate and aggressive laity who represented a new generation of the old Catholic Action movements. By the mid-1950s these movements had matured beyond clerically dominated lay assistance programs such that a well-educated and articulate corps of Catholic laypersons existed in the Milwaukee archdiocese who were interested and informed in many areas of Catholic life. Many of these suburbanites and professional types compelled Meyer to pay attention to them and impressed him with their obvious devotion to the mind of the Church.[23]

Although Meyer was often consumed with the sheer pace of work this busy era was demanding, he took note of the significant changes occurring in the Catholic commu-

Meyer receiving the obedience of one of his priests as he is enthroned as Archbishop of Milwaukee.

—*Photo compliments of the Archives of the Archdiocese of Milwaukee*

nity. He made this clear in an address at a church dedication:

> The challenge of modern times . . . is not only or even principally met by the creation of new facilities . . . important as these are. The moral and spiritual fiber of a community are determined indeed in part by the material environment in which people have to live; but that environment is itself subordinate to the religious life of the people, and their realization of the place of God in their lives. Catholic confidence is founded not in ourselves, but in our understanding and acceptance of the plan of Christ: 'Thou art Peter and upon this rock I will build my church.'[24]

Yet there were limits to what he could do in Milwaukee. Neither the times nor the generally conservative temperament of Milwaukee's priests and larger community (after all he was a hometown boy) allowed the fullest flowering of this spirit of confidence. The experience of Chicago Catholicism and Vatican II would provide the necessary stimulus to a fuller expression of this confidence.

To Chicago

In January of 1958, at the age of seventy, an ailing Samuel Cardinal Stritch was appointed proprefect of the Roman Congregation for the Propagation of the Faith. The reasons for this move are still shrouded in mystery. Whatever the rationale, Stritch went to Rome unwillingly and died before he could assume his new duties. Pius XII, himself in his final days, personally intervened in the choice of a successor to Stritch and selected Albert Gregory Meyer for the Chicago post in September 1958.

Chicago's Catholic establishment dwarfed that of its neighbor to the north. Two million Catholics lived in the two-county archdiocesan boundaries out of a total of four million total residents. There were over two thousand priests, four thousand sisters, and five hun-

Meyer entering Chicago as archbishop in 1959. Flanking him at the left is Msgr. George Casey and at right Auxiliary Bishop William O'Brien.
—Photo by The New World, *courtesy of the Archives of the Archdiocese of Chicago*

dred parishes. Like Milwaukee, Chicago had been in the process of massive population shifts to the western suburbs since the end of the war. Indeed Stritch had told a group of priests in the early 1950s: "A whole new diocese is being built on the outskirts of the city."[25] The needs of this growing body of Catholics engaged Meyer's attention in Chicago as it had in Milwaukee with parochial, institutional, and seminary expansion at the top of the list.

But serious problems in urban Chicago addressed an even more significant challenge to Meyer's social conscience and compelled him to articulate a clear vision of the Church's response. The paramount challenge for many large northern cities was racial relations. Since 1940, Chicago's black population had been steadily increasing, standing at 852,000 by 1960. The inexorable advance of the black residential district southward and westward brought a familiar pattern of white resistance and ultimately white flight. For the Church this meant that once thriving urban parishes and schools were soon abandoned as parishioners fled to the suburbs.[26] Moreover, Catholic laypersons and priests often supported and even led movements to keep blacks out of Catholic schools and white neighborhoods.

The shifting racial composition of neighborhoods was only one agent of change. In the 1950s, the administration of Mayor Richard J. Daley launched a major program of urban renewal. These coordinated efforts of government and private developers sought to reclaim blighted areas of the city by tearing down dilapidated housing and replacing it with more expensive dwellings. Hence the plight of many displaced citizens (many but not all of them black) tugged at the sympathies of local pastors and archdiocesan officials. Local priests found themselves the natural leaders of disparate movements to control or resist these urban plans.[27]

When Meyer moved to Chicago, he stepped into a moving stream of clerical and lay activism encouraged by his predecessors Mundelein and Stritch to address the needs of the changing city. Since the 1930s, two Chicago clerics in particular had energized and marshaled the efforts of committed priests to address the problems: Bishop Bernard J. Sheil and Msgr. Reynold Hillenbrand.

The Sheil Legacy

Because of his work in organizing the Catholic Youth Organization (CYO), Bernard J. Sheil's name was more familiar to the average Catholic.[28] He had become an auxiliary bishop and vicar general of the diocese in 1928 under Cardinal Mundelein and used his office as a bully pulpit for some very progressive and even courageous stands on labor organization, racial relations, community organization, and New Deal politics. One of the most stimulating projects to come out of Sheil's active mind was the establishment in 1943 of a school of social studies (named for himself) that offered a program of adult education intended to relate the church to the needs of the times. The Sheil School of Social Studies shared the Congress Street building with the CYO and was initially directed by James Shannon. Later, George Drury and then Viatorian Father Edward Cardinal directed the organization. The Sheil School attracted considerable talent to its roster of volunteer faculty and provided a number of high quality adult education programs on a diversity of issues related to Chicago Catholic life.[29] When it collapsed in the early 1950s, with much of Sheil's empire, it was succeeded by the equally innovative adult education centers conceived by Msgr. Daniel Cantwell and headed by layman Russell Barta.[30]

Hillenbrand's Influence

The Sheil School provided a strong undercurrent of intellectual vitality to the Catholic Church in Chicago, a vitality complemented by the less visible but perhaps more efficacious work of Msgr. Reynold Hillenbrand.[31] The son of a Chicago dentist, Hillenbrand was ordained in 1929 and in 1936 appointed rector of St. Mary of the Lake Seminary. Mundelein introduced him to the seminarians by saying, "The seminary can be a dull place so I've brought you a man with imagination."[32] Nothing could have been truer. Hillenbrand linked a passionate attachment to papal social teaching to an equally strong interest in the liturgical movement and was able to influence a generation of priests to be actively engaged in the social ministry of the Church. Moreover, since 1938 he had been a devoted follower of the methodology of Specialized Catholic Action pioneered by Canon Joseph Cardijn of Belgium, and this enthusiasm rubbed off on the impressionable young clerics under his charge. Later, Hillenbrand was instrumental in developing the program of the Christian Family Movement, perhaps one of the most successful family organizations in American Catholicism. Hillenbrand was eventually removed from the seminary in 1944, but the effect he had on students like Daniel Cantwell, John Egan, William McManus, George Higgins, and William Quinn was of inestimable value for the Catholic Church. It is important to note that the theological and philosophical backgrounds of these activists were remarkably similar to Meyer's. (Hillenbrand would later be castigated in postconciliar years as an outdated curmudgeon because of his deep-seated attachment to papal teaching.) Here were people grounded in the same basics of Catholic teaching and theology, successfully and confidently applying the lessons of those truths to the evolving conditions of Church life.

Despite tensions and difficulties Stritch experienced with both Sheil and Hillenbrand, he generally tolerated their activities as long as they did not create problems for him. At times he even funded some of the projects from his own pocket or archdiocesan funds. By 1956 *Jubilee* magazine lauded the Chicago church as "the center of an amazing rebirth of the Christian spirit."[33] Meyer caught the Chicago spirit, and even more than Stritch who allowed events to lead him, soon moved to the forefront in dealing with the knotty problems confronting the Church in the changing urban and suburban environments.

Confronting Racial Issues

Chicago's tense racial situation enjoined his attention early on because of its significant impact on urban Catholic life. Although Meyer was no stranger to the conditions in urban ghettos he determined to study the problems of Chicago firsthand. Throughout 1959 he traveled with the city archdiocesan urban affairs director Msgr. John Egan, seeing both the slums and the Gold Coast, talking to people on the street, and hearing of the effects of discrimination.[34] It did not take him long to realize the massive problems confronting the city and the Church, nor did he long hesitate in acting on behalf of racial justice. He actively elicited the advice of veteran priests active in the black apostolate, including men such as Msgr. Daniel Cantwell, the chaplain of the Catholic Interracial Council since its foundation in 1946, as well as successful pastors of black parishes, Joseph Richards and Martin Farrell. In mid-1959 he allowed Msgr. Egan to draft a statement in his name to the President's Commission on Civil Rights, which made a strong appeal to end the housing shortage for blacks and to encourage black community organization.[35] In addition, Meyer quietly challenged and at times removed pastors who resisted racial integration.

Cantwell would write of Meyer's decisiveness in racial matters: "Happily we have in Archbishop Meyer the most aggressive leadership that we have ever enjoyed. He does it, of

Meyer was reluctant to become overtly involved in urban politics. Here he makes a rare joint appearance with Chicago Mayor Richard J. Daley at a television panel session.
—*Photo by* The New World, *courtesy of the Archives of the Archdiocese of Chicago*

course, very quietly, but he has already insisted that certain embarrassing situations of long standing had to be corrected without any further delay."[36] In the following year, again under the advice of Cantwell, Farrell, Egan, and Superintendent of Schools William E. McManus, a major clergy conference on the Church and the Negro was convened. In a widely acclaimed speech entitled "The Mantle of Justice," Meyer revealed the basis for his thinking on the proper Catholic response to race. Paraphrasing the 1958 Episcopal Conference Statement on Race, he stated:

The heart of the race question is moral and religious. No one who bears the name of Christian can deny the universal love of God for all mankind. Our Christian faith is of its nature universal; it knows not the distinction of race, color or nationhood.

We must accept these conclusions: First, we must repeat the principle that all men are created equal in the sight of God. By equal we mean that they are created by God and redeemed by His Divine Son, that they are bound by His Law and that God desires them as His friends in the eternity of heaven. This fact confers upon all men human dig-

nity and human rights. . . . The second important conclusion is: we are bound to love our fellow-man. This Christian love is not a matter of emotional likes or dislikes. It is a firm purpose to do good to all men, to the extent that ability and opportunity permit.

From these clear principles, Meyer insisted, "Every Catholic child of the Negro race, whether his parents be Catholic or not, has free access to our schools as any other Catholic child on all levels of academic training, elementary and secondary, as well as higher levels."[37] Following up on this rhetoric Meyer mandated the preaching of a series of sermons on racial justice in all Chicago parishes, pressed forcefully for admission of blacks into Catholic high schools, and continued to pressure pastors who were dragging their feet on admitting black children to their schools and parishes. Moreover, he granted liberal permission to his clergy to participate in national and local civil rights demonstrations. The culmination of his efforts came in early 1963 when the historic Chicago Conference on Religion and Race was convened. So great had his confidence in the efficacy of Catholic thinking become that now he could even sit down with Protestants and Jews in an epochal joint endeavor.

Community Organization

Housing and community organization also became an opportunity for the application of Church teaching. Ecclesiastical interest in the preservation of Chicago's neighborhoods arose in the wake of the city's urban renewal program after World War II. In 1953 Cardinal Stritch formed the Cardinal's Conservation Committee (later changed to the Archdiocesan Office of Urban Affairs), an advisory board of leading pastors that would discuss and act on issues affecting the Church and urban renewal. In 1957 Stritch appointed Msgr. John Egan as executive secretary of the same committee that Egan had drifted away from in his earlier work with the popular Cana Conference, and with Stritch's permission, became an intern with the Industrial Areas Foundation of community organizer Saul D. Alinsky. Alinsky's success in organizing the famous Back of the Yards community in the 1930s had convinced Egan of the significant role the Church could play by providing natural leadership for community organization.[38] Stritch had offered as much support and money as he could afford, but Meyer dramatically expanded the investment of the Church in the process of community organization. Under the influence of Egan and Msgr. Edward Burke, Meyer approved a liberal use of his archiepiscopal prestige and church funds in the establishment of community organizations. In 1959, he lent his endorsement to the newly-formed Organization of the Southwest Community. In 1961, he convoked a memorable meeting of the Polish pastors of Chicago's Northwest Side and all but ordered them to contribute substantial sums from their parish treasuries to the Northwest Community Organization.[39] In that same year he committed support and subsidies from Catholic Charities to the all-black Woodlawn Organization spearheaded by Fr. Martin Farrell and two Protestant ministers. His personal feelings for Alinsky aside (he did not like or really trust him), Meyer saw in these efforts a practical application of the virtue of justice and, once convinced, supported them as completely as his time and energies allowed.

Theological Renewal and Vatican II

This background of Meyer's confident response to Chicago Catholicism's problems makes it easier to understand his activities at Vatican II. As early as 1959, Meyer's ideas on the correct exegesis of scripture had begun to change as the result of presentations at a Summer Biblical Institute for priests held at Glen Ellyn, Illinois, by Passionist Barnabas Mary Ahern. Ahern's respectful and convincing exposition of the historical-critical method together with extended correspondence with his old teacher Augustine Cardinal Bea, S.J., gave Meyer a whole new outlook on understanding and use of scripture.[40] But if Ahern and Bea incited thoughtful curiosity in Meyer's mind, the opening address of Pope John XXIII at the Council positively energized him. John urged the council fathers not to get bogged down in debates over doctrine; those points were settled. Instead the mission of the council was to apply those timeless teachings to the exigencies of modern times:

> The greatest concern of the ecumenical council is this: that the sacred deposit of Christian doctrine should be guarded and taught more efficaciously. . . . In order, however, that this doctrine may influence the numerous fields of human activity . . . it is necessary . . . that the Church should never depart from the sacred patrimony of truth . . . but at the same time she must ever look to the present, to the new conditions and new forms of life introduced into the modern world which have opened new avenues to the Catholic apostolate.[41]

Meyer taking possession of his titular Church in Rome, St. Cecilia in Trastevere after his elevation to the rank of cardinal in 1960.
—*Photo courtesy of T. Benedetti, Via Pietro Giannone, Rome*

Meyer emerged as a leader of the American bishops at Vatican II. His impeccable ecclesiastical Latin, his grasp of the major theological issues at the council, and his cardinalitial rank allowed him to stand out as one of the major American prelates at the gathering. Here he confers with his successor in Milwaukee, William E. Cousins.
—*Photo compliments of the Archives of the Archdiocese of Milwaukee*

Nothing more perfectly articulated Meyer's evolving position, vis-à-vis the Church and the world. His alliance with the moderate-progressive faction of the Council that included Cardinals Bea, Alfrink, and Suenens was a linkage with a like-minded group of confident prelates who had also seized on John's vision for the Council. He opposed old teachers and friends like Ernesto Cardinal Ruffini and Alfredo Cardinal Ottaviani because they were not confident enough that Catholic teaching would eventually triumph. Indeed, his first intervention on the council floor was a call to rework the proposed document on Divine Revelation that had been crafted by Ottaviani's preconciliar doctrinal commission. In subsequent interventions Meyer offered support and amendments to key conciliar documents, including *The Constitution on the Church* and *The Church in the Modern World* as well as *The Decree on Christians and Jews* and *The Decree on Priestly Life and Formation*, not to mention *The Degree of Religious Liberty*.

The sense of euphoria that characterized the Council and the immediate postconciliar era bears witness to the high hopes and expectations that these meetings held. The Church would shed its defensive posture and allow its clear and confident teaching to affect humanity. The confidence inspired by a strong neoscholastic Catholic ideology was the midwife of the postconciliar era. American Catholicism's "Indian summer" was not a period of liberal ferment, of revolutionaries waiting in the wings to seize power. Rather it represented the maturation of a basically conservative approach to social and theological issues. Albert Gregory Meyer was typical of that era. The Church of the 1950s was an age of transitions. Meyer never saw or imagined what it was in transit to.

7

The Beginning and the End of an Era: George William Mundelein and John Patrick Cody in Chicago

by Edward R. Kantowicz

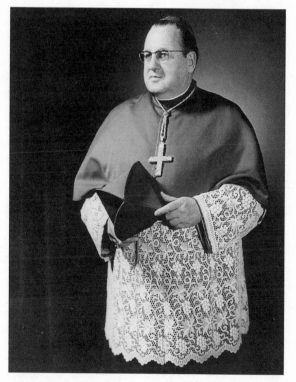

The beginning of an era. George William Cardinal Mundelein, third archbishop of Chicago, 1916–1939.
—Photo by The New World, *courtesy of the Archives of the Archdiocese of Chicago*

The end of an era. John Patrick Cardinal Cody, sixth archbishop of Chicago, 1965–1982.
—Photo by Fabian Bachrach, courtesy of the Archives of the Archdiocese of Chicago

When George William Cardinal Mundelein of Chicago was buried on October 6, 1939, the administrator of the archdiocese declared all three and a half million Chicagoans, Catholic and non-Catholic alike, honorary pallbearers. So closely had the cardinal identified himself with his adopted city (he came from New York) that this unusual gesture seemed perfectly appropriate. Mundelein's influence extended far beyond Chicago, however, to Rome and Washington. The eulogist at his funeral noted: "Cardinal Mundelein was not a man to confine himself to the sacristy, but, exercising his franchise as a free American citizen, he played a man's part in public life." A *Chicago Tribune* columnist styled Mundelein "the most influential Catholic in the world . . . next to the Pope." Both Mundelein's contemporaries and later observers have concluded that the Chicago cardinal "put the Catholic Church on the map" in the United States.[1]

Forty years and three archbishops later, John Patrick Cardinal Cody was laid to rest on April 29, 1982. Hundreds of dignitaries and thousands of mourners attended the splendid obsequies for Cody, but nonetheless a cloud seemed to hover over the proceedings. Controversy had swirled about Cody's seventeen-year stewardship of the Chicago archdiocese. Many observers believed that both Pope Paul VI and Pope John Paul I were on the verge of removing him in 1978 when death felled them both. The *Chicago Sun-Times* revealed in 1981 that the United States atttorney had instructed a grand jury to investigate Cody's diversion of funds to a woman who turned out to be his stepcousin. The eulogist at Cody's funeral delivered an eloquent address on the Christian meaning of death, but he barely mentioned the deceased cardinal. Chicagoans seemed more relieved than saddened by Cardinal Cody's death.[2]

Why the vast difference in reputation between those two cardinals, whose administrations in Chicago spanned nearly half the twentieth century? The simplest explanation is that Mundelein ushered in the beginning of a distinct era in church history and identified himself with it, whereas Cody came in at the end of that era and, unfortunately for him, outlived it. Mundelein's administration marked a rising sun, Cody's signaled sunset. There were important differences in management style and personnel policy between the two men as well, but in order to understand the contrast between them, we must first delineate the beginning and the end of their era.

Consolidating Bishops and an Era of Institutional Maturity

The years from 1910 to the Second Vatican Council of the 1960s mark a distinct period in American Catholic history, though this has been insufficiently noted by Church historians.[3]

Prior to the turn of the century, American Catholicism was weak and disorganized. Catholic bishops had their hands full simply building churches and schools for the millions of immigrants pouring into America and had no time for fine points of administration. The laity took the initiative in shaping their own brands of immigrant Catholicism, priests were often undisciplined and always independent-minded, and American Catholics lacked status and respect both in Rome and in America. Roman authorities considered the United States a mission territory as late as 1908, and in 1899 the pope condemned a vague set of doctrines he called "Americanism." American Protestants, for their part, feared and mistrusted the Catholic Church as an un-American invader of the republic. American Catholics were too Roman for the native Protestants but also too American for Rome.

Then in the years surrounding World War I, a generation of American-born but Roman-trained bishops came to power in the largest urban dioceses of the United States. Men such as William Cardinal O'Connell in Boston, George Cardinal Mundelein in Chicago, and Francis Cardinal Spellman in New York were "consolidating bishops" who, like their counterparts in business and government, saw a need for greater order and efficiency. They centralized and tightened the administrative structure of their dioceses and put them on a firm financial footing; they built the beginnings of a national Catholic administration in Washington; and they tied American Catholicism more closely to headquarters in Rome.

The consolidating bishops also gained new respect for the American Catholic Church, both in Rome, where their financial support became the Vatican's mainstay, and in the United States, where their highly visible leadership bolstered the self-image of American Catholics and earned the grudging respect of non-Catholics. The careers of O'Connell, Mundelein, and Spellman spanned the entire period from the turn of the century to Vatican II. Their leadership and that of similar bishops in other cities brought the American Catholic Church to institutional maturity and earned for it self-confidence and power at home and in the Vatican.[4]

This period of institutional maturity and satisfied self-confidence ended with astonishing swiftness after the Second Vatican Council, when priests, nuns, and laity openly challenged their bishops and then left the Church in droves. Yet, for about fifty years, from 1910 to 1960, the American church seemed monolithic and unchanging. Having overcome the administrative disorder and psychological insecurity of an immigrant church, the Catholic community in the first half of the twentieth century felt fully Catholic and fully American—an enormous achievement for the leadership of the consolidating bishops. Their leadership had many facets, but three aspects of their episcopal style—Romanism, triumphalism, and centralization—will illuminate the comparison between Mundelein and Cody.

Romanism, Triumphalism, and Centralization

Born in 1872 in New York City, George William Mundelein entered priestly studies for the Brooklyn diocese, whose bishop, Charles McDonnell, handpicked him for a Roman education. Mundelein studied at the Urban College of the Propaganda from 1892 to 1895 and was ordained in Rome by Bishop McDonnell on June 8, 1895. One acquaintance he made in the Eternal City, John Bonzano, proved crucial to his later career. A few years older than Mundelein, Bonzano later served as rector of the Urban College and, more important, as apostolic delegate to the United States from 1912 to 1922, where he was instrumental in Mundelein's appointment to Chicago.[5]

Mundelein remained a thoroughgoing Romanist all his life. In 1907 he wrote an essay defending the pope's condemnation of modernism, a Latin literary effort that earned him entrance into the ancient Roman Academy of the Arcadia. As archbishop of Chicago, he made the Peter's Pence collection a top priority, raising over $120,000 a year in the 1920s, more than the entire American church had collected at the turn of the century. When he built a new major seminary for Chicago, he chose early American, neoclassical architecture for the façades, but he designed the seminary rules from Roman models. The interior of the seminary library was patterned after the Barberini Palace in

Rome, and the focal point of the seminary plan centered on a Roman column with a statue of the Virgin atop it. Under Mundelein's leadership, the Catholic Church in Chicago became American on the outside but Roman to the core.[6]

The cardinal cultivated a special relationship with Pope Pius XI, who appreciated Chicago Catholic financial support and encouraged Catholic Action social experiments. Each of the major consolidating bishops—O'Connell, Mundelein, and Spellman—was close to a particular pope: O'Connell to Pius X, Mundelein to Pius XI, and Spellman to Pius XII. Mundelein's special relationship to the pope who reigned during most of his administration in Chicago earned him a reputation as a kingmaker, with a decisive voice in the naming of American bishops.

Mundelein conducted all his public activities with an imperial flair, which is nowadays called triumphalism. Affecting the manner of a Renaissance prince, he collected old coins and manuscripts, purchased gigantic paintings from the school of Rubens and Titian, and assembled a collection of famous men's autographs. Clerical wags referred to him as the "late Cardinal Mundelein" for he often arrived slightly late at a public ceremony, sweeping in swiftly for maximum effect with horns blowing and police sirens blaring.

Mundelein believed that the Church should "go first class," in order to overcome its immigrant defensiveness.[7] He hired the best law firm in the city to defend the Church's interests and worked with the speaker of the Illinois House of Representatives as his personal agent in the legislature. When he built his new seminary, St. Mary of the Lake, he designed a lavish plan, sprawling over a thousand acres, with a private golf course and lake. Each seminarian enjoyed his own room with a bath. Mundelein provided first-class facilities for his seminarians, then demanded a lot in return. He expected them to be giants—physically, intellectually, spiritually.

The high point of Mundelein's triumphalism came in 1926 when he brought the International Eucharistic Congress to the United States for the first time. Prelates and pilgrims gathered from all over the world at the lakefront Soldier Field from July 20 to 24. Then,

on the final day, close to one million worshipers attended an outdoor procession at Mundelein's seminary outside the city. The Chicago Catholic newspaper *The New World* cautioned its readers: "Let there be no mistaking the fact that the Eucharistic Congress is no endeavor to demonstrate strength. There is no thought behind it of a flaunting of vast numbers before non-Catholics." Yet a "flaunting of vast numbers" is precisely what Chicago's Eucharistic Congress accomplished. It was a flamboyant, slightly arrogant proof that American Catholics had arrived.[8]

Such triumphal display may seem like megalomania, but it was more than personal vainglory. Mundelein was trying to carry a whole institution—a whole generation of immigrant outsiders—upward with him. Acutely aware that Catholics in America lacked self-confidence and social status, he tried to burnish the image of the Catholic Church. Triumphal display carried risks. It could, and probably did, evoke Protestant fears of the Church's foreign and antirepublican connections. Yet, on the other hand, Americans love spectacle, and they frequently fawn over royalty. In a country without a royal family, cardinal princes filled a psychological vacuum and raised the status of the Catholic minority.

Mundelein, however, earned his greatest accolades not for ceremonial excess but for businesslike management.[9] The cardinal centralized fundraising for Catholic Charities and other causes and levied assessments on the parishes to finance the seminary and the Eucharistic Congress. He took all crucial brick-and-mortar decisions away from the individual pastors. Before a pastor could build, he had to negotiate a nine-step bureaucratic process that included the bishop's approval of the architect, a full discussion of the parish finances by the board of consultors, and the constant supervision of the project by a two-man subcommittee of consultors. He removed a handful of priests from parish work and named them diocesan directors for charities, schools, cemeteries, and the missions, thus creating the beginnings of an administrative bureaucracy in the chancery office.

In order to shift capital internally within the archdiocese, Mundelein used his corporate bonding power to create a central banking mechanism. Legally constituted as a corporation sole, the Catholic Bishop of Chicago had the power to issue bonds. Mundelein required parishes that showed a surplus to invest the money in Catholic Bishop of Chicago bonds, and then he loaned this money to poorer parishes at a low rate of interest. In effect, he had created a diocesan bank that shifted money from wealthy parishes to those in need and permitted rational planning and management. Cardinal Spellman of New York is often credited with devising the first central bank in a Catholic diocese, but Mundelein's system predates Spellman's by twenty years.[10]

Centralized management put the Catholic Church in Chicago on a firm financial footing and gained the respect of American businessmen. The archdiocese's credit survived the depression intact, and Catholic Bishop of Chicago bonds rarely dropped below par. There was an oft-repeated comment, variously attributed either to Julius Rosenwald of Sears, Roebuck or Frederick Eckert of Metropolitan Life as well as to other business leaders, that Mundelein missed his calling by going into religion rather than business.

Thirty-five years younger than Mundelein, John Patrick Cody grew up during the heyday of the consolidating bishops and apprenticed with one of their number, Archbishop John Glennon of St. Louis.[11] Born in St. Louis in 1907, Cody entered the seminary at age thirteen, receiving an even more thorough Roman indoctrination than Mundelein had. He spent nearly ten years in Rome, first as a student at the North American College from 1927 to 1931, then as vice rector of the college and staff member of Cardinal Pacelli's Secretariat of State from 1932 to 1938. One of his fellow workers in the Vatican Secretariat was a young papal diplomat named Giovanni Montini. Later, as Pope Paul VI, Montini would assign Cody to Chicago, name him a cardinal, then hesitate indecisively over the possibility of removing him. Cody liked to joke about his closeness to Paul VI: "Whenever the Pope sees me, he always reminds me that I was ordained a bishop seven years before he was."[12]

Indeed, Cody's Roman training brought him rapid ecclesiastical advancement.

Archbishop Glennon recalled him to St. Louis in 1938 to serve as his personal secretary. Cody then became chancellor of the St. Louis archdiocese in 1940 and auxiliary bishop in 1947. The Roman authorities moved Cody frequently before finally assigning him to Chicago. Between 1954 and 1965 he served in three different dioceses—St. Joseph, Missouri; Kansas City, Missouri; and New Orleans, Louisiana. In each case, he started out as coadjutor to an aging bishop, then swiftly ascended to full authority as ordinary.

Cody had already proved his complete Romanism and his primary loyalty to the Church before he was consecrated bishop. In February 1946 he accompanied Archbishop Glennon to Rome when the ailing, elderly prelate belatedly received a cardinal's red hat. After the conclave, Glennon retired to his boyhood home in Ireland to die, posing Cody with a thorny dilemma. Cody's mother also lay mortally ill at this time, so he had to choose which deathbed to sit by, Cardinal Glennon's or his mother's. He chose the cardinal's. On March 9, 1946, Glennon died with Cody at his side; that very same day, Mrs. Mary Cody was buried in St. Louis.[13]

Once appointed to Chicago, Cody continued the imperial style of his predecessors. Indeed, he stage-managed a triumphal entrance into the Windy City worthy of a prince or a president. To the surprise of his advisers, Cody decided to travel from New Orleans to Chicago by train, not by air. He set off with the mayor of New Orleans aboard, then picked up the mayors of St. Louis and Kansas City along the way. South of Chicago, he changed trains and made the final run into Union Station flanked by Chicago Mayor Richard J. Daley and Illinois Governor Otto Kerner. Thousands of priests and nuns, with flag-waving schoolchildren, cheered him at each stop.[14]

Cody's physical appearance also seemed a throwback to a more imperial age. The *Chicago Tribune* called him, tactfully, "a man of great scale," and the *New York Times* described him as "a man who might have been a Notre Dame tackle in the [Knute] Rockne days but has since lost his battle with the scales." The archbishop liked to assert his authority in the time-honored Chicago practice of demonstrating clout. The editor of the archdiocesan newspaper reported that "he would boast about being able to get his plane in—if he was coming in and planes were all stacked up, he could get the plane he was aboard landed ahead of the others at O'Hare. . . . If he wanted something, he could always find people to do it."[15]

Cody also continued and completed the work of bureaucratic centralization and administrative consolidation that Mundelein had begun. Mundelein's immediate successors had not much changed the administrative structures of the Chicago archdiocese. Samuel Cardinal Stritch (1939–1958) was a gregarious, outgoing person who gave speeches and shook hands but left administration to his chancellor and vicar general, men handpicked and trained by Mundelein. Albert Cardinal Meyer (1958–1965) was so preoccupied with the proceedings of the Vatican Council in Rome that he had little time to make changes in Chicago. But Cody hit the city like a whirlwind, summarily dismissing a handful of old pastors and proceeding to shore up the central bureaucracy of the archdiocese.

He instituted life and health insurance plans for priests, funded a pension plan for both lay and clerical employees, and organized a personnel board to standardize appointment procedures. He greatly expanded the number of central archdiocesan agencies, housing them under one roof in a downtown office building. Not even his official newspaper was certain how many new offices and agencies he opened, but it was "at least sixteen," the newspaper reported.[16]

Cody's administrative improvements were overdue, and his Roman imperial style was no different from that of Mundelein or dozens of other bishops; but, unfortunately for him, times had changed. To put the matter bluntly, a rotund potentate in red robes, exercising

Cardinal Cody addresses the founding meeting of the Association of Chicago Priests in 1966. This "priests union" became Cody's nemesis.
—*Photo by* The New World, *courtesy of the Archives of the Archdiocese of Chicago*

personal prerogative and centralized authority, seemed out of place in the Age of Aquarius and the era of democratic reform in the Church.

Shortly after Cody's arrival in Chicago, an ad hoc group of younger clergy formed a coordinating committee that led to the founding of the Association of Chicago Priests (ACP) on October 24, 1966. This unofficial body representing several hundred Chicago priests avoided the word *union*, but it acted much like one, constantly pressuring Cody on personnel matters and demanding consultation with him on major policy decisions. The high point of ACP militance came on June 15, 1971, when the association, by a narrow vote, censured Cody and all his auxiliary bishops for failing to represent adequately the Chicago clergy's views on celibacy at the annual meeting of the U.S. bishops.[17]

It is not hard to imagine what Cardinal Mundelein would have done to a group like the ACP. He would have disbanded it immediately and exiled its leaders to parishes in steel-mill and coal-mining towns. Cody broke off all contact with the ACP after its censure vote, but he took no reprisals against individuals. As Fr. John Fahey, who later delivered the eulogy at Cody's funeral, once remarked: "This is a rough era to be in a position of authority in the Catholic Church."[18]

Cody Changes with the Times

The Archdiocese of Chicago seemed to have come full circle. Mundelein was sent to Chicago in 1915 to impose discipline on a fractious, unruly group of priests with a tradition of rebellion against their bishops.[19] He succeeded in disciplining them and instilling a remarkable esprit de corps. Yet, after the Second Vatican Council, Chicago priests became restive and assertive again, unwilling to defer to authority unquestioningly. Even if John Patrick Cody were an exact clone of George William Mundelein, he still would have experienced difficulties with the clergy of Chicago. But he was not an exact clone of Mundelein. He compounded his difficulties with a secretive, obsessive style of management. Yet, in fairness to him, we must also admit that Cody did change with the times in some areas, advancing far beyond Mundelein on some important policy matters.

In 1970 Cardinal Cody laid aside one of the more visible tokens of triumphalism, Illinois license plate No. 1, which had traditionally been assigned to the archbishop of Chicago since Mundelein's day. Cody characterized the No. 1 plate as "ostentatious." Thereafter, the secretary of state of Illinois assigned the first license to the wife of the governor.[20]

More important, Cardinal Cody completely reorganized the major seminary, replacing the old rector, greatly liberalizing the rules, and reforming the curriculum. He enthusiastically promoted the ordination of married men to the permanent diaconate and thus created the largest corps of married clergy in the Roman church. He implemented the liturgical reforms of the Second Vatican Council and thoroughly renovated Holy Name Cathedral in the spirit of the new liturgy. Not content simply to turn the altar around, Cody's architects stripped away nearly all devotional pictures and graven images from the cathedral, leaving it starkly modern and bare, much like a Protestant church. Characteristically, the ACP complained about the $3 million cost of the cathedral renovation, avowing that the money might have been better spent on social action or charity. They did not, however, object when Cody deposited $12 million into the priests' pension account to compensate for unfunded liabilities.[21]

Cody's most strikingly progressive actions, however, came in the field of race relations. Cardinal Mundelein had been socially and politically liberal, openly supporting Franklin Roosevelt's New Deal, defending the rights of labor unions, and encouraging the activities of Bishop Bernard J. Sheil, Msgr. Reynold Hillenbrand, and many other social action pioneers. But Mundelein had a blind spot on race relations. He admitted early in his administration that he felt "quite powerless" to change racial segregation in his city, and he accordingly assigned all black Catholics to a handful of segregated parishes conducted by missionary priests. By employing missionaries to deal with the blacks, Mundelein succeeded in ignoring them.[22]

Cody had experienced the folly of a similar policy in his own archdiocese of St. Louis, where archbishop Glennon was even more segregationist than Mundelein, and the scandal of racial exclusion in the St. Louis church delayed his election to the College of Cardinals until he was virtually on his deathbed.[23] Cody learned this lesson well and vigorously promoted desegregation of Catholic churches and schools in all the dioceses he headed. In New Orleans he had earned a national reputation for racial liberalism and personal courage in the cause of desegregation.

Cody was named coadjutor to New Orleans archbishop Joseph Francis Rummel on August 14, 1961. The following spring, Rummel issued an order decreeing that all parochial grammar schools and high schools would be desegregated in September. It is unclear whether Rummel or Cody made the decision, but Cody took the blame for it as an "outside agitator." He also took the responsibility for implementing the decision; the ailing, nearly blind Rummel, having excommunicated three archsegregationists, petitoned Rome to relieve him of authority. Cody was named apostolic administrator in June 1962; and in September of that year he courageously defied pickets and protests in pushing Catholic school desegregation to a successful, and largely peaceful, conclusion.[24]

Cody continued support for the civil rights movement in Chicago. He met privately with Martin Luther King, Jr., on February 2, 1966, to discuss King's upcoming northern city campaign; and at a July 10 mass rally in Soldier Field, he sent an auxiliary bishop to read what King's biographer has called a "surprisingly strong message of support." He participated

Despite his conservative style, Cardinal Cody did embrace many reforms of the Second Vatican Council. He ordained so many permanent deacons that Chicago now has the largest corps of married clergy in the country. Here he is shown with the 1974 deacon class.
    —Photo by The New World, *courtesy of the Archives of the Archdiocese of Chicago*

personally in a "summit conference" with Mayor Daley and Dr. King to work out procedures for ensuring order on King's open housing marches in Chicago.[25]

Later in Cody's administration, Chicago priests criticized the cardinal for closing some inner city schools and consolidating black parishes. One priest even called Cody an "unconscious racist." This was the most unfair charge ever leveled at Cody. He may have been abrupt and undiplomatic in the way he proposed parish consolidation, but the work of consolidation needed to be done and has been carried on vigorously by his successor. Furthermore, Cody was not abandoning inner city parishes. Throughout his administration, he allocated approximately $3 million a year in subsidies to about fifty black and Hispanic parishes. In 1976, he also established a "twinning" or "sharing" program, whereby wealthy white parishes held monthly collections for a "sister parish" in the inner city.[26]

Significantly, when Cardinal Cody came under attack in 1981 from the *Chicago Sun-Times* for alleged improprieties and misuse of funds, the first group to openly defend him was the Black Catholic Clergy of Chicago. Black priests held a news conference at Holy Angels Church on September 16, 1981, and Rev. George Clements announced that the group was grateful for the "spiritual and material support" the cardinal had given to black parishes. The black clergy sponsored a support rally for Cody on September 18 at the International Amphitheatre. Thousands of black schoolchildren cheered as Cody accepted a plaque at the rally.[27]

Cardinal Cody did not neglect the inner city. In fact, just the opposite was true—he neglected the suburbs. From the start of his administration in Chicago, he declared a moratorium on construction of suburban Catholic schools. A rational bureaucratic management would have gradually withdrawn resources from the inner city, which was no longer Catholic, and applied them to the increasingly Catholic suburbs. Cody did not do this; and, as a result, a whole generation of Catholic parishioners is growing up without Catholic schooling. This may well be the most permanent effect of Cody's stewardship in Chicago.[28]

Cardinal Cody with African-American schoolchildren.
   —*Photo by* The New World, *courtesy of the Archives of the Archdiocese of Chicago*

An Insecure Autocrat

Cardinals Mundelein and Cody shared a general style of leadership—Romanist, triumphalist, centralizing—but a closer analysis reveals that their management techniques and their choices of subordinates differed greatly. These differences in respect to process and people ultimately account for the great disparity in their reputations.

Mundelein was an authoritarian manager. He laid down the law to his clergy and enforced it vigorously. He made large plans and drove them forward single-mindedly. He always remained the boss, and he swiftly demoted anyone who failed to live up to his standards. Yet he was not an autocrat, for he never tried to do everything himself. Mundelein delegated authority extensively and chose his subordinates wisely. He not only permitted subordinates to take responsibility, he demanded it; he would not let them pass major decisions back to him. If his subordinates proved able and competent, they might go for months or even years without seeing him. He did not look over their shoulders.

Mundelein even tolerated divergent personalities and competitive management styles. For example, his auxiliary bishop and vicar general, Bernard J. Sheil, was constantly hatching new social action schemes before yesterday's plans were final, and he rarely counted costs or consequences. Mundelein gave Sheil his head, but he also hemmed him in with cautious, conservative priests such as Msgr. Robert Maguire, the chancellor. As long as Sheil and Maguire battled each other in private, he let them fight it out, hoping that somehow the result would be a plan both visionary and practical.[29]

Cody, on the other hand, hated to delegate authority and thus lose control, especially control over money. He insisted on signing all checks for more than two dollars, he read every piece of incoming and outgoing mail at the chancery office, and he personally sent birthday and anniversary cards to hundreds of priests and lay acquaintances. Journalists compared him to the insecure Captain Queeg in the novel *The Caine Mutiny*. Queeg was so obsessed with trying to figure out who stole the strawberries that he neglected his duty and never noticed the growing mutiny on his ship. So too, Cody immersed himself in trivial details, often letting more important matters pile up and ignoring the disaffection of his clergy.[30]

The subordinates with whom Cody surrounded himself tended to be yes-men, cronies, or soulless bureaucrats. He purchased diocesan insurance through a St. Louis broker, David Dolan Wilson, who was the son of his stepcousin, the woman to whom he allegedly diverted large sums of money. His closest lay financial adviser, Francis O'Connor, was also a St. Louis friend.[31] Even when these subordinates made the right decisions, the manner in which they acted lost respect for the archdiocese.

Cody's secretive, obsessive management is partly explained by his background. He had served in the delicate post of coadjutor bishop on three separate occasions, and he certainly must have observed how painful it was for the aging and infirm bishops whose authority he was taking over. Finally on his own in a major see, he probably wanted to ensure that no one ever took over from him. Hence his obsession with total control of detail. Ironically, his insecure, autocratic management techniques nearly produced the result he most feared.

The history of Cody's pet project, the Catholic Television Network of Chicago (CTN/C), aptly illustrates the various strands of his administrative style and how this style differed from Mundelein's. The concept of the Catholic Television Network, linking all the parishes of the Chicago archdiocese, was a brilliant idea, fully in accord with the Second Vatican Council's decree on modern communications. When Cody opened the four-channel, closed circuit network on February 3, 1975, it was not the first such Catholic media facility, but clearly the largest and most ambitious.[32] The concept, then, was visionary, a proof of Cody's ability to move with the times.

Yet the way Cody executed the CTN/C plan was clearly old school. He announced the project to the Priests' Senate (a canonical consultative body mandated by Rome, not to be confused with the ad hoc ACP) in January 1974 as a fait accompli, without any request for consultation or advice. When priest senators questioned the $4 million investment in studio equipment, Cody replied: "Let me worry about the money, you just give it your blessing."[33] His response resembled a saying in the Vatican: *Roma locuta est, causa finita est* (Rome has spoken, the case is closed).

Furthermore, Cody made abysmal personnel choices to run CTN/C. Charles Hinds, the station manager, moved CTN/C away from its prime mission of religious programming and devoted most of the studio resources to production of TV commercials. Fr. James Moriarty, the priest-director at the station, failed to stop this deviation from the primary mission. Despite the growing commercialism, CTN/C still required an annual subsidy averaging $1.2 million between 1975 and 1981. Finally, Cardinal Cody's successor, Joseph Bernardin, commissioned a consultant's study of CTN/C, which concluded sharply: "Clearly, the original intentions concerning primary function have been lost along the way—actually, quite some time ago. The commercial production has become virtually an end in itself. And, apparently, not a profitable one, even in just a commercial sense, for the Archdiocese."[34]

It is interesting to speculate how Cardinal Mundelein might have managed CTN/C. Actually the cardinal contemplated the founding of a similar Catholic radio station in the 1920s, but he abandoned the idea "due to the flatness of our purse."[35] Mundelein rarely risked the Church's money on projects that were peripheral to the Church's primary mission of worship, education, and charity. Had he gone ahead and found the project straying from its religious purpose, he would have fired the lay manager (and possibly sued him) and exiled the priest director to North Chicago for life.

Four dusty red hats hang from the ceiling in the sanctuary of Holy Name Cathedral, fading pennants of past glory, like NBA championship banners in the Boston Garden. George Mundelein was the "First Cardinal of the West," the first American named a cardinal from a city west of the Appalachians; and each of his successors in turn has been nominated to the College of Cardinals. Yet John Patrick Cody's hat is the last to hang in the cathedral, for Pope Paul VI terminated the custom as an unnecessary bit of triumphalism. Four hats—Mundelein's at the beginning, Cody's at the end—symbolize an era in Church administration.

Neither Mundelein nor Cody was well loved by priests or people. Each was too aloof and authoritarian for that. Yet Mundelein was universally respected by priest and layman, Catholic and non-Catholic. His imperial style served an important purpose: it put the Catholic Church on the map. When I was interviewing priests for my biography of Cardinal Mundelein in the mid-1970s, I found that most priests would rather gossip about their present archbishop, Cody, than reminisce about Mundelein. To my astonishment, I discovered that not a single priest I talked to—from the youngest "Young Turk" to the most elderly monsignor—expressed any respect for Cody.

I have a hunch why Cardinal Cody, at the end of an era, failed to win the respect of his clergy. He seems to have lost track of the distinction between ends and means. Mundelein, for all his authoritarianism and triumphal display, always used money and power as means to an end, the advancement of his Church and its spiritual mission in America. Cardinal Cody, whose administration came along when the Church was well established in Chicago, seems to have pursued power largely for its own sake. The former editor of *The Chicago Catholic*, A. E. P. Wall, has stated that he believes Cody was an agnostic, uninterested in God or religion but only in the material, institutional apparatus of the Church.[36] This is an extreme, and unverifiable, assertion, but it points to a possible truth. Cody mistook the means that Cardinals Mundelein and Glennon had employed for ends in themselves.

Cardinal Cody manipulated the structure of power and authority that Cardinal Mundelein had painstakingly constructed forty years earlier. But the structure had become a hollow shell. An era had ended.

8

Sacred Space: Parish and Neighborhood in Chicago

by Ellen Skerrett

With their colorful banners, American flags, and marching bands, parish parades in the 1890s contributed to the high profile of Chicago Catholicism. School graduations in Holy Family parish became neighborhood events, intensifying the connection between church and turf.

—*Holy Family Church, courtesy Jane Addams Hull-House*

One of the hallmarks of Chicago Catholicism has been the abiding link between parish and neighborhood, between church and turf. Much more than mere lines on a map marking the divisions of an episcopal diocese or a city, parishes and neighborhoods constitute the heart of the Chicago Catholic experience. For more than 150 years, parishes have been sacred places in the lives of Chicago Catholics, continuing sources of pride, self-esteem, and respectability. It is no exaggeration to say that from the earliest days in Chicago, parishes challenged the conventional wisdom that Catholic immigrants threatened the fabric of city life. The existence of parish complexes in neighborhoods throughout Chicago refuted the idea that immigrants were somehow less than equal, less deserving of respect, dignity, and beauty than more prosperous native-born Americans. As the Chicago experience makes abundantly clear, Catholics used the very process of church-building to create community in the city. Built with the nickels and dimes of poor people, Catholic churches and schools became landmarks in Chicago, visible signs that Catholics were establishing a place for themselves in the city. Not only did parishes transform the physical landscape of Chicago, even more important, they profoundly shaped the way in which Catholics thought about themselves.

Whether based on language or territory, Catholic parishes conferred a sense of belonging—religiously, socially, and geographically. To the immigrant newcomer, the Catholic Church was a link with the homeland, a place to worship, receive the sacraments, and make friends. In addition to being anchors in immigrant districts, parishes formed the heart of Catholic life in new residential areas throughout the city. So successful was this process of parish formation that to this day, Catholics in Chicago and many of its suburbs instinctively identify themselves as belonging to a particular parish. While the Catholic custom of parish identity is not unique to Chicago, in no other American city has it persisted so intensely. Chicagoans' continuing fascination with ethnicity has been matched only by the familiar Catholic greeting, "What parish are you from?" The desire to locate oneself precisely in the metropolitan region is neither a sign of romanticism or nostalgia. It is a continual reminder that place is important, that people desire and need community, and will create and recreate it wherever they move.

More than any other institution, the Catholic parish humanized Chicago, transforming it from an alien to a familiar place. This process had far reaching consequences for Chicago Catholicism. First and foremost, the Church early on assumed an urban identity. In contrast with mainline Protestant denominations that found the city a difficult place to maintain congregational life, Catholic parishes quickly took root. Equally important for the future of the Church in Chicago is that from its very beginning it has been responsive to the needs of diverse ethnic groups. While its parishes, schools, hospitals, charitable organizations, and cemeteries were originally organized along national lines, these institutions changed to meet the needs and aspirations of American-born children and grandchildren as they entered the ranks of the middle class. Third, and perhaps most important for the vitality of Chicago Catholicism, the Church has been rooted in its parishes.

Brick-and-mortar Catholicism

Although Catholics formed the largest denomination in the city from the 1840s on, numbers alone did not guarantee that the Church would become a powerful presence in Chicago. Indeed, so great was the poverty of Chicago's Irish immigrants that historian Bessie Pierce has charged that "they brought to the new community the beginning of a slum district."[1] Considering the limited resources of Chicago's Catholic immigrants, it is nothing short of remarkable that they invested so heavily in "brick-and-mortar Catholicism." But as the history of of the Chicago diocese makes clear, far from restricting institutional development, the complex process of church-building actually led to higher levels of commitment among urban dwellers. In parish after parish, the campaign to complete a church and school demanded cooperation among Catholics living in a particular area. While the debts incurred were often enormous, fundraising became an important component of parish life, bringing together members of a congregation in a way that worship alone could not. Built of brick and mortar, these parish complexes provided incontrovertible evidence that immigrants and their children were creating a place for themselves in the city. Indeed, the genius of the Chicago Catholic experience is that the institutional Church maintained its urban identity even as its parishes put down deep roots in the neighborhoods. Catholic church-building not only kept pace with the growth and development of Chicago, its parishes laid the foundation for the expansion of the Church into suburban areas.

In addition to shaping the physical landscape of the city, Catholic churches also challenged accepted notions of class. In the nineteenth century, conventional wisdom held that monumental church-building was a proper activity for the middle class, most of whom were native-born Protestants. But poor Catholic congregations—now *that* was a different story. Instead of building beautiful churches and establishing separate schools, many critics felt that Catholics should concentrate on improving the lot of their impoverished members. In 1857, for example, the *Chicago Tribune* suggested that the bishop's house could be used as a residence for "the widows and orphans of his flock" and that the unfinished cathedral of the Holy Name be turned into "a workshop for the unemployed."[2] Despite such criticism, Chicago Catholics continued to finance the construction of substantial churches throughout the city because they met fundamental needs for identity and community. In the sixty-year period between the incorporation of the city and the World's Fair of 1893, immigrants and their children established nearly one hundred parishes in Chicago, each with its own distinctive house of worship and usually a school as well. The history of the diocese is filled with examples of the way diverse ethnic groups used their churches to establish identity and turf in the city. St. Mary, the first Catholic parish in Chicago, is a case in point.

Church and Turf: St. Mary's

In 1833, French, Irish, and German Catholics petitioned Bishop Joseph Rosati of St. Louis to send them a pastor, "before other sects obtain the upper hand, which very likely they will try to do."[3] Religious competition has been an important dimension of Chicago's history, and Catholics were eager participants. While Chicago's Methodists, Presbyterians, and Baptists shared worship quarters, the city's small band of Catholics set about to establish a church of their own. The original St. Mary's was a modest affair, a low frame structure built by local carpenter Augustine Deodat Taylor near the corner of State and Lake streets in September 1833. According to historian Perry Duis, the Catholic church was the first balloon-frame building in Chicago, perhaps in the world. By substituting inexpensive lighter boards for massive timbers and "nails for interlocking mortise work," Taylor pioneered a method of construction that revolutionized domestic architecture.[4]

Although St. Mary's was enlarged over the next few years to meet the needs of the growing Catholic population, it soon began to look shabby in comparison with newer houses of worship. Indeed, as Daniel Bluestone documents in his fine book, *Constructing Chicago*, the city's most prominent Protestant churches all built imposing structures along Washington Street in the 1840s.[5] Well aware of Protestant progress in Chicago, St. Mary's parishioners enthusiastically supported the construction of a brick church at the southwest corner of Wabash and Madison. It was no coincidence that A. D. Taylor adopted the neoclassical style of rival congregations nor that sketches of the new Catholic church began to appear in advertisements and entries in Chicago directories, complete with dimensions: "Length, 112 feet, including 12 feet portico; width, 55 feet; height of walls 34 feet."[6]

When Bishop William J. Quarter arrived in Chicago on May 5, 1844, he found the cathedral of the new diocese to be "a respectable building," but far from habitable:

> The building was not plastered; a temporary altar was stuck up against the western wall. There was no vestry; the sanctuary was enclosed with rough boards; the children were seated on benches, on either side . . . There were neither columns, nor steps, nor doors . . . and worse than all, even that much of a church was burdened with about three thousand dollars of debt . . . bearing interest at from 10 to 12 per cent.[7]

Anticipating Daniel Burnham's dictum, "Make no little plans," by half a century, Quarter's vision for the fledgling Chicago diocese included a university and seminary, schools for girls and boys, and a hospital and orphan asylum. But his first order of business was to call a meeting to discuss the completion of the cathedral. The bishop's plans for dividing the city into districts and appointing parishioners to collect funds door-to-door succeeded so well that by November 1844 the

new spire of the steeple could be raised. Quarter asserted, with a touch of pride, that "The steeple . . . . [is] the first and only spire, as yet, in the city of Chicago." In its account of the dedication ceremony on October 5, 1845, the *Chicago Democrat* noted that the cathedral had been "completed in the most beautiful manner with a splendid organ and bell." A visible sign of the Catholic presence in Chicago, the new St. Mary's was also a city landmark. According to Dr. John E. McGirr, the cathedral bore the only cross in Chicago, and it "is the first object that presents itself to the traveller approaching the harbour from the lakes, or far away upon the prairie."[8]

Just months after dedicating St. Mary's Cathedral, Bishop Quarter made two policy decisions that changed forever the character of Chicago Catholicism: he established parishes based on language as well as territory, and he invited the Sisters of Mercy to make a foundation in the city. In an early letter to Bishop John B. Purcell of Cincinnati, Quarter had expressed his belief that "the prospects everywhere are . . . bright for Catholicity."[9] The new cathedral with its stately portico and Ionic columns was a powerful symbol of Catholic cooperation. But as Quarter was well aware, a single structure could not meet the needs of diverse immigrant groups. In 1845 he expressed concern that

> as yet the Germans have no church of their own, which is indeed a great drawback. The faithful of every nationality gather in one and the same church; this condition does not permit of special religious instructions for the German children and people in their own language . . . [10]

Although the bishop recognized the competing demands of other missions in his vast diocese (which was encumbered with a debt of nearly $5,000), he decided that "first assistance" should be devoted to Chicago, where Catholics constituted 10 percent of the city's thirteen thousand residents. In his own words, Chicago immigrants were "new arrivals [who] have scarcely brought enough with them to begin life anew."[11] Convinced of the absolute necessity of churches for immigrants, Bishop Quarter organized three

St. Mary's Cathedral, St. Xavier Academy, and the Convent of the Sisters of Mercy on Wabash Avenue, a powerful example of "brick-and-mortar" Catholicism in early Chicago. Destroyed in the Great Fire of 1871 and reestablished at other locations, St. Mary parish and St. Xavier University recall the pioneer days of the Chicago diocese.
—Archives Center of the Sisters of Mercy/Chicago Regional Community

new parishes in the spring of 1846. Using the river as a dividing line, he established St. Peter's for Germans living on the South Side; St. Joseph for Germans on the North Side; and St. Patrick's for the Irish who had moved west of the cathedral. The creation of separate parishes for the rapidly expanding German and Irish populations was a pragmatic solution to the thorny problem of cultural diversity, and it firmly established the Catholic Church's reputation as a dynamic force in the city. In a process that has been repeated hundreds of times since 1846, the new parishes of St. Joseph, St. Patrick, and St. Peter developed their own identities, their own customs and traditions, and their own modern church complexes. In addition to extending the presence of the Catholic Church to all sections of Chicago, these new parishes were eloquent reminders that Catholic parochial life could flourish in an urban setting.

Without the commitment of religious orders it is unlikely that parishes would have become such prominent features of the Chicago Catholic experience. Long before the Third Plenary Council of Baltimore mandated parochial schools in 1884, Catholic grammar schools and academies were a tradition in Chicago. Far from being a luxury that immigrants could ill afford, these local schools helped to solidify Catholic identity as they prepared children for jobs in the larger society.

The Sisters of Mercy Put Down Roots

In a very real sense, a new era in the history of Chicago Catholicism began on September 23, 1846, with the arrival of the Sisters of Mercy. So determined was Bishop Quarter to secure the services of this Irish order for charitable and education work that he had met their boat when it docked in New York in December 1843—months before he ever set foot in Chicago.[12] When the small band of sisters finally made their way to Chicago from their community in Pittsburgh, they found neither convent nor school awaited them. Undaunted, twenty-four-year old Sr. Agatha O'Brien, R.S.M. and her Irish companions established a "select school," known as St. Francis Xavier Academy on October 12, 1846, in the rear of the old frame church of St. Mary. Proceeds from the boarding school and tuition were used to finance a free parochial day school for girls. In reporting on their foundation in Chicago, a national Catholic magazine noted that the Sisters of Mercy

> also visit the sick and distressed, and dispense mercies to the wretched. . . . They will also soon establish a hospital in the city, and take the entire burden of nursing the sick, and management of such charity upon themselves.[13]

Just as parishes played a crucial role in creating Catholic communities throughout the city, so too religious orders left their imprint on Chicago. When it came to making wise real estate investments, few congregations equaled the Sisters of Mercy. In addition to their convent and schools in St. Mary parish downtown, they purchased property on the outskirts of the city for future development. St. Agatha Academy (1854) at Twenty-sixth Street and Calumet Avenue paved the way for such Catholic institutions as Mercy Hospital and St. James parish, with its large grammar school and high school for girls. Despite disputes with several early Chicago bishops over the right of their order to hold title to property, the Mercy sisters continued their educational and charitable work, confident in the future of the city and its Catholic population. Their trust was not misplaced. In 1867, when the Chicago diocese was still heavily in debt, the Sisters of Mercy owed "not a cent of debt on any property held by the community, and the academy and grounds at Wabash Avenue and Madison street were valued at over a quarter of a million."[14]

Revising Stereotypes: Holy Family Parish

By all accounts, the institution that really put Chicago Catholicism on the map was Holy Family parish, established by Jesuit Arnold Damen in 1857. Right from the start, this parish challenged contemporary notions about poor immigrants and their neighborhoods. In a move that surprised many Chicagoans, Fr. Damen refused Bishop Anthony O'Regan's invitation to staff Holy Name parish on the North Side where the Jesuits had recently preached missions to overflowing crowds. Damen also rejected a valuable site known as the Bull's Head at Madison Street and Ogden Avenue. Instead, he chose to establish Holy Family parish at Twelfth Street and Blue Island Avenue, a "desolate and uninviting locality" judging from the "riots and ructions" that occurred regularly among the Irish squatters who occupied shanties on the prairie.[15]

Its unfavorable location notwithstanding, the *Chicago Tribune* waged a vigorous campaign to derail Fr. Damen's plans for a church and college. Reflecting nativist sentiments of the day, the newspaper implored its readers to withhold financial contributions and begged Protestants "to think twice before they aid in any way the founding of Jesuit institutions in this city." The *Tribune* claimed that: "We do this not in a spirit of intolerance, but upon the warrant of facts which show that the Society of Jesus is the most virulent and relentless enemy of the Protestant faith and Democratic government."[16]

As things turned out, Fr. Damen experienced more difficulty with his own Jesuit superiors over plans for Holy Family parish than he did with the *Chicago Tribune*. The financial panic of 1857 was an inauspicious time to begin raising funds for a massive church, but Damen remained undeterred. Within weeks of his arrival in the city, he wrote to his provincial in St. Louis that "people are aston-ished that I can get money at all." By the time workers laid the cornerstone of Holy Family Church on August 23, 1857, however, the depression had widened. Damen's correspondence with his superiors is a financial litany: the difficulty of collecting $30,000 in subscriptions for the new church; the increasing cost of materials and labor; and the size of the parish debt. His letter of July 19, 1858, was by turns plaintive and pragmatic. "Had I $6,000 I could make all payments and put the roof on the church," he wrote Rev. John Druyts, S.J., reminding him, "If the people see that nothing is done at the church, it will be impossible for me to make collections."[17]

Holy Family parish, founded in 1857 at Twelfth Street (Roosevelt Road) and Blue Island Avenue, put Chicago Catholicism on the map. Built on a grand scale, the Victorian Gothic church (1860) and St. Ignatius College (1870), revised prevailing stereotypes about Catholic immigrants and their commitment to American urban life. Recently restored to their former beauty, Holy Family Church and St. Ignatius College Prep continue their mission on Chicago's Near West Side.

—Photo by Thomas J. Gobby

Not only did Damen have a shrewd understanding of human behavior but he was well aware that the construction of Holy Family Church was a matter of pride and self-respect for Catholics who lived in frame shanties without running water or indoor plumbing. His choice of John Van Osdel, Chicago's first registered architect, signaled his intention to build a church that would inspire the loyalty of his poor Irish parishioners and compare favorably with existing Protestant houses of worship. Damen specified that the brickwork on the front of Holy Family Church be "of best possible character, every joint filled solid with good lime and clean lake shore sand mortar." And he insisted that the stained glass crafted by Robert Carse "be equal to that of the windows in St. James' [Episcopal] church, North Side."[18]

Holy Family did more than set the standard for Catholic church architecture in Chicago, it became the undisputed symbol of Catholic confidence and respectability. Shortly before its dedication on August 26, 1860, the *Tribune* proclaimed its interior "the finest by far in this city, if indeed it has a superior in the United States" and predicted that Holy Family "will ever be one of the most marked and prominent objects of interest in our city, for its size and costliness."[19] High praise, indeed, coming from the newspaper that had railed against Damen's plans for Holy Family parish!

No other parish church in Chicago—Holy Name Cathedral included—did more to alter the physical landscape of its neighborhood and revise popular images of immigrant Catholics. What happened in Holy Family Church was reported by all the daily papers—column inch after column inch detailing the richness and complexity of Catholic life in an American urban neighborhood. Whereas news of local Protestant churches was confined almost entirely to reprinted texts of Sunday sermons, Chicago readers enjoyed first-hand reports of feast day celebrations, May crownings, first communions and confirmations, Christmas and Easter Masses, school plays and graduations. Considered especially noteworthy by city editors were ceremonies in conjunction with the interior decoration of Holy Family Church. The blessing of the fifty-two-foot Gothic altar carved by Anthony

Buscher, the communion railing of solid walnut crafted by Louis Wissmer, the side altars, oil paintings, statues, and magnificent pipe organ from Montreal—all were reported in great detail. Indeed, contemporary accounts make it clear that within the walls of the Gothic church on Twelfth Street, thousands of working-class Catholics encountered sacred music and art of a very high order, this at a time when Chicago lacked its own symphony orchestra and art museum. A conspicuous feature of the dedication ceremony in 1860, for example, was the production of Mozart's *Twelfth Mass*. And on Christmas 1863, the *Chicago Times* reminded its readers that Holy Family had taken the lead among Chicago churches in presenting Haydn's *First Mass*.[20]

Fr. Damen's preferential option for the poor involved two main ideas: worship and education. At the same time that he financed the construction and decoration of Holy Family Church, the Jesuit pastor created an entire school system within the parish, providing instruction from grade school through college. Nearby on Taylor Street, the Madames of the Sacred Heart established an academy in 1858, the nucleus of the present Barat College in Lake Forest. By 1865, Holy Family School for Boys on Morgan Street enrolled nine hundred students and in 1867, the Sisters of Charity of the Blessed Virgin Mary opened a grammar school and secondary school for girls, their first foundation in Chicago.

The original plans for Holy Family parish included a college that would "eventually rival that of Georgetown,"[21] but nearly ten years passed before ground was broken for St. Ignatius College. Although financial advisers warned Damen that the time was still not right, he forged ahead. When his Jesuit superior in St. Louis traveled to Rome in the summer of 1867, Damen seized the opportunity to invite the acting provincial, Rev. Joseph Keller, S.J., to come to Chicago. Impressed with Holy Family Church and its network of schools, Fr. Keller enthusiastically endorsed Damen's plans. By the time Rev. Ferdinand Coosemans, the provincial, returned from Rome, the foundation and first story of the college building had been completed. Then funds ran out. Not willing to let such a project die, the provincial interceded on

Damen's behalf with Father General Peter Beckx, stressing the role the college would play in the life of Chicago and the Jesuit order. He noted that:

> The building has been begun on a large scale to make it possible to compete with the Protestant colleges and the public schools, which are like palaces. It was necessary to do this so as to induce parents to give us the preference; external appearances do much to impress Americans.[22]

When St. Ignatius College opened its doors on September 5, 1870, it was widely regarded as the crowning glory of the Jesuit educational enterprise in Chicago. Indeed, one local paper referred to it as "the noble college standing side by side and a companion to the great Church of the Holy Family."[23] The forerunner of Loyola University, the institution is known today as St. Ignatius College Prep.

Catholic Community Building

Contemporary newspaper accounts as well as Damen's own correspondence confirm that Holy Family parish exerted a profound effect on the Near West Side of Chicago, transforming a prairie into an urban neighborhood. In a letter to the Father General of the Jesuit order in Rome in 1865, Damen reported that nearly two thousand homes had been constructed in the parish recently and that the "alms of the faithful" had built a complex valued at $250,000. Increasingly, real estate developers advertised "Lots for Sale Near the Jesuit Church," and newspapers began to acknowledge the positive link between parish and neighborhood. On a tour in Dublin in 1869, Rev. Thaddeus J. Butler, D.D., entertained large audiences with his tales of Chicago and its marvelous progress. In singling out Holy Family parish as an example of Catholic success, he noted that, "No better location can now be found for a family where boys and girls can both be educated than this locality, which was twelve years ago the scandal of the city." Echoing Fr. Butler's views, a Chicago newspaper argued a few years later that Holy Family parish was a great benefit to the city. Far from being a burden upon taxpayers, its church and schools were responsible for "filling up that district with a dense and closely settled population—thus swelling the assessed value of the property by many millions and increasing the revenues of the city and county in a corresponding ratio."[24]

Catholic success in creating community in the city was not lost on Protestant reformers. In 1869, Catharine E. Beecher, daughter of the famous New England Presbyterian minister Lyman Beecher, compiled a popular manual on domestic economy with the assistance of her married sister, Harriet Beecher Stowe. In addition to providing hundreds of pages of advice on the proper organization of a Christian home and family, Beecher devised a bold plan for Protestant women to organize Christian neighborhoods. Drastic action was necessary, she believed, because Catholic nuns under the direction of "a highly educated priesthood, with no family ties to distract attention" were now taking the lead in education and charity work. Beecher's solution, illustrated on the opening page of *The American Woman's Home*, was the construction of combination church-school-and-residence buildings that would form the nucleus of Christian neighborhoods. She argued that this scheme was "so economical and practical that two or three ladies, with very moderate means, could carry it out." From such humble beginnings, Beecher believed, "central church[es] would soon appear," complete with meeting rooms for social events and literary gatherings.[25]

Rebuilding the Catholic City

In the Chicago Catholic experience, it was not unusual for parishes to invest substantial sums of money in building permanent churches. Indeed, Catholics suffered an estimated $1.5 million loss in property, the largest of any denomination, during the Great Fire that began on October 8, 1871, at Desplaines and DeKoven streets at the east end of Holy Family parish. Although the parish complexes of Holy Family, St. Patrick, and St. Peter escaped destruction, six other Catholic churches, several schools, convents, rectories, and charitable institutions were consumed in the flames. *The Chicago Evening Journal* later recalled that "the ghostly ruins" of local churches were often the only landmarks "by which the awe-struck and amazed visitors who came here by the thousands were able to tell their whereabouts as they wended their way through the vast wilderness of desolation."[26]

As Daniel Bluestone has documented, Chicago's mainline Protestant churches began to move out of the downtown business district in the 1850s, a process "dramatically concluded" by the Great Fire of 1871.[27] Virtually all of Chicago's "First" Protestant churches sold their valuable downtown property and followed their congregations to newer residential districts. It is no coincidence that St. Mary, St. Peter, and St. Patrick parishes remained in the commercial district and continued to flourish long after leading Protestant churches had departed for the boulevards. Perhaps because Chicago's Catholics had fought so hard to create sacred space in the city, they were reluctant to give up turf. Then too, parishes were not simply Sunday affairs. Catholic churches opened every day for Mass and devotions, and parochial schools played a critical, if unacknowledged role, in sustaining community life. The increasing commitment of Catholics to churches and schools in the wake of the Great Chicago Fire of 1871 suggests that parishes had become holy places, in their lives and in their neighborhoods.

Not only were Catholics faced with the daunting task of rebuilding church and school complexes in such parishes as Holy Name, St. Joseph, St. Michael, and Immaculate Conception, but their limited resources were desperately needed by religious orders who ran hospitals and charitable institutions. The Sisters of the Good Shepherd, for example, had depended on contributions from local parishes to offset the cost of building a new convent and enlarging their Magdalen Asylum at Hill and Orleans streets where they cared for orphans, destitute mothers, and former prostitutes. On December 20, 1871, Mother Mary of Nativity wrote her superior in Angers, France that:

> Our loss is valued at One Hundred and Eighteen Thousand Dollars. No portion of the building remains, no, not even the foundation, which was literally baked by the burning of 90 tons of coal which we had stored in our cellar. Six [weeks] after the fire, this coal was still burning in the kitchen cellar, so much so that the laboring men were obliged to cover their wheelbarrows with tin to remove the cinders; oftentimes they warmed their dinner over these burning coals.[28]

In contrast to Chicago's mainline Protestant congregations, Catholics rebuilt older city parishes as well as forming new ones in the expanding metropolis. Throughout the 1870s, Catholic cornerstone layings became regular events, each one a vivid reminder that immigrants and their children were creating a place for themselves in Chicago. Instead of being congratulated for reinvesting in the city, however, Catholics were lambasted for their "willingness to expend too much money upon ostentatious churches, and costly adornments." The *Chicago Times* argued that "true charity would be better exemplified, and true Christianity more beautifully illustrated by the erection of plain, substantial, unadorned churches . . ." and the newspaper suggested that money earmarked for oil paintings, statues, and stained glass windows be used instead "for the enlargement and erection of orphan asylums and reform schools."[29]

What critics of brick-and-mortar Catholicism failed to understand was the fundamental connection between church and community. Nineteenth-century Chicago Catholics did not consider their houses of worship as impediments to their faith or their economic well-being. On the contrary, they regarded church-building as the most natural—and practical—method of creating community in the city. Unlike wealthy Protestant congregations that increasingly favored fashionable areas for their houses of worship, Catholics made no such distinctions. They erected magnificent churches wherever they lived, from grimy industrial districts dominated by the smoke and smell of factories, to sparsely settled prairies.

The Catholic Parish on the Prairie: Our Lady of Sorrows

The memoirs of Rev. Austin Morini, O.S.M., provide striking evidence that the creation of new parishes and churches was an act of confidence, as much as faith. This fascinating document, recently translated and annotated by Servite archivist Conrad Borntrager, also sheds new light on the role Catholic church-building played in the creation of an urban neighborhood.[30] When Morini began organizing Our Lady of Sorrows parish in May 1874, there were only a few Catholic families living on the prairie west of Western Avenue, the city's limit. As the Italian immigrant priest recalled the event years later, Bishop Thomas Foley simply instructed him to "Go west, as far as you want." Although he had only been in the United States four years, Morini had experienced the diversity of American Catholic life. In addition to preaching missions in Wisconsin to Germans, Indians, French-Canadians, and Irish, he had tried, unsuccessfully, to organize a parish for Chicago's small Italian community. Bolstered by the Servites' conviction "that if we want to start something good in Chicago we must contract debts," Morini lost little time in negotiating the purchase of an entire block of property with frontage on Jackson Street between Troy and Albany. Although the site was remote, its location near the city's new West Side park (later renamed Garfield) guaranteed that Our Lady of Sorrows parish would anchor the neighborhood as it developed over time. Indeed, so conscious was Morini of the link between Catholic parish formation and urban development that he set two conditions on the sale. He refused to pay pending taxes on the property and he insisted that real estate developer William Kerfoot solicit substantial donations for the new church—from local Protestant property owners! Morini argued that Our Lady of Sorrows Church "would be a focal point for the Catholics and therefore the owners of nearby property could expect to gain from it." While the extent of Protestant contributions is not clear, the "simple but elegant" brick church was completed in time for Mass on Christmas Day 1874. A landmark on the open prairie, Our Lady of Sorrows provided "a pleasing sight to those coming from the city."[31]

In his memoirs, Morini asserts that from the beginning he made plans for a parish school, "which, as they say in America, makes the church." A local Catholic woman, Margaret Carroll, instructed the children of the parish until 1886 when a permanent building was completed and opened under the leadership of the Sisters of Providence from St. Mary of the Woods, Indiana. Enrollment figures confirm that Our Lady of Sorrows school soon became an important component of parish life and played a significant role in the creation of a Catholic community. By 1889, parish membership numbered 435 families with nearly an equal number of students in the school.[32] When construction began on the present house of worship in 1890 this part of the West Side was still sparsely settled. But the Servite pastors who succeeded Fr. Morini built on the grand scale, confident that it was only a matter of time before the Garfield Park area would be filled up with brick homes and apartments. Indeed, the parish's peak years in terms of population were decades away when Our Lady of Sorrows was dedicated in 1902. Completed according to the plans of architect

William J. Brinkmann, the Renaissance-style church with its barrel-vault coffered ceiling was one of Chicago's ecclesiastical wonders, a sign of Catholic commitment to the city.[33]

Concern about the proper relationship between church-building and charity work was the subject of much debate in the nineteenth century. In 1880, Bishop John Lancaster Spalding, one of the American Catholic Church's most respected leaders, compared the magnificent churches financed by immigrants to the pyramids of Egypt, built by slaves. In his view, the construction of urban Catholic churches represented "the absence of home and a future for God's people." Indeed, the bishop went so far as to argue that:

Half a dozen churches serve the purpose of an episcopal city as well as a hundred; and, in fact, one of the chief difficulties in the administration of the large dioceses of this country is the necessity of maintaining, at great outlay of money, asylums and orphanages which are always crowded. Institutions of this kind would be hardly needed had the masses of our people settled upon the fertile lands which were to be had for nothing.[34]

In the experience of Chicago Catholics church-building reflected hope in the future of the city and its neighborhoods. The churches and schools built by immigrants of very different ethnic backgrounds became

Constructed between 1890 and 1902, the magnificent Renaissance church of Our Lady of Sorrows at Jackson Boulevard and Albany Avenue anticipated the phenomenal growth of Chicago's West Side. Nationally acclaimed as the birthplace of the Sorrowful Mother Novena in 1937, Our Lady of Sorrows Church was raised to the status of a basilica in 1957.

—*Photo by Joan Radtke*

important sources of identity, pride, and community. Not only were parish complexes powerful symbols of faith and cooperation but also they exerted a tremendous influence on the day-to-day lives of working people. From an administrative and financial standpoint, fewer churches might have appeared to be the best use of limited resources. But in practical terms, the proliferation of Catholic parishes meant that families had more opportunities to practice their religion. In contrast to houses of worship in the country, the Church was a real presence in the daily lives of urban Catholics.

As the history of Chicago parishes makes clear, under very difficult circumstances, Catholics used their churches to create holy places, in their lives and in their neighborhoods. The stockyards on Chicago's South Side, for example, provided immigrants with opportunities to work, but its future as a residential district left much to be desired. The surrounding area had originally been low and swampy, and decades passed before the streets were improved and paved. While annexation to Chicago in 1890 brought better services in terms of police and fire protection, its housing stock of modest frame and brick cottages ensured that this area would develop as a working-class district. Yet few parts of Chicago have been as profoundly shaped by sacred space. Between 1879 and 1910 Catholics of diverse ethnic backgrounds established twelve parishes in a district less than two square miles bounded roughly by Forty-third Street on the north; Fifty-fifth Street on the south; Stewart Avenue on the east; and Western Avenue on the west.

St. Gabriel's: Sacred Space in Canaryville

When Maurice J. Dorney began organizing St. Gabriel parish just east of the stockyards in 1880, the cabbage fields were fast disappearing, along with the wild pigs (nicknamed "canaries") that had roamed freely in the area. Despite its lyrical name, Canaryville was a rough-and-tumble district. Unsanitary working and living conditions, compounded by the seasonal nature of packinghouse employment, left their mark on families in the neighborhood. So, too, did alcohol consumption. "Rushing the can" was a familiar sight in Canaryville, as men, women, and children carried pails to be filled with beer in the forty-odd saloons that lined Halsted Street between Fortieth and Forty-fifth streets. Now Dorney realized that this area would never be an exclusive residential district, but he believed his Irish parishioners deserved a stable neighborhood as well as a beautiful church. About the same time that he hired the noted architectural firm of Burnham and Root (of Rookery fame) to design a permanent house of worship, he spearheaded a campaign to keep saloons off the side streets of Canaryville. With support from neighboring Protestant ministers, the Catholic priest successfully petitioned local authorities to establish a prohibition district that corresponded almost exactly with the boundaries of St. Gabriel parish. All went well until Dorney took a vacation in the spring of 1888, just about the time the new church was nearing completion at the corner of Forty-fifth Street and Lowe Avenue. In his absence, a number of local residents in favor of saloons on the side streets signed a petition to abolish the prohibition district.

When Dorney returned to Canaryville, he took to the pulpit to explain the philosophy behind the prohibition campaign, and he implored his parishioners to see the important connection between St. Gabriel Church and its neighborhood. Not only did he remind his fellow Irish Catholics "that the church property belonged to the people of the congregation," but he made it clear that the new church of St. Gabriel's "had given value to property in the neighborhood." Just to make sure that parishioners understood the gravity of the situation, Dorney read the names and addresses of the sixty-four signers of the petition, according to the local newspaper, "applying many caustic remarks to the names as he read them, and bringing out some hard hits at the social status of some of those who had signed." In the hushed silence that followed, the pastor argued forcefully for the improvement of local streets, some of which "were little better than mud holes," and he concluded by announcing the formation of a parish temperance organization.[35]

Two weeks later, on May 27, 1888, Archbishop Patrick A. Feehan traveled to Canaryville to dedicate St. Gabriel Church in an impressive ceremony that was widely covered in the daily press. The local stockyards paper recounted Fr. Dorney's campaign against saloons and stressed the speed with which the new church had been completed, an unusual accomplishment for a parish that was only eight years old. The physical appearance of St. Gabriel's was of particular interest to the downtown papers. According to the *Chicago Times,* the edifice boasted "all the modern improvements," including electric lights, and the *Tribune* went so far as to call it "a public ornament . . . an addition to the artistic structures of the city."[36] But it was Archbishop Feehan's dedication sermon that came closest to describing the role St. Gabriel Church would play in the lives of Canaryville residents.

A man of few words, Feehan took the opportunity to discuss the legacy of sacred space and Catholic tradition. Beginning with the dedication of Solomon's temple, he quickly moved down to the present day, explaining the right of Catholics "to come here when we please . . . whether old or young, rich or poor, strong or feeble." Conscious that many St. Gabriel parishioners were immigrants, he reminded them that "no place on earth brings such sacred memories as the church" and that "the holiest and best recollections of our lives" are connected to the church.[37] In stressing the link between sacred space, personal experience, and memory, the archbishop acknowledged the vital role parish churches played in connecting people with their past even as they rooted them in the present.

A landmark in the Canaryville neighborhood since 1888, St. Gabriel Church at Forty-fifth Street and Lowe Avenue is a classic example of the way in which church-building created community and improved the surrounding neighborhood. In his dedication sermon Archbishop Patrick A. Feehan praised architect John Wellborn Root's design for St. Gabriel's and predicted that "in the churches yet to be built [in the Chicago diocese] the splendor of art will be revived."

—*Courtesy,* The New World

Church-building and Catholic Identity

Against overwhelming odds, Catholic parishes such as St. Gabriel did become holy places in the lives of ordinary Catholics and their neighborhoods. The existence of beautiful churches and modern schools, especially in poor sections of Chicago, challenged contemporary notions about immigrant life and provided compelling evidence that Catholics were creating a future for themselves in the city. The extent of Catholic investment in Chicago was highlighted in 1890 when Archbishop Feehan celebrated his twenty-fifth jubilee as a bishop. In addition to a special Mass at Holy Name Cathedral, festivities included a banquet for clergy and visiting bishops, a children's gathering in the new Auditorium building downtown, and a torchlight parade on Michigan Avenue with thirty thousand Irish, German, French, Polish, African-American, Italian, and Bohemian marchers. This Catholic show of strength also constituted a protest against the recently enacted compulsory school legislation known as the Edwards Law. As written, the law provided for state control of private schools and mandated the teaching of elementary school subjects in English. Chicago Catholics used their archbishop's jubilee as a way to showcase their ethnic diversity and demonstrate their loyalty to America.[38]

In his address to the 333 priests of the diocese, Vicar General D. M. J. Dowling characterized the 1880s as "the church-building . . . [and] also the Catholic school-building epoch of our history." According to Dowling, twelve distinct national groups worshiped each week in more than eighty Catholic churches in Chicago, and he informed his listeners that, "We have comparatively the largest parochial school attendance of any diocese in our land . . ." Echoing this theme, Archbishop Feehan asserted that the Catholic Church "has kept pace with even the wonderful growth and material prosperity of this great city," and he reminded his fellow priests that: "In promoting religion and education, you advance also the highest interests of Chicago and of all the people."[39]

Throughout the nineteenth century and well into the twentieth, church-building remained a high priority for Catholics of many different ethnic backgrounds because it met fundamental human needs for respect, dignity, spirituality, and community. Part of the continuing appeal of "brick-and-mortar Catholicism" was its very physicality. The church and school complexes built by immigrants and their American-born children and grandchildren were tangible signs of Catholic progress, and sometimes competition as well. Although parish histories rarely mention such things, church-building was a pragmatic way to proclaim identity—and leave an indelible mark on the surrounding neighborhood. Churches financed by German Catholics on the North Side, for example, not only rivaled German Lutheran edifices in terms of size and beauty, they often overshadowed the parish churches of local Irish Catholics as well. On the South Side, Protestant-Catholic conflict shaped many parishes established by upwardly mobile Irish families who left industrial areas for middle-class residential districts. In neighborhoods such as Oakland, Englewood, and Beverly Hills, local residents waged vigorous campaigns to keep Catholic churches off certain fashionable streets. It is no coincidence that the Irish reacted by constructing monumental churches and schools that dominated the boulevards.

Yet another important dimension to "brick-and-mortar Catholicism" was the sense of place it engendered. Whether they were located near lumberyards, stockyards, and steel mills, in apartment house districts, or residential areas of single family homes, parish church and school complexes became focal points of Catholic neighborhood life. In addition to providing opportunities for worship and education, they enlarged a family's circle of friends and acquaintances beyond the immediate block. Parish membership not only fostered a sense of belonging to a particular place, it intensified the connection between church and turf. Indeed, to a degree unparalleled in other denominations, Chicago Catholics superimposed their experience of sacred space on their surroundings, often referring to their neighborhood by the parish name.

Parish and Neighborhood in Polonia

Nowhere was this link between sacred space and neighborhood more richly illustrated than on the city's Near Northwest Side, the heart of Chicago's Polonia. Depending upon whether they belonged to St. Stanislaus Kostka or Holy Trinity parish—located three blocks from each other on Noble Street—Polish Catholics called their neighborhood "Stanislawowo" or "Trojcowo." The mother church of Polish Catholicism in Chicago, St. Stanislaus Kostka grew so rapidly after its founding in 1867 that a second house of worship was constructed nearby in 1873. Resurrectionist pastor Rev. Vincent Barzynski's refusal to establish the new church of Holy Trinity as a separate parish provoked a firestorm of controversy among lay trustees. The ensuing battle, waged over the next twenty years, involved serious issues of Polish identity, lay control of church finances, and the right of congregations to maintain title to parish property. While scholarly studies have enlarged our understanding of this difficult chapter in the history of Chicago's Polonia, less attention has been paid to the role church-building played in creating the city's largest Polish neighborhood.[40]

In terms of sheer size and monumentality, Polish Catholic churches on the Near Northwest Side surpassed the parish churches constructed by most German, Bohemian, and Irish congregations. Ten years after St. Stanislaus Kostka parish was organized, the cornerstone of the present church was laid. Despite their poverty, members contributed generously to the erection of a Renaissance-style structure designed by Patrick C. Keely of Brooklyn. The choice of Keely was no accident. The best known Catholic architect of his day, he had designed hundreds of churches in the United States, most recently Holy Name Cathedral and St. James Church at Twenty-ninth Street and Wabash Avenue. Modeled after a church in Krakow, and dedicated in 1881, St. Stanislaus Kostka was a landmark for newcomers, a symbol of the dynamic Polish community on the Near Northwest Side. Although a single church could not put the city's Polish immigrants on an equal footing with earlier waves of Irish,

Germans, and Bohemians, it nevertheless proclaimed that Poles were creating a place for themselves in Chicago. By the time the twin towers were completed in 1892 at a cost of $100,000, the parish was the largest in the world with 40,000 members.

After two decades of controversy during which Holy Trinity Church had been closed and reopened several times, a compromise was reached. When Apostolic Delegate Francis Satolli visited Chicago in 1893, he had two important items on his agenda: attending the World's Columbian Exposition and resolving the crisis in Polonia by placing the parish under the direction of the Congregation of the Holy Cross from South Bend, Indiana. Within just a few years, Holy Trinity became one of Polonia's most influential institutions. But more churches were needed to serve the rapidly expanding Polish neighborhoods on the Near Northwest Side.

In 1893, the Resurrectionists purchased property on Carpenter Street near Chicago Avenue for another parish, but so densely populated was the neighborhood that twenty homes had to be demolished to make way for the new house of worship. Despite its ready-made congregation of two thousand families from St. Stan's, the new parish of St. John Cantius still faced the daunting task of establishing an identity distinct from that of the mother church. Contemporary newspaper accounts suggest that the church building itself—with its 240-foot tower—played an important role in creating parish identity and a sense of place. According to the *Tribune*, architect Adolphus Druiding's design ensured that St. John Cantius Church would be "fully in keeping with the conditions and progress of the times." More than twenty-five thousand people attended the cornerstone laying ceremony on September 3, 1893, a strong indication that the daughter church was off to a promising start. Indeed, the music provided by twenty-seven Polish singing societies "filled the air to the remote edges of the crowd half a mile in each direction," prompting the *Chicago Times* to declare that: "There was never before in Chicago such a gathering."[41]

A pattern that emerges throughout the history of different ethnic groups in Chicago is the way in which national parishes based on language shaped the character of Catholic neighborhood life. When Rev. Francis Gordon, a leading priest of the Resurrectionist order, purchased an entire city block for the new Polish parish of St. Mary of the Angels in 1899, he chose a a site on North Hermitage Avenue practically in the shadow of Annunciation Church at Wabansia Avenue and Paulina Street. Gordon hired the talented architect Henry J. Schlacks to design a three story brick combination church-and-school building, completed at a cost of $65,000. A powerful sign of the expansion of Chicago's Polonia, St. Mary of the Angels soon became the center of a flourishing Polish neighborhood. The effect on Annunciation parish was immedi-

ate: church membership and school enrollment declined dramatically as Polish newcomers displaced older Irish residents.

As a newspaper editor and former pastor of St. Stanislaus Kostka Church, Gordon was well aware of the important role church-building had played in the creation of Chicago's Polonia. As early as 1909, he began to plan for a massive house of worship that would become a fitting symbol of Polish Catholic progress in Chicago. He hired the architectural firm of Worthmann & Steinbach to draw up plans for a Roman Renaissance structure with a terra cotta dome modeled after Michelangelo's design for St. Peter's in Rome. Although work began in 1911 and the cornerstone was laid in 1914, there followed many delays due to strikes, the outbreak of World War I, and the shortage of building

Widely regarded as the finest example of Roman Renaissance architecture in the United States, St. Mary of the Angels symbolized the tremendous growth and vitality of Chicago's Polish community in 1920. Rededicated on October 11, 1992, after a major restoration campaign, St. Mary's continues to anchor the Bucktown neighborhood on the Near Northwest Side.

—Photo, Holabird and Root

supplies. A powerful reflection of the growing confidence and commitment of Polish Catholics to city life, St. Mary of the Angels dramatically altered the physical landscape of its neighborhood. In his dedication sermon in 1920, Archbishop George W. Mundelein compared the construction of St. Mary's to the great cathedrals of Rheims, Amiens, and Cologne, noting that "the people in this neighborhood were satisfied to contribute from their slender earnings in order that God's house might rise gigantic, majestic and beautiful, while about it clustered their poorer and unpretentious homes. . ." To the charge that church-building on this scale "waste[d] the poor people's money," Mundelein acknowledged that Jesus himself had been similarly criticized. The bishop congratulated St. Mary of the Angels parishioners

> for among all of the churches of this great city, they have added one of the most beautiful. It will stand here as a monument of the zeal, the deep faith and the generous spirit of self-sacrifice of the children of the Polish race in this city. . . . [42]

Although national parishes such as St. Mary of the Angels often spelled the end of the "glory days" of older territorial parishes such as Annunciation, English-speaking parishes soon adapted to ethnic changes in the larger neighborhood. In Old Town, Bridgeport, Back of the Yards, South Chicago, and other neighborhoods, territorial parishes performed a valuable role in expanding the choices available to Catholics for worship and education. Moreover, as the history of individual parishes makes clear, another characteristic of Chicago Catholicism was an unwillingness to give up turf in the city, even in the wake of profound economic, ethnic, and racial change. Far from closing its doors, for example, Annunciation parish financed a new school at 1645 North Hermitage Avenue in 1902—the better to recruit new students of Eastern European descent (and hence their parents) who now lived in the neighborhood.

Staying Put in Downtown Chicago

By the 1890s, Catholic parish formation was in full swing, in ethnically diverse neighborhoods as well as newer residential districts along the city's boulevards and lakefront. Whereas many Chicago denominations elected to spend limited resources on houses of worship in stable middle-class areas, Catholics attempted to maintain a delicate balance between older parishes in economically distressed areas and new parishes. By all accounts, the historic downtown parishes of St. Mary, St. Peter, and St. Patrick had fallen on hard times in the twenty years since the Great Chicago Fire of 1871. The *Tribune* characterized St. Mary's as the parish of great contrasts, embracing the levee district where prostitution and gambling flourished just blocks from the city's cultural institutions and downtown skyscrapers:

> . . . the parish that once had all the glory of the Catholic Church in Chicago is left today with the dregs. Nearly every Protestant church—and there were many in what is now the First Ward—has been abandoned. St. Mary's . . . remains to hold the torch of faith to the denizens of the down-town slums. It remains with the poor in spirit—those who are poor indeed.[43]

While conceding that the *Tribune's* description of St. Mary's was accurate, Rev. Edward A. Murphy protested in an interview that, "This is a good parish." The Franciscans who staffed nearby St. Peter Church expressed much the same feelings about sacred space in the city. Although they labored "Midst Vice and Squalor," they refused all attempts by the railroads to purchase the parish property at Polk and Clark streets. At the time of the parish's golden jubilee in 1896, *The New World* noted that St. Peter's "stands out with startling vividness among the shanties surrounding it . . ." many of which dated to the early 1860s. In characteristic Catholic fashion, the Franciscans continued to staff their church downtown while creating a new German parish, St. Augustine, "Back of the Yards."[44]

By 1899, St. Patrick's days as a *bon ton* Irish parish were only a memory. Irish families had been moving out of the parish for years in their quest for better housing along Chicago's West Side boulevards. Although cheap lodging houses and factories nearly engulfed the old church on Adams Street, the parish continued to support its grammar schools and commercial academies. The situation was much the same in Holy Family parish, which had become a port of entry for thousands of Eastern European immigrants. The east end of the parish around Maxwell Street had developed a reputation as the city's largest Jewish community, and Italian families had begun to settle around Halsted Street. The response of the Jesuits to the tumultuous changes in the neighborhood was to reorganize the parish schools and redecorate the old Gothic church with elaborate Victorian stenciling. Moreover, the installation of fifteen hundred incandescent lights on the main altar in 1899 ensured that Holy Family "glowed with a new brilliancy" as it began to serve generations of Italian Catholics who, in turn, claimed the church as their own.[45]

The Catholic Church's impressive record in maintaining its urban identity even as it put down roots in new residential neighborhoods garnered praise from the city's newspapers at the turn of the century. Indeed, even the *Tribune* was forced to concede that: "There is no instance on record where a Catholic church, which had suddenly found itself in an unfashionable neighborhood on account of the growth of the city, has been dismantled to become a gymnasium, dance hall, or saloon."[46]

Parish Formation and Urban Development

At the time James E. Quigley began his tenure as Archbishop of Chicago in 1903, parishes had become familiar institutions in the city, the center of neighborhood life for more than five hundred thousand Catholics of diverse ethnic backgrounds. Although the diocese covered ten thousand square miles of territory in Northern Illinois, it drew its numerical strength—and much of its identity and vigor—from city churches. In seventy years, the Catholic Church in Chicago had expanded dramatically, from a single parish in 1833 to 157 parishes, 80 percent with schools. While much of Chicago's population of nearly 2 million remained concentrated in older neighborhoods, vast tracts of land remained to be developed within the city's 185-square mile limits. Thanks to Quigley's policy of parish formation, the Catholic Church was present, right from the beginning, in new apartment house districts and residential areas of single family homes.

Conscious of the success of brick-and-mortar Catholicism in Chicago, the new archbishop divided older territorial parishes to form new parishes one-square mile in territory. This size, he believed, promoted closer ties between priest and parishioners, as well as between Catholic families living in a circumscribed area. Although a few wealthy Chicagoans owned automobiles by 1910, most city dwellers depended upon public transportation, notably streetcars and the "L." Well into the 1950s, Chicago was still very much a neighborhood-based walking city. And its network of Catholic parishes every mile—or less—served to intensify the connection between church and turf, between parish and neighborhood.

In establishing parishes for upwardly mobile Catholic families who were settling in outlying areas of the city, Quigley did not neglect the needs of new Italian, Lithuanian, Slavic, and Polish immigrants. He divided older national parishes such as St. Joseph Back of the Yards, thereby insuring that the expansion of Chicago's Polish community would remain parish-centered. Likewise, one of Quigley's top priorities was to establish new parishes for Chicago's Italians who had come to Chicago by the thousands since the 1890s. For decades, the city's only Italian parish was

Assumption, B.V.M. on Illinois Street, organized by the Servites in 1880 to meet the needs of immigrants from northern Italy. The process of parish formation among newly arrived Sicilian immigrants was compounded by poverty and the shortage of Italian priests. Although efforts at organizing a second Italian parish began in 1892, it was not until 1899 that Holy Guardian Angel Church at 717 West Forquer (Arthington) Street was dedicated. Rev. Edmund M. Dunne, the parish's first pastor, had learned Italian during his seminary days at the North American College in Rome and wrote extensively about the experience of Italian immigrants in Chicago. As had happened so often in the history of Chicago Catholicism, the organization of a new parish provided tangible proof that another group was creating a place for itself in the city. Located two blocks from the old church of St. Wenceslaus, the "mother parish" of Chicago's Bohemians, Holy Guardian Angel Church also signaled the changing ethnic character of the neighborhood. While the new edifice with its stately Romanesque arches recalled the parishioners' Italian origins, they "strenuously objected to its Celtic [cross]," and regarded its destruction by lightning in 1904 as a divine omen! A few years after a Latin cross was installed, the parish took on new life under the direction of the Scalabrini Fathers, a religious order founded in Italy in 1887.[47]

Between 1903 and 1915, seven more Italian Catholic churches opened for worship in Chicago, a sign of the increasing diversity of the city and the diocese. In establishing new national parishes in older city neighborhoods, Quigley continued the pragmatic approach to ethnicity pioneered by his predecessor, Archbishop Feehan. When he visited Rome in 1906 to report on the progress of the Chicago archdiocese, *The New World* noted that: "In no other diocese in the world are all the foreign populations so well provided with churches, hospitals, and schools."[48]

Sacred Space in the Industrial Slum

In industrial districts such as Back of the Yards, national parishes did more than meet the spiritual and educational needs of diverse Catholic ethnic groups, they extended traditional concepts of sacred space. In middle-class neighborhoods, churches often occupied prominent locations—Michigan and Wabash avenues on the South Side; Washington and Jackson boulevards on the West Side; and Fullerton Parkway and Sheridan Road on the North Side. Although there were no boulevards in Back of the Yards, Hermitage Avenue emerged as the choice location for Catholic churches. Unlike the architectural competitions for skyscrapers downtown, the campaign to create beautiful houses of worship was financed by immigrant laborers who earned approximately fifteen cents an hour in the stockyards. Between 1913 and 1915, Bohemians, Poles, and Lithuanians all built magnificent churches on Hermitage Avenue, transforming this bleak section of the neighborhood.

The Bohemians of SS. Cyril and Methodius parish led the church-building boom with their stately Corinthian-style structure at Fiftieth Street, dedicated in 1913. The following year, Polish families celebrated the completion of St. Joseph Church at Forty-eighth Street, a masterpiece of Renaissance Revival architecture. The Lithuanian Church of the Holy Cross, dedicated in 1915 at Forty-sixth and Hermitage, did more than match St. Joseph's, tower for tower. In terms of its scale and design, Holy Cross also eclipsed St. George Church in Bridgeport, the "mother parish" of Chicago's Lithuanians. Although immigrant Catholics invested nearly $1 million in their Hermitage Avenue houses of worship Back of the Yards, their remarkable accomplishment was all but invisible to the larger city. While language barriers no doubt contributed to the lack of coverage in the English-speaking press, the fact remains that Catholic church dedications in Chicago were routine events by the time of World War I. According to *The New World,* parishes had become such an integral part of Chicago life that their tremendous contributions to the health and well-being of the city "passe[d] almost unnoticed."[49]

Since the early days of the Chicago diocese, parish development in the city had been uneven at best, reflecting differences in the numerical strength of immigrant groups, residential patterns, and economic backgrounds, as well as natural cycles of growth and decline.

Paradoxically, the parochial schools that rooted families in a neighborhood also promoted social and economic mobility among the children of immigrants. The effect of all this was a steady movement of Catholic families from older city neighborhoods to outlying areas, where the process of parish and school formation began all over again.

Recreating the Parish: The Suburban Experience

"Parishes, like cities, grow by immigration," *The New World* proclaimed in 1907, noting that a family's decision to move was also influenced by "the character of parish, church, and school." For upwardly mobile Catholics

who settled in Protestant-dominated areas, parish formation and church-building took on added meaning, as the history of St. Edmund's in Oak Park illustrates. Whereas Catholics regarded the formation of this

St. Edmund's Church, dedicated in 1910 at Oak Park Avenue and Pleasant Street, constituted a visible sign of the Catholic presence in Oak Park. At the turn of the century, Catholics used their churches and schools as a means of establishing identity and community in middle-class Protestant suburbs.

—*Author's collection*

parish in 1907 as a new beginning, a sign of progress and faith in the future, for some Protestants it represented a serious fissure in the fabric of suburban life. According to James F. Bundy, the Catholics of St. Edmund's constituted "the most definite symbol of an 'alien' presence in Oak Park. . ." and while there was little overt opposition to the new parish, he notes that "the Protestant leadership almost completely ignored the existence of the Roman Catholic Church in Oak Park."[50]

Accounts differ as to the reception Rev. John J. Code and his parishioners received when they built their new church in 1910 at the corner of Oak Park Avenue and Pleasant Street, but there is no question that the very existence of St. Edmund parish challenged accepted notions about Catholics. In his first sermon, Fr. Code had thrown down the gauntlet:

> What others have done here Catholics can surpass. Let it not be said that we shall take second place in works that glorify God. The Catholic Church is the mother of art . . . we will build here, with God's blessing, a church and school that shall be a glory to God, a credit to ourselves, an ornament to our village and a source of pride to every citizen.[51]

The experience of St. Edmund parishioners suggests that brick-and-mortar Catholicism was not a luxury but a necessary condition of their survival in a middle-class Protestant district. English-speaking Catholics of Irish and German descent routinely broke the religion barrier in outlying Chicago neighborhoods and suburbs. Considering the religious climate of the times, it was no coincidence that Catholics recreated parishes and schools as a means of preserving their faith and identity. Nowhere was this more evident than in the erection of St. Edmund School, built in 1917 according to plans by the well-known architect Henry J. Schlacks. Designed after the medieval Palace of Justice in Rouen, France, the elegant structure symbolized Catholic confidence, power, and identity. Archbishop Mundelein described St. Edmund's new school building as "the children's church," and he assured the residents of Oak Park

> irrespective of creed, race or position . . . that there is no building in the confines of the village that will work harder or more effectively for the common welfare than the school we have blessed today.[52]

The Golden Age of Catholic Church-building

Catholic identity and monumental church-building reached new heights during the tenure of Archbishop Mundelein (1916–1939). His first address to the Catholic laity on February 13, 1916, at the Auditorium Theater was a curious blend of confidence and one-upmanship. Acknowledging the diversity of the million Catholics in the Chicago archdiocese, Mundelein asserted that: "This great crowd of people . . . represents more nations and tongues than were gathered in Jerusalem's streets on Pentecostal day. . ." In addition to characterizing Chicago Catholicism as "one of the greatest churches in Christendom," he argued that the Catholic Church represented "the great bulwark against anarchy, the great preventative agency against crime in our cities. . ." Linking the future of their city and

its 215 Catholic parishes, Mundelein exhorted the laity to support charitable and educational efforts and "to make Chicago more beautiful in its religious edifices."[53]

One of Mundelein's first priorities was to organize new parishes and expand church and school facilities in the apartment house districts and "bungalow belts" on the city's North, West, and South sides. While some reformers and social scientists doubted that community life could flourish amidst steam-heat "flats," Catholics entertained no such qualms. In record time, parish churches and schools were distinguishing features of lakefront neighborhoods, the city's boulevards, and new residential areas of bungalows and apartments. Edward Kantowicz's research confirms that Mundelein favored the Colonial

St. Anselm's Church, immortalized in James T. Farrell's classic novel, Studs Lonigan, *was built in 1924–25 at Sixty-first Street and Michigan Avenue to keep Irish Catholics in the Washington Park neighborhood. In designing the $350,000 Romanesque church, architect Charles L. Wallace incorporated Celtic crosses and shamrocks inlaid in marble.*

—*Courtesy,* The New World

style of architecture and insisted that school quarters precede a permanent house of worship.[54] Still, individual pastors and congregations enjoyed wide latitude in constructing parish complexes. The 1920s represented a high-water mark in terms of ecclesiastical architecture and Catholics were eager, willing participants in the creation of parish churches and schools that marked the center of neighborhood life.

Perhaps no other pastor in the early twentieth century believed as fervently in church-building as Rev. Michael S. Gilmartin. When he began organizing St. Anselm parish on the

South Side in 1909, the Washington Park district was experiencing a building boom. *Prairies* (the Chicago term for vacant lots) disappeared almost overnight, replaced by modern brick apartment buildings and greystones. The Irish-born pastor found a substantial number of Catholic families living in the area, and within months they had contributed generously to the erection of a combination church-school building and rectory. St. Anselm parishioners were proud of the speed with which their parish complex took shape, and in 1911 they financed a spacious convent for the Sisters of Providence. It was only a matter

The graduating class of St. Anselm's grammar school in the depression year of 1938. Founded by Irish Catholics in 1909, the parish took on a new life and identity as a cradle of African-American Catholisim in the 1930s. Rev. Joseph Eckert, S.V.D. (seated) baptized more than fifteen hundred men, women, and children during his eight-year tenure as pastor.

—*Courtesy*, The Divine Word Missionaries/St. Anselm's Parish

of time, they knew, before a permanent church would be constructed. What happened next in this parish has been immortalized by James T. Farrell in his classic novel, *Studs Lonigan*.[55]

By the end of World War I, St. Anselm parishioners were on a collision course with one of the great mass migrations in American history. In search of jobs and a better life, thousands of Southern blacks had traveled north to Chicago, many recruited by the packinghouses as strikebreakers. The promised land turned out to contain segregated neighborhoods, poor housing, and tenuous em-

ployment.[56] Among the Irish of St. Anselm's, racial change was a frequent topic of conversation as adults and children struggled to comprehend the tremendous growth and expansion of Chicago's "Black Belt." Not only did Fr. Gilmartin refuse to believe that his parish would become a black neighborhood, but he insisted that a new St. Anselm Church would keep the neighborhood white. In 1924, he secured permission from Cardinal Mundelein to build a $350,000 edifice at the corner of Sixty-first Street and Michigan Avenue, hiring architect Charles Wallace of Joliet to draw up plans. As Farrell recounted the story in *Studs Lonigan,* many parishioners desperately wanted to believe "Gilly" when he preached that St. Anselm's was indeed "a coming parish." Although opinion on the future of the neighborhood was sharply divided, a number of parishioners clung to the hope that:

Michigan Avenue is going to be made a boulevard. Property values around here will skyrocket. The new church will clinch the matter . . . it'll make people stay here, and [Catholics] of the right kind with money will move in and buy property.[57]

By the time the new Romanesque structure with its distinctive twin towers was dedicated in 1925, however, the exodus of white parishioners was well underway. Although St. Anselm's was built for all the wrong reasons, it did indeed fulfill Fr. Gilmartin's hopes—for the city's growing black Catholic population. As often happened in the history of Chicago parishes, another group claimed the church as its own, infusing it with new life and meaning. Beginning in 1932 under the direction of Rev. Joseph Eckert of the Divine Word Fathers and Sisters of the Blessed Sacrament, St. Anselm's became a center of convert work, a cradle of African-American Catholicism in Chicago.

In a city shaped by immigration, Catholics were no strangers to social and economic dislocation. Since the 1840s, immigrant groups in Chicago had vied with each other for jobs and housing, and sometimes sacred space as well. Although the transitions were often painful, what is remarkable is the degree to which individual Catholic parishes adapted to changes in the larger neighborhood. On a scale unmatched by any other religious denomination, Catholic churches and schools remained in the city in the wake of tumultuous demographic and ethnic change. As Steven Avella has documented, enlightened social policies at the chancery office played a crucial role in the persistence of Catholic institutions throughout the worst years of the Great Depression and well into the World War II era.[58]

Despite wrenching dislocations wrought by ethnic, economic, and racial change, Chicago Catholics shared a belief that churches constituted holy places in their lives and in their neighborhoods. By the 1920s, this attitude was so widespread that families often called their neighborhood by the parish name. The tendency to envision the city in parochial terms was inextricably linked with the tradition of Catholic parish formation and church-building. From the nineteenth century on, the institutional Church had kept pace with the tremendous physical expansion of Chicago. The forty-seven city parishes established between 1916 and 1929, for example, not only extended the presence of the Catholic Church to virtually every corner of Chicago, they guaranteed the continuity of Catholic neighborhood life. The scope of this achievement became clear in 1930 when the Social Research Committee at the University of Chicago mapped Protestant and Catholic churches. Thanks in large measure to the mile-square parish model advocated by Quigley and Mundelein, the city's 257 Catholic parishes revealed a "planned distribution." The haphazard clustering of Chicago's 1,128 Protestant churches, on the other hand, was attributed to the "principle of the self-chosen parish."[59]

So effective was the mile-square parish in creating Catholic community—as well as a sense of place—that it remained the preferred model of parish formation throughout the 1950s. As a result, Chicago Catholics who moved from older neighborhoods to the city's edge or suburbs after World War II encountered a familiar institution amidst ranch-style homes and cul-de-sacs. Although few parishes financed the construction of monumental edifices, churches and schools continued to be an important feature of neighborhood life in Chicago suburbs. Ironically, the ecclesiastical building boom in the post-World War II era was so great that *The New World* did not have space enough for feature stories about each new parish complex.

The shrine to Our Lady of Guadalupe, featuring the colors of the Mexican flag, provides incontrovertible proof of ethnic change in the old Lithuanian parish of Holy Cross at Forty-sixth Street and Hermitage Avenue. No matter what the weather, thousands of Mexican immigrants and their American-born children gather to celebrate the feast of Our Lady of Guadalupe on December 12.

—Photo by Joan Radtke

Urban Parishes in a Declining City

In the early days of the Chicago diocese, bishops were forced to balance the competing needs of country missions and immigrant city churches. After World War II, the pendulum swung between parishes in older industrial neighborhoods and new suburban growth. Archbishop Samuel A. Stritch realized the precarious position of urban parishes shortly after his appointment to head the Chicago diocese in 1940. Convinced that neighborhood parishes had an important role to play in the future of the city, Stritch supported the organization of groups such as the Back of the Yards Neighborhood Council, the Organization for the Southwest Community, and the Cardinal's Conservation Committee. The first grass-roots community group in America, the Back of the Yards Neighborhood Council was organized with the help of local businesses, the C.I.O. United Packinghouse Workers, and financial assistance from the Archdiocese of Chicago. Under the inspired leadership of Saul Alinsky and Joseph Meegan, the council attacked problems of juvenile delinquency, substandard housing, and inadequate recreational facilities.[60] Whereas earlier generations of social reformers had regarded the churches Back of the Yards as luxuries that immigrants could ill afford, Alinsky and Meegan recognized their inherent power to create and sustain community life. In a very real sense, the Back of the Yards Neighborhood Council succeeded precisely because it rekindled powerful connections between church and turf.

In a speech to local Catholic pastors in 1952, Cardinal Stritch acknowledged that "As things are going now, we are building a new archdiocese on the perimeter of Chicago." While the needs of Catholics in suburban areas remained a priority, he maintained his belief that Chicago parishes "can not only reclaim some of the blighted areas . . . but we can prevent other areas from becoming blighted."[61]

In East Humbolt Park neighborhood, for example, Catholic parishes were important community anchors, serving many different ethnic groups. A port of entry since the 1880s for waves of German, Irish, Scandinavians, Italians, Poles, Eastern European Jews, and Ukrainians, this port of the Northwest Side was widely regarded as a deteriorating neighborhood. In the 1960s, Catholic parishes played an important role in the formation of the Northwest Community Orginization (NCO), aimed at improving condions in the area.[62]

The commitment of the Catholic Church went beyond social programs. Three new churches were constructed within blocks of each other, underscoring the important link between sacred space and neighborhood. St. Mark's parish led the way with a modern church on the corner of Thomas Street and Campbell Avenue, which included beautiful

In 1958, the Back of the Yards Neighborhood Council assisted homeowners in renovating the area's aging housing stock.

—Photo by The New World, *courtesy Archives of the Archdiocese of Chicago*

Suburban-style picture windows and cement steps gave old immigrant housing a modern look and contributed to the stability of one of Chicago's most ethnically diverse neighborhoods.

—Photo by The New World, *courtesy Archives of the Archdiocese of Chicago*

*At a time when many religious denominations were leaving the East Humboldt
Park neighborhood in the wake of ethnic change, St. Mark's parish financed
a modern church complete with art glass windows crafted by Gabriel Loire of
Paris. Dominating the corner of Thomas Street and Campbell Avenue, the new
St. Mark's symbolized "courage and confidence in the future of the inner city"
when it was dedicated by Albert Cardinal Meyer in 1963.*

—Courtesy, St. Mark's parish

faceted windows crafted by Gabriel Loire of Paris. The new St. Mark's (which came to be known as the Puerto Rican Cathedral) was dedicated on St. Patrick's Day, March 17, 1963. A few months later, members of the old German parish of St. Aloysius broke ground for a new edifice at LeMoyne Street and Claremont Avenue, and in 1964, work began at the corner of Augusta and Oakley boulvards for a contemporary church in the Polish parish of St. Helen.

Although expressway construction, urban renewal, and profound ethnic and racial change sorely tested the fabric of city life in the 1950s and 1960s, Catholic parishes continued to exert a powerful influence on Chicago neighborhoods. Their distinctive church and school complexes symbolized hope in the future of the city, eloquent reminders of the Catholic Church's urban mission.

The Loss of Sacred Space

The massive parish closings that occurred recently in the Archdiocese of Chicago had been a long time in the making. The decline of the stockyards and steel mills, the exodus of industry to suburban areas, along with "white flight," had all left their mark on older city neighborhoods. In the 1950s, for example, Catholics living in the Englewood and West Englewood neighborhoods on Chicago's South Side supported twelve Catholic parishes and schools. But thirty years later, rapid racial and economic changes prompted the Catholic Community of Englewood to initiate a planning process that resulted in the consolidation of eight parishes in the area roughly bounded by Garfield Boulevard (Fifty-fifth Street) on the north, Seventy-fifth Street on the south, the Dan Ryan Expressway on the east, and Western Avenue on the west. In a homily on May 27, 1989, Joseph Cardinal Bernardin hailed the restructuring of the Catholic community in Englewood as "a creative moment" that held "much promise for the future." Indeed, the new St. Benedict the African Church at Sixty-sixth Street and Stewart Avenue, with its immersion baptismal font, is a symbol of new life in the Englewood neighborhood. But its dedication on June 10,

A symbol of Polish Catholic reinvestment in the neighborhood, Sacred Heart Church at Forty-sixth Street and Wolcott Avenue was designed by a Polish architect, John Flizikowski, and completed in 1911 by skilled Polish craftsmen. In the 1930s, Sacred Heart parish hosted the first national congress of the Polish Highlanders Alliance of North America.

—Courtesy, the Polish Highlanders Alliance of North America

No matter how poor the neighborhood, there has always been an unwritten agreement that churches constitute sacred space. Virtually untouched by graffiti in its eighty-year history, Sacred Heart has become a target of gangs since its closing by the Archdiocese of Chicago in 1990.

—*Author's collection*

1990, was nearly eclipsed by the many parish closings announced six months earlier. The diocese that pioneered the urban neighborhood parish was now engaged in the difficult process of retrenchment.[63]

While most Catholics understood the need for restructuring urban parishes, especially in a time of financial crisis, the scale of the closings still came as a shock. In 1990, thirty-five Catholic parishes and missions in the city and suburbs were canonically suppressed, a watershed event in the history of the Chicago diocese.[64] In contrast with other religious dominations who sold their houses of worship in response to dramatic shifts in neighborhood population, for more than a century the Catholic Church had avoided giving up

turf. The loss of sacred space is never easy, but the experience has been doubly painful in the city where Catholics often refer to their neighborhoods by the parish name. One of the unintended consequences of the recent archdiocesan closings is that Catholics—and Chicagoans at large—are beginning to understand the complex role parishes played in fostering dignity, respect, and sense of place in neighborhoods throughout the city. The line between stability and decay in urban areas has always been a fine one, and time will tell whether the loss of sacred space accelerates neighborhood change.

While the future growth of the Chicago archdiocese is clearly in the suburbs, there is compelling evidence that parish identity is as important for "mega-churches" such as St. Michael in Orland Park and St. Mary in Buffalo Grove as it was for neighborhood parishes in the city.[65] Unlike the "walking" parishes familiar to generations of Chicagoans, however, newer suburban parishes often cover eight square miles of territory. The task of creating community in such a vast area is a daunting one, compounded by the design of subdivisions and the reliance on the automobile. But in spite of such obstacles, parishes continue to put down roots and transform the physical landscape. Moreover, in recent years there has been renewed interest among pastors and parishioners in constructing churches that will be focal points of suburban life. Likewise, the campaigns to restore Holy Family and St. Patrick's on the Near West Side and St. Mary of the Angels in Bucktown have captured the imagination of thousands of Chicagoans and refuted the contemporary wisdom that beautiful churches built by immigrants have outlived their usefulness. The challenge of creating community in the city is as difficult today as it was in the nineteenth century. Without sacred spaces, it may well be impossible.

Detail of a stained glass window in Holy Name of Mary Church, 112th and Loomis streets in the East Morgan Park neighborhood. Designed by an African-American architect, Raymond Broady, and financed entirely by a local black congregation, Holy Name of Mary illustrates the continuing role church-building plays in creating community, identity, and a sense of place in an urban neighborhood.

—Photo by Joan Radtke

The annual Via Crucis (Way of the Cross) procession on Good Friday, 1990,
illustrates the enduring link between parish and neighborhood in Chicago.
Thousands of Mexican Catholics in the Pilsen neighborhood participate in the
reenactment of the Passion of Christ, which begins at Providence of God Church
and winds it way along Eighteenth Street to Harrison Park. The ceremony
concludes at St. Adalbert Church, visible in the background.

—Author's collection

Notes

Introduction. What Has Made Chicago Catholicism Distinctive?

[1] Margery Frisbie, *An Alley in Chicago: The Ministry of a City Priest* (Kansas City, Mo.: Sheed and Ward, 1991), *viii*.

[2] New York City has never ranked number one in this census sweepstakes since it has always been divided into two separate ecclesiastical divisions, the archdiocese of New York and the diocese of Brooklyn. The two together would outrank Chicago and Los Angeles in population.

Chapter 1. The Ethnic Church

[1] H. Richard Niebuhr first made this point in his pioneering study, *The Social Sources of Denominationalism* (New York: Henry Holt and Company, 1929). See particularly chap. 8, "The Churches of the Immigrants," 200–235. After the ethnic revival of the 1960s, church historians became more attentive to the ethnic factor. Martin E. Marty reviews the historiographic issues in "Ethnicity: The Skeleton of Religion in America," *Church History* 41 (March 1972): 5–21. The quotations at the head of this chapter are taken from these two sources.

[2] Jay P. Dolan, "The Immigrants and Their Gods: A New Perspective in American Religious History," *Church History* 57 (March 1988), 66.

[3] I have relied on the account in Sydney E. Ahlstrom, *A Religious History of the American People* (Garden City, N.Y.: Doubleday Image, 1975), vol. 2, 215–23.

[4] Robert C. Wiederaenders, "A History of Lutheranism in Chicago," vol. 2 of the *Chicago Lutheran Planning Study* (National Lutheran Council, 1965), 3–5; Ulf Beijbom, *Swedes in Chicago: A Demographic and Social Study of the 1846–1880 Immigration* (Uppsala, Sweden: Studia Historica Upsaliensa, 1971), 231–65; Odd S. Lovoll, *A Century of Urban Life: The Norwegians in Chicago before 1930* (Northfield, Minn.: Norwegian-American Historical Association, 1988), 54–58.

[5] Lovoll, *Century of Urban Life*, 109.

[6] *Polk's Directory of Chicago, 1923* (Chicago: R. L. Polk & Co., 1923), vol. 1, 162–69.

[7] Lovoll, *Century of Urban Life*, 61.

[8] Niebuhr, *Social Sources of Denominationalism*, 223.

[9] Beijbom, *Swedes in Chicago*, 231.

[10] Ahlstrom, *Religious History*, vol. 2, 467–80; Morris Gutstein, "The Roots and Branches: A Survey of the Chicago Jewish Community, 1845–1976," in *Faith and Form: Synagogue Architecture in Illinois* (Chicago: Spertus College Press, 1976), 21.

[11] Much of the extensive literature on Jewish immigration focuses on New York City. For settlement background in Chicago, see Edward H. Mazur, *Minyans for a Prairie City* (New York: Garland Publishing, 1990), 1–78.

[12] Hyman Meites, *History of the Jews of Chicago* (Chicago: Jewish Historical Society of Illinois, 1924), 116, 489–90.

[13] Edward R. Kantowicz, "Church and Neighborhood," *Ethnicity* 7 (1980): 349–66; Ellen Skerrett, "The Catholic Dimension," in Lawrence McCaffrey et al., *The Irish in Chicago* (Urbana, Ill.: University of Illinois Press, 1987), 49.

[14] Though there is no overall narrative history of the Catholic Church in Chicago, Harry C.

Koenig, ed., *A History of the Parishes of the Archdiocese of Chicago,* 2 vols. (Chicago: Archdiocese of Chicago, 1980) is a rich, encyclopedic source of information. Ellen Skerrett did most of the research for these volumes.

[15] Kantowicz, "Church and Neighborhood," 351–61.

[16] The parish population figures were drawn from the annual reports of the parishes, at the Archives of the Archdiocese of Chicago.

[17] The territorial parishes and their founding dates are: St. Bridget, 1850; Nativity, 1868; All Saints, 1875; St. David, 1905; the German parishes are St. Anthony of Padua, 1873, and Immaculate Conception, 1883.

[18] Edward R. Kantowicz, *Corporation Sole: Cardinal Mundelein and Chicago Catholicism* (Notre Dame, Ind.: Notre Dame University Press, 1983), 71–72.

[19] I gathered these statistics at the Archives of the Archdiocese of Chicago while researching *Corporation Sole.* I analyzed them more thoroughly in a paper entitled "Men, Money, and Masonry: The Maturing of American Catholicism," delivered at the Perspectives on American Catholicism Conference at Notre Dame, on November 19, 1982.

[20] Skerrett, "The Catholic Dimension," 41–42.

[21] Kantowicz, *Corporation Sole,* 129–31, 197–202.

[22] Ibid., 68–69.

[23] Mary Cygan, "Ethnic Parish as Compromise: The Spheres of Clerical and Lay Authority in a Polish American Parish, 1911–1930," Charles and Margaret Hall Cushwa Center for the Study of American Catholicism, Working Paper Series 13, No. 1, Spring 1983.

[24] Kantowicz, *Corporation Sole,* 69–71.

[25] Ellen Skerrett has made this point very eloquently in "Whose Church Is It, Anyway?," *Commonweal,* November 18, 1988, 622–29.

[26] Edward R. Kantowicz, "To Build the Catholic City," *Chicago History* 14 (Fall 1985): 4–27.

[27] A word is in order about the Romanesque, the simple, rounded style of the early middle ages that preceded the Gothic. No ethnic pattern is detectable in the use of Romanesque. Chicago Romanesque tended to be a modest, utilitarian style chosen most frequently by the less wealthy parishes in each ethnic league.

[28] George Cardinal Mundelein, who was a vigorous Americanizer in the Catholic Church, instructed his architect, Joseph McCarthy, to use this English model, as filtered through colonial New England, when he designed the seminary of St. Mary of the Lake.

[29] Wiederaenders, in "History of Lutheranism in Chicago," 46–47, adopted this description of the transition process from Sharvy G. Umbeck, "The Social Adaptations of a Select Group of German-Background Protestant Churches in Chicago," (Ph.D. diss., University of Chicago, 1940), 74–83.

[30] Ahlstrom, *Religious History of the American People,* outlines the torturous process of synodal consolidation in a long footnote, vol. 2, 222–23. The statistics are from *Lutheran Annual,* 1989, of the *Lutheran Church–Missouri Synod,* 657, and *1988 Yearbook: Evangelical Lutheran Church in America,* 496.

[31] Kantowicz, *Corporation Sole,* 72–83. A number of Polish priests in several cities had broken away from the Catholic Church in the 1890s and organized a separate Polish National Catholic Church. This was the only major schism in American Catholicism, but it served as a warning to strong bishops like Mundelein.

[32] Ibid., 72–74; Charles Shanabruch, *Chicago's Catholics: The Evolution of an American Identity* (Notre Dame, Ind.: University of Notre Dame Press, 1981), 181–85, 210–11; Koenig, *History of the Parishes,* vol. 1, 285–86, 444–47, 691–95.

[33] *Chicago Tribune,* January 22, 1990, 1, 4; January 23, 1990, sec. 2, 1; *The New World,* January 26, 1990, 9–16.

[34] *Chicago Tribune,* June 29, 1990, sec. 2, 8; *The New World,* July 6, 1990, 2–6.

Chapter 2. The Irish in Chicago: The Catholic Dimension

This chapter derives from research begun under a Youthgrant awarded by the National Endowment for the Humanities.

[1] Jay P. Dolan, *The Immigrant Church: New York's Irish and German Catholics, 1815–1865* (Baltimore: Johns Hopkins University Press, 1975), 4. For background information on Chicago parishes, see Charles Shanabruch, *Chicago's Catholics: The Evolution of an American Identity* (Notre Dame, Ind.: University of Notre Dame Press, 1981) and James W. Sanders, *The Education of an Urban Minority: Catholics in Chicago, 1833–1965* (New York: Oxford University Press, 1977).

[2] Dolan, *Immigrant Church,* 9.

[3] Ibid., 71.

[4] Chicago Catholic parish statistics in this essay are based on Rev. Msgr. Harry C. Koenig, ed., *A History of the Parishes of the Archdiocese of Chicago,* 2 vols. (Chicago: Archdiocese of Chicago, 1980). Between 1844 and 1900, sixty-one English-speaking (territorial) parishes were organized in Chicago. The sixty-seven national parishes formed during the same period were divided as follows: German, twenty-seven; Polish, sixteen; Bohemian, eight; French, five; Italian, four; Lithuanian, three; Negro, one; Slovak, one; Slovene, one; Dutch, one.

[5] Population statistics in this essay are based on *The People of Chicago: Who We Are and Who We Have Been* (Chicago: City of Chicago Department of Planning, 1976), 10, 11, 13, 17; and U.S. Bureau of the Census, *Eleventh Census of the United States: 1890,* "Population," Part 1 (Washington, D.C.: Government Printing Office, 1895), 671, 708, 714, 720, 726, 728.

[6] Bessie Louise Pierce, *A History of Chicago,* 3 vols. (New York: Alfred A. Knopf, 1937–1957), 1:72.

[7] For a full treatment of nativism and the *Chicago Tribune's* anti-Catholicism, see Thomas M. Keefe, "Chicago's Flirtation with Political Nativism, 1854–1856," *Records of the American Catholic Historical Society of Philadelphia* 82 (1971): 131–58; and "The Catholic Issue in the Chicago Tribune before the Civil War," *Mid-America* 57 (1975): 227–45.

[8] *Chicago Tribune,* February 26, 1855.

[9] *Chicago Tribune,* March 19, 1855.

[10] *Chicago Times,* November 7, 1875.

[11] Cited by Shanabruch, *Chicago's Catholics,* 12.

[12] *Chicago Daily Journal,* January 18, 1855. Contemporary newspaper accounts question the bishop's financial dealings, and they dispute the allegation that the banished faculty left O'Regan with a $45,000 debt on unauthorized projects as well as an embezzlement of $30,000. (Cited by Shanabruch, *Chicago's Catholics,* 13.) Six days after his installation as bishop of Chicago, O'Regan hired the city's leading architectural firm to design an episcopal residence at a cost in excess of $15,000. See the *Daily Democratic Press,* September 9, 1854, and the *Chicago Tribune,* May 21, 1857; August 15, 20, 25, 1857. Significantly, Kinsella, Clowry, Breen, and Hoey all achieved prominence in the East.

[13] *Daily Democratic Press,* November 2, 3, 5, 6, 1855.

[14] Cited by Robert Trisco, "Bishops and Their Priests in the United States," *The Catholic Priest in the United States: Historical Investigations,* ed. John Tracy Ellis (Collegeville, Minn.: St. John's University Press, 1971), 128.

[15] For information on the character of Catholicism in nineteenth-century Ireland see S. J. Connolly, *Priests and People in Pre-Famine Ireland, 1780–1845* (Dublin: Gill and Macmillan, 1982); James O'Shea, *Priest, Politics and Society in Post-Famine Ireland: A Study of County Tipperary, 1850–91* (Atlantic Highlands, N.J.: Humanities Press, Inc., 1983); Emmet Larkin, *The Historical Dimensions of Irish Catholicism* (Washington, D.C.: Catholic University of America Press, 1984); Patrick J. Corish, *The Irish Catholic Experience* (Dublin: Gill and Macmillan, 1985); K. Theodore Hoppen, *Elections, Politics and Society in Ireland, 1832–1885* (Oxford: Oxford University Press, 1984); and Desmond J. Keenan, *The Catholic Church in Nineteenth Century Ireland* (Totowa, N.J.: Barnes and Noble, 1983).

[16] *Daily Chicago Times,* July 1, 1859.

[17] *Chicago Tribune,* August 10, 1862.

[18] The Irish Legion was one of the oldest Union regiments in the field, having joined Gen. William T. Sherman's army at Vicksburg, Mississippi, in 1863. The 90th Volunteers fought in campaigns from Mission Ridge, Tennessee, to Resaca, Georgia and Jonesboro, Arkansas. Three hundred enlistees died in battle, and more than four hundred succumbed to "the various casualties of war." On their return to Chicago, the *Tribune* commented that: "Their

fine, soldierly bearing and bronzed appearance attracted general attention." Alfred T. Andreas, *History of Chicago*, 3 vols. (Chicago: A. T. Andreas Co., 1884–1886), 2: 249–52; and *Chicago Tribune*, June 12, 14, 1865.

[19] *Chicago Times*, December 27, 1868.

[20] James P. Gaffey, "Patterns of Ecclesiastical Authority: The Problem of Chicago Succession, 1865–1881," *Church History* 42 (1973): 257–70.

[21] *Chicago Times,* September 28, 1868.

[22] *Chicago Times,* September 22, 27, 1868.

[23] *Chicago Tribune,* October 13, 1868.

[24] Eyewitness account of Rev. L. L. Laitner cited by Gaffey, "Patterns of Ecclesiastical Authority," 263–64. The *Chicago Times*, April 16, 1869, traced the bishop's "mental malady" to the deathbed confrontation with Dunne.

[25] *Chicago Times*, January 30, 1870.

[26] *Chicago Tribune*, February 20, 1879.

[27] *The New World*, April 14, 1900.

[28] *Chicago Times,* June 22, 1873.

[29] Newspaper article, "Our Religious Orders, the Jesuits in Chicago," March 27, 1875, St. Ignatius College Prep Archives.

[30] *Chicago Times*, August 21, 1876.

[31] *Chicago Times*, August 20, 1876.

[32] Rev. Thomas L. Harmon, *Church of the Annunciation, a Parish History, 1866–1916* (Chicago: D. B. Hansen and Sons, 1916), 16.

[33] *Western Catholic*, September 15, 1877.

[34] "More Waldrons Wanted," *Chicago Times,* October 3, 1875, reprinted in *Western Catholic,* September 15, 1877.

[35] *Western Catholic,* September 15, 1877.

[36] Joseph J. Thompson, ed., *The Archdiocese of Chicago, Antecedents and Development* (Des Plaines, Ill.: St. Mary's Training School Press, 1920), 345.

[37] *Chicago Times,* December 18, 1868 and June 22, 1873.

[38] Michael Funchion has argued that although most Irish immigrants in 1900 were manual laborers, if the second generation had been included in labor statistics prior to 1890 "one would have seen a gradual increase in the number of Irish white-collar workers from 1870 onward, as the children of Irish immigrants entered the work force." "Irish Chicago: Church, Homeland, Politics, and Class—The Shaping of an Ethnic Group, 1870–1900," *Ethnic Chicago*, eds. Melvin G. Holli and Peter d'A. Jones (Grand Rapids, Mich.: William B. Eerdmans Publishing Co., 1981), 26–27. Indeed, according to the 1890 "foreign-stock" classification, Chicago's second-generation Irish (113,816) outnumbered foreign-born Irish (70,028).

[39] Emmet Larkin, "The Devotional Revolution in Ireland, 1850–75," *American Historical Review* 77 (June 1972): 625–52, and *The Making of the Roman Catholic Church in Ireland, 1850–60* (Chapel Hill, N.C.: University of North Carolina Press, 1980).

[40] *Chicago Times,* June 3, 1888.

[41] Thompson, *Archdiocese of Chicago,* 345.

[42] Gerald Sullivan, ed., *The Story of Englewood, 1835–1923* (Chicago: Foster and McDonnell, 1924), 112.

[43] *Chicago Sun*, September 5 and 12, 1896.

[44] Michael F. Funchion, *Chicago's Irish Nationalists, 1881–1890* (New York: Arno Press, 1976), 38–41.

[45] For a full account of the nationalist controversy which split Chicago's Polonia, see Joseph John Parot, *Polish Catholics in Chicago, 1850–1920* (DeKalb, Ill.: Northern Illinois University Press, 1981).

[46] School statistics in this essay are based on Sanders, *Education of an Urban Minority*, 5; *Sadlier's Catholic Directory* (New York: D.J. Sadlier and Co., 1876), 341–42; "Province of Chicago," published in James J. McGovern, *Souvenir of the Silver Jubilee in the Episcopacy of His Grace the Most Rev. Patrick Augustine Feehan, Archbishop of Chicago* (Chicago: privately printed, 1891),

250–52; and *Chicago Daily News Almanac and Year-Book for 1907* (Chicago: Chicago Daily News Co., 1906), 429.

[47] Timothy G. Walch, "Catholic Education in Chicago and Milwaukee, 1840–1890" (Ph.D. diss., Northwestern University, 1975), 83.

[48] *The New World,* June 29, 1895.

[49] *The New World,* May 15, 1897 and July 2, 1898. St. James's High School also claimed the distinction of having the first extension courses ever given in a Chicago school, with instructors from the University of Chicago. Extension courses from St. Ignatius College (later Loyola University) were conducted at St. Mary's High School as early as 1911.

[50] *The New World,* September 2, 1911.

[51] *Reverend Hugh McGuire: A Memorial* (Chicago: privately printed, [1911?]), n.p.

[52] *The New World,* July 12, 1902.

[53] *The New World,* June 25, 1920.

[54] Thomas N. Brown makes this point about Irish identity in his classic work, *Irish-American Nationalism, 1870–1890* (Philadelphia: J. B. Lippincott Co., 1966), 34.

[55] *The New World,* August 26, 1911.

[56] *The New World,* February 17, 1906.

[57] Information on the Knights of Columbus is based on Joseph J. Thompson, *A History of the Knights of Columbus of Illinois* (Chicago: Universal Press, 1922), 342–45, 506, 768, 824.

[58] *The New World,* September 22, 1906 and July 10, 1909.

[59] Paul Frederick Cressey, "Population Succession in Chicago: 1898–1930," *The Social Fabric of the Metropolis,* ed. James F. Short (Chicago: University of Chicago Press, 1971), 116.

[60] Ibid.

[61] *The New World,* December 19, 1908.

[62] *Chicago Record-Herald,* July 7, 1909.

[63] *Chicago Inter-Ocean,* March 13, 1902.

[64] Shanabruch, *Chicago's Catholics,* 99–102.

[65] Based on August 1975 interview with John Jordan, a 1924 graduate of Visitation grammar school who later became head basketball coach at Notre Dame University. Rev. Thomas Tormey, an assistant at Visitation from 1924 to 1930, was first athletic director of the CYO.

[66] Based on personal interviews conducted in August 1975 as part of an NEH Youthgrant.

[67] ACLU report on Englewood disorder, November 7, 1949, cited by Arnold Hirsch, "Making the Second Ghetto: Race and Housing in Chicago, 1940–1960" (Ph.D. diss., University of Illinois, 1978), 214.

[68] Ibid., 30.

[69] *The New World,* September 17, 1915.

[70] Andrew M. Greeley, *The Irish Americans: The Rise to Money and Power* (New York: Harper and Row, 1981), 146–47.

[71] Under orders from Archbishop John P. Cody, who headed the Chicago diocese from 1965 to 1982, no new parish schools were established in the archdiocese after 1967.

[72] Of 81,251 students enrolled in Chicago's Catholic elementary schools in 1982, 22,210 were black and 14,074 were Hispanic. The city's Catholic high school enrollment of 33,048 included 6,034 blacks and 3,856 Hispanics. Based on Chicago Archdiocese Office of Catholic Education, "Fall Enrollment Survey, October 1982." See also Alfredo S. Lanier, "Let Us Now Praise Catholic Schools," *Chicago* (October 1982): 147–53.

[73] Lawrence J. McCaffrey, *The Irish Diaspora in America* (Bloomington, Ind.: Indiana University Press, 1976), 176.

[74] Although the number of Irish-American novelists is increasing, only a few such as Elizabeth Cullinan have mined what Andrew Greeley calls the rich lode of American Irish Catholicism, *Irish Americans,* 183–98.

Chapter 3. Cardinal Mundelein of Chicago and the Shaping of Twentieth-Century American Catholicism

[1] The novelist Wilfrid Sheed has made this point very well in a book of essays. Wilfrid Sheed, *Three Mobs: Labor, Church, and Mafia* (New York: Sheed and Ward, 1974), 2–3.

[2] For general histories of American Catholicism, see John Tracy Ellis, *American Catholicism* (Chicago: University of Chicago Press, 1956); John Cogley, *Catholic America* (New York: Dial Press, 1973); Thomas T. McAvoy, *A History of the Catholic Church in the United States* (Notre Dame, Ind.: University of Notre Dame Press, 1969); Andrew M. Greeley, *The Catholic Experience: An Interpretation of the History of American Catholicism* (Garden City, N.Y.: Doubleday, 1967).

[3] The best description of the Americanist controversy is in Robert D. Cross, *The Emergence of Liberal Catholicism in America* (Cambridge, Mass.: Harvard University Press, 1958). But see also Thomas T. McAvoy, *The Great Crisis in American Catholic History, 1895–1900* (Chicago: Henry Regnery, 1957); John Tracy Ellis, *The Life of James Cardinal Gibbons: Archbishop of Baltimore, 1834–1921* (Milwaukee, Wis.: Bruce Publishing, 1952); and James H. Moynihan, *The Life of Archbishop John Ireland,* 2 vols. (New York: Harper Bros., 1952).

[4] Of the bishops mentioned, William Cardinal O'Connell, John Cardinal Glennon, and Francis Cardinal Spellman are reasonably well served by biographies and diocesan histories. See James Gaffey, "The Changing of the Guard: The Rise of Cardinal O'Connell of Boston," *Catholic Historical Review,* LIX (July 1973): 225–44; Robert H. Lord, John E. Sexton, and Edward T. Harrigan, *History of the Archdiocese of Boston in Various Stages of Its Development: 1604 to 1943,* 3 vols. (New York: Sheed and Ward, 1944), 3: 499–633; Dorothy Wayman, *Cardinal O'Connell of Boston* (New York: Farrar, Straus, 1955); Nicholas Schneider, *The Life of John Cardinal Glennon* (Liguori, Mo.: Liguori Publications, 1971); William Barnaby Faherty, *Dream by the River: Two Centuries of Saint Louis Catholicism, 1766–1967* (St. Louis, Mo.: Piraeus Publishers, 1973), 130–80; Robert I. Gannon, *The Cardinal Spellman Story* (Garden City, N.Y.: Doubleday, 1962). Only a few brief articles discuss Philadelphia's Denis Cardinal Dougherty. See Hugh L. Lamb, "Catholicism in Phil-adelphia," *Records of the American Catholic Historical Society of Philadelphia* LXII (March 1951): 5–14; Hugh J. Nolan, "Cardinal Dougherty: An Appreciation," ibid. (September 1951): 135–41. The only attempt at a biography of George Cardinal Mundelein was a commemorative volume for his twenty-fifth anniversary as a bishop, written when he was still alive. See Paul R. Martin, *The First Cardinal of the West: The Story of the Church in the Archdiocese of Chicago under the Administration of His Eminence George Cardinal Mundelein, Third Archbishop of Chicago and First Cardinal of the West* (Chicago: New World, 1934). For general biographical information on all these major bishops, see Francis B. Thornton, *Our American Princes: The Story of Seventeen American Cardinals* (New York: A. P. Putnam's Sons, 1963); Brendan A. Finn, *Twenty-Four American Cardinals* (Boston: Bruce Humphries, 1947).

[5] The consolidating bishops are a good example of the major themes suggested in Robert Wiebe, *The Search for Order: 1877–1920* (New York: Hill and Wang, 1967). For further discussion of this point, see Edward R. Kantowicz, "Cardinal Mundelein of Chicago: A Consolidating Bishop," in *An American Church: Essays on the Americanization of the Catholic Church,* ed. David J. Alvarez (Moraga, Calif.: St. Mary's College of California, 1979), 63–72.

[6] "Putting the Church on the map" is a phrase encountered repeatedly in interviews with surviving clergy who knew Mundelein; it was used by contemporaries as well. See, for example, Charles O'Hern to George William Cardinal Mundelein, January 23, 1917, doc. no. 4-1917-M-268, Archives of the Archdiocese of Chicago (St. Mary of the Lake Seminary, Mundelein, Ill.).

[7] For biographical details, see Martin, *First Cardinal of the West,* 25–43; Finn, *Twenty-Four American Cardinals,* 150–68; Thornton, *Our American Princes,* 121–36; Menceslaus J. Madaj, "First Cardinal of the Archdiocese of Chicago," *The New World* (Chicago archdiocesan newspaper), August 30, 1974, 7–9; U. S. Bureau of the Census, 1880 manuscript census schedules, New York County, New York, Enumeration District no. 141, 23 (Midwest Regional Federal Records Center, National Archives, Chicago).

[8] George L. Duval to Mundelein, March 25, 1915, doc. no. 2-1915-M-37, Archives of the Archdiocese of Chicago.

[9] Population data are from *The Official Catholic Directory, 1916* (New York: P. J. Kenedy, 1916); U.S. Bureau of the Census, Religious Bodies, 1916, 2 vols. (Washington, D. C.: Government Printing Office, 1916), 2: 644–59. Biographical information is from Joseph B. Code, *Dictionary of the American Hierarchy* (New York: Joseph F. Wagner, 1964).

[10] Schneider, *Life of Cardinal Glennon*, 43–54; Mundelein to Rev. Adalbert Furman, March 31, 1916, doc. no. 2-1916-F-19, Archives of the Archdiocese of Chicago.

[11] *The New World*, May 12, 1916, 1; July 23, 1916, 1; Mundelein to Joseph M. Cudahy, November 25, 1916, doc. no. 2-1916-C-52, Archives of the Archdiocese of Chicago.

[12] Harry Koenig, "University and Seminary of St. Mary of the Lake," undated typescript (St. Mary of the Lake Seminary Library, Mundelein, Ill.); *The New World*, April 30, 1920, 1; J. Gerald Kealy, interview with author, May 21, 1976; Reynold Hillenbrand, interview with author, October 13, 1975; Harry Koenig, interview with author, May 10, 1976.

[13] Mundelein to Rodolfo A. Correa, November 23, 1918, doc. no. 4-1918-C-14, Archives of the Archdiocese of Chicago.

[14] For the official version of the bequest, see *The New World*, April 30, 1920, 1. The Speedway Hospital affair can be followed in the *The New York Times*, January 26, 1919, 17; February 19, 1919, 24; July 16, 1919, 17; July 18, 1919, 4; March 1, 1920, 16; March 3, 1920, 10; March 16, 1920, 5; October 25, 1921, 16. For Mundelein's behind-the-scenes maneuvers, see Mundelein to Joseph Tumulty, April 20, 1919, doc. no. 5-1919-T-1, Archives of the Archdiocese of Chicago; Mundelein to Tumulty, May 13, 1919, doc. no. 5-1919-T-2, ibid.; Mundelein to J. Ogden Armour, November 1, 1919, doc. no. 5-1919-A-5, ibid.; Armour to Mundelein, November 4, 1919, doc. no. 5-1919-M-19, ibid.

[15] George William Mundelein, "Address at the Dedication of the Church-School St. Thomas of Canterbury, Chicago, June 24, 1917," *Two Crowded Years* (Chicago: Extension Press, 1918), 58.

[16] Kealy interview; Hillenbrand interview; Koenig interview; F. X. McMenamy to Mundelein, July 27, 1920, doc. no. 6-1920-M-48, Archives of the Archdiocese of Chicago; Vladimir Cardinal Ledochowski to Mundelein, January 6, 1921, doc. no. 6-1921-M-18, ibid.

[17] W. M. Ryan to Mundelein, May 26, 1924, doc. no. 8-1924-M-151, Archives of the Archdiocese of Chicago; Bernard J. Sheil to Ryan, June 4, 1924, doc. no. 8-1924-R-9, ibid.; *The New World*, December 23, 1921, rotogravure supplement.

[18] *The New World*, March 19, 1926, 3; April 16, 1926, 1; April 23, 1926, 4; April 30, 1926, 1; June 18, 1926, 13; *Twenty-Eighth International Eucharistic Congress*, June 20–24, 1926 (Chicago: unpublished, 1926); Milton Fairman, "The Twenty-Eighth International Eucharistic Congress," *Chicago History* V (Winter 1976–1977): 202–12.

[19] Fairman, "Twenty-Eighth International Eucharistic Congress," 212; *America*, June 26, 1926, 245; July 3, 1926, 275–77; "Editorial of June 16, 1926," in James O'Donnell Bennett, *The Eucharistic Congress as Reported in the Chicago Tribune* (Chicago: Chicago Tribune, 1926), 4.

[20] A good description of the seminary regime was provided by the first rector, J. Gerald Kealy, *The New World*, May 23, 1924, 9–10.

[21] The tax case was decided by the Illinois Supreme Court. See *People ex rel. Ira E. Pearsoll, County Collector v. Catholic Bishop of Chicago*, October 1923, doc. no. 7-1923-C-21, Archives of the Archdiocese of Chicago. See also Perry Patterson to Mundelein, February 20, 1924, doc. no. 8-1924-M-267, ibid.; Samuel Holmes to D. F. Kelly, March 9, 1924, doc. no. 8-1924-K-5, ibid.; Patterson to Kelly, April 21, 1924, doc. no. 8-1924-K-3, ibid.; Mundelein to Patterson, July 24, 1924, doc. no. 8-1924-P-11, ibid.

[22] Patrick J. Hayes, interview with author, November 26, 1975; Kealy interview.

[23] Hayes interview; Kealy interview; Charles C. Kerwin, interview with author, July 14, 1976. The cardinal's testimony for Harold Stuart is covered in the *New York Times*, November 10, 1934, 1.

[24] *The New World*, June 11, 1920, 2; June 13, 1924, 1; February 6, 1925, 1; February 13, 1925, 1; April 16, 1926, 1; April 13, 1928, 1; Mundelein

to Kelly, November 3, 1919, doc. no. 5-1919-K-44, Archives of the Archdiocese of Chicago. Especially helpful on financial matters were Hayes interview; Kealy interview; Kerwin interview; and Cletus F. O'Donnell, interview with author, June 1, 1976.

25 An example of an emergency assessment before Mundelein's time was the levy to rebuild St. Mary's Training School, which burned down in 1899. See doc. no. 1-1900-F-4, Archives of the Archdiocese of Chicago. The 1924 assessment was billed as a free will offering in *The New World,* May 16, 1924, 1. But it is clear from the annual parish financial reports in bound volumes at the Archives of the Archdiocese of Chicago that this and similar assessments were mandatory.

26 Edward F. Hoban to "Rev. dear Father," June 5, 1916, and "Manner of Procedure in all Building Operations" [1924?], doc. no. 2-1916-H-84, Archives of the Archdiocese of Chicago.

27 For the legal status of "corporation sole," see Patrick J. Dignan, *A History of the Legal Incorporation of Catholic Church Property in the United States (1784–1932)* (Washington, D.C., 1933). For a copy of the 1861 Illinois act authorizing such a corporation sole, see doc. no. 8-1924-H-162, Archives of the Archdiocese of Chicago. The forms used by pastors to file their annual reports with the chancery office contained the instruction: "All funds should be invested in Catholic Bishop of Chicago Securities." The standard study in Catholic Church finances mistakenly identifies Spellman as the originator of central banking in a diocese. James Gollin, *Worldly Goods: The Wealth and Power of the American Catholic Church, the Vatican, and the Men Who Control the Money* (New York: Random House, 1971), 138.

28 *The New World,* January 7, 1921, 4; May 16, 1924, 1.

29 Mundelein to E. B. Ledvina, February 10, 1920, doc. no. 6-1920-L-6, Archives of the Archdiocese of Chicago. Mundelein's personal lawyer attributed the business quote to Rosenwald, Msgr. Harry Koenig attributed it to Eckert. William J. Campbell, interview with author, November 21, 1975; Koenig interview.

30 Studies of the Americanist controversy are cited in note 3. See also Greeley, *Catholic Experience,* 150–215.

31 *Chicago Tribune,* December 3, 1915, 11. On Mundelein's Americanization policy, see James W. Sanders, *The Education of an Urban Minority: Catholics in Chicago, 1833–1965* (New York: Oxford University Press, 1977), 105–20; Edward R. Kantowicz, "Polish Chicago: Survival through Solidarity," in *The Ethnic Frontier: Essays in the History of Group Survival in Chicago and the Midwest,* eds. Melvin G. Holli and Peter d'A. Jones (Grand Rapids, Mich.: William B. Eerdmans, 1978), 179–209; Charles H. Shanabruch, "The Catholic Church's Role in the Americanization of Chicago's Immigrants" (Ph.D. diss., University of Chicago, 1975), 458–543; Joseph John Parot, "The American Faith and the Persistence of Chicago Polonia" (Ph.D. diss., Northern Illinois University, 1971), 310–40. For the "English only" order, see *The New World,* June 23, 1916, 1; *New York Times,* May 12, 1916, 22; and doc. no. 3-1916-R-40, Archives of the Archdiocese of Chicago.

32 *The New World,* April 13, 1917, 1; April 20, 1917, 1; April 27, 1917, 1.

33 Ibid., June 1, 1917, 1; March 29, 1918, 1; May 3, 1918, 1; May 17, 1918, 1; October 18, 1918, 1; March 28, 1919, 1.

34 Mundelein to Theodore Roosevelt, June 5, 1916, doc. no. 3-1916-R-21, Archives of the Archdiocese of Chicago.

35 Mundelein to David E. Shanahan, April 18, 1919, doc. no. 5-1919-S-42, ibid.; Mundelein to William Hale Thompson, April 25, 1917, doc. no. 4-1917-T-8, ibid.

36 Pieces of the Mundelein-Franklin Roosevelt relationship can be found in David J. O'Brien, *American Catholics and Social Reform: The New Deal Years* (New York: Oxford University Press, 1968); George Q. Flynn, *American Catholics and the Roosevelt Presidency, 1932–1936* (Lexington, Ky.: University Press of Kentucky, 1968); George Q. Flynn, *Roosevelt and Romanism: Catholics and American Diplomacy, 1937–1945* (Westport, Conn.: Greenwood Press, 1976). The first contact between the two men can be followed in these letters: David I. Walsh to Marvin H. McIntyre, April 18, 1933, President's Personal File no. 321, Franklin D. Roosevelt Papers, [Franklin D. Roosevelt Library, Hyde Park, N.Y.]; Franklin Roosevelt to Mundelin, April 15, 1933, ibid.; Mundelein to Franklin Roosevelt, April 26, 1933, ibid.; Franklin Roosevelt to Mundelein, August 15, 1933, ibid.

[37] Hayes interview; Campbell interview; Thomas Corcoran, interview with author, November 7, 1975.

[38] Harold L. Ickes, *The Secret Diary of Harold L. Ickes*, 2 vols. (New York: Simon and Schuster, 1953), 1: 479–80, 2: 214–22, 458; Flynn, *American Catholics and the Roosevelt Presidency*, 183–84; Charles J. Tull, *Father Coughlin and the New Deal* (Syracuse, N.Y.: Syracuse University Press, 1965), 203; *The New World*, October 13, 1933, 1; July 26; 1935 1; November 22, 1935, 1; December 13, 1935, 1; November 20, 1936, 1; October 8, 1937, 1; October 15, 1937, 4; John F. O'Hara to Franklin Roosevelt, November 18, 1935, President's Personal File no. 2329, Franklin D. Roosevelt Papers; O'Hara to McIntyre, November 26, 1935, ibid.; O'Hara to McIntyre, December 5, 1935, ibid.; Mundelein to Franklin Roosevelt, September 23, 1937, President's Personal File no. 1321, Franklin D. Roosevelt Papers.

[39] George Q. Flynn, "Franklin Roosevelt and the Vatican: The Myron Taylor Appointment," *Catholic Historical Review* LVIII (July 1972): 171–94; Flynn, *Roosevelt and Romanism*, 98–101.

[40] Mundelein's most noteworthy pro-labor speech was delivered on January 2, 1938, to the annual assembly of the Chicago Holy Name Society. He stated: "The trouble with us in the past has been that we were too often allied or drawn into an alliance with the wrong side. . . . Our place is beside the poor, behind the working man." *The New World*, January 7, 1938, 1.

[41] Flynn, *American Catholics and the Roosevelt Presidency*, 50–51; Corcoran interview.

[42] *The New World*, September 16, 1938, 1; October 28, 1938, 1; November 4, 1938, 1; November 11, 1938, 1, 2; November 18, 1938, 2; William Phillips to Franklin Roosevelt, November 10, 1938, container 58, President's State Department File— Phillips, Franklin D. Roosevelt Papers; Mundelein to Franklin Roosevelt, November 10, 1938, ibid.; Sumner Welles to Franklin Roosevelt, October 11, 1938, container 95, President's State Department File—Welles, Franklin D. Roosevelt Papers.

[43] Wayman, Cardinal O'Connell, 183–91; Gannon, *Cardinal Spellman Story*, 249–72.

[44] Winthrop S. Hudson, *American Protestantism* (Chicago: University of Chicago Press, 1961), 130.

Chapter 4. Reynold Hillenbrand and Chicago Catholicism

[1] This touching scene is recounted in Robert McClory, "Hillenbrand: U.S. Moses," *National Catholic Reporter*, September 7, 1979.

[2] See Joseph John Parot, *Polish Catholics in Chicago, 1850–1920* (De Kalb, Ill.: Northern Illinois University Press, 1981); Edward R. Kantowicz, *Corporation Sole: Cardinal Mundelein and Chicago Catholicism* (Notre Dame, Ind.: University of Notre Dame Press, 1983); Charles Shanabruch, *Chicago's Catholics: The Evolution of an American Identity* (Notre Dame, Ind.: University of Notre Dame Press, 1981).

[3] Charles Harbutt, "Chicago," *Jubilee* 4 (September 1956): 8.

[4] Dennis J. Geaney, O.S.A., "The Chicago Story," *Chicago Studies* (Winter 1963): 287–300.

[5] Dennis Robb, "Specialized Catholic Action in the United States, 1936–1945: Ideology, Leadership, Evaluation" (Ph.D. diss., University of Minnesota, 1972).

[6] Jeffrey Mark Burns, "American Catholics and the Family Crisis 1930–1962, The Ideological and Organizational Response" (Ph.D. diss., University of Notre Dame, 1982).

[7] Robert L. Tuzik, "The Contribution of Msgr. Reynold Hillenbrand (1905–1979) to the Liturgical Movement in the United States: Influences and Development" (Ph.D. diss., University of Notre Dame, 1989).

[8] One of the first attempts at a biography of Hillenbrand was my own 1982 seminar paper " 'I've Brought You a Man With Imagination': The Life and Career of Reynold Hillenbrand until 1944." This seminar paper was delivered at the annual meeting of the College Theology Society in 1985 at Salve Regina College, Newport, Rhode Island, and was used by Fr. Tuzik in his doctoral dissertation. A sampling of other sources where Hillenbrand's name and accomplishments appear include: James Hennesey, S.J., in *American Catholics: A History of the Roman Catholic Community in the United States* (New York: Oxford University Press, 1981), 263, 269; Jay P. Dolan, *The American Catholic Experience: A History from Colonial Times to the Present* (Garden City, N.Y.: Doubleday,

1985), 415–16; R. Scott Appleby, "Present to the People of God: The Transformation of the Roman Catholic Parish Priesthood," in Jay P. Dolan, R. Scott Appleby, Patricia Byrne, and Debra Campbell, *Transforming Parish Ministry: The Changing Roles of Catholic Clergy, Laity, and Women Religious* (New York: Crossroad, 1989), 26, 29, 30–31, 34, 51, 322.

9 Andrew M. Greeley, *The Catholic Experience: An Interpretation of the History of American Catholicism* (Garden City, N.Y.: Doubleday, 1967), 250.

10 Hillenbrand to parents, September 17 [no year] Hillenbrand Papers, Archives of the University of Notre Dame. (Hereafter cited as AUND).

11 Often those who see Hillenbrand as a kind of "closet liberal" of the preconciliar era neglect to take into account the power that neoscholastic philosophy and theology had on him and his positions. The best discussion of neoscholasticism's ideological impact is Philip Gleason's, "Neoscholasticism and Preconciliar Ideology," *U.S. Catholic Historian* 7 (Fall 1988): 401–12.

12 Hillenbrand Diary, Epiphany, 1929 [no pagination] Hillenbrand Papers, AUND.

13 Robert McClory, "Hillenbrand: U.S. Moses."

14 Reynold Hillenbrand, "De Modo quo Deus Justificatos Inhabitat" (S.T.D. diss., St. Mary of the Lake Seminary, 1931).

15 See Henri Rondet, trans. Tad Guzie, *The Grace of Christ, A Brief History of the Theology of Grace* (New York: Newman Press, 1967).

16 This theme continually reappears in Hillenbrand's discourses. A good example of it is found in his talk "The New Life" delivered at the 1948 Liturgical Week in Boston. See *Proceedings of the National Liturgical Week* (Conception, Mo.: The Liturgical Conference, Inc., 1949), 28–35.

17 Msgr. John Hayes, interview with author, October 29, 1982. Letter of Msgr. Stanislaus Piowowar to the author, October 23, 1987.

18 Letter of Msgr. George G. Higgins to the author, October 29, 1982.

19 Details of Chicago's bout with the depression can be found in Roger Biles, *Big City Boss in Depression and War: Mayor Edward J. Kelly of Chicago* (DeKalb, Ill.: Northern Illinois University Press, 1984), 21–23. See also Harold M. Mayer and Richard C. Wade, *Chicago: Growth of a Metropolis* (Chicago: University of Chicago Press, 1969), 358–64.

20 Hayes interview.

21 "Seminary Social Thoughts, 1936," quoted in Tuzik, 41.

22 Sr. Mary Eva McCarty, *The Sinsinawa Dominicans: Outlines of Twentieth Century Development* (Dubuque, Iowa: Hoermann Press, 1952), 478.

23 Msgr. Daniel Cantwell, interview with author, December 14, 1983.

24 Reynold Hillenbrand, "With One Another At Mass," *Proceedings of the National Liturgical Week*, Portland, Ore., August 18–21, 1947 (Boston: National Liturgical Conference, 1948), 64.

25 Virgil Michel, "The Basis of Social Regeneration," *Orate Fratres* 9 (1935): 545.

26 *Philosopher's Chronicle 1937–1938* (no pagination), Feehan Library, St. Mary of the Lake Seminary, Mundelein, Ill.

27 This mode of teaching liturgy was quite different from the standard seminary course in the United States that continued to rely on the classic *Sacrae Liturgiae Compendium* of Innocent Wapelhorst first published in 1887. See Joseph M. White, *The Diocesan Seminary in the United States* (Notre Dame, Ind.: University of Notre Dame Press, 1989), 253.

28 This was not warmly received by many of the faculty members who disliked the additional time the Ferial Mass took. Interview with Msgr. Harry S. Koenig, October 23, 1986.

29 Gerald Ellard, S.J., "Progress on the Dialogue Mass in Chicago," *Orate Fratres* 14 (1939): 19–25.

30 Michael Ducey, O.S.B., "The National Liturgical Weeks and American Benedictines," *American Benedictine Review* 6 (Summer 1955): 156–57.

31 "Liturgy School Opens Monday," *The New World*, July 11, 1941; "Three Day Liturgical Meeting Opens at Cathedral Tuesday," *The New World*, October 8, 1943.

32 William Edward Wiethoff, "Popular Rhetorical Strategy in the American Catholic Debate Over Vernacular Reform" (Ph.D. diss., University of Michigan, 1974).

33 Reynold Hillenbrand, "The Liturgical Revival Today," in *Proceedings of the National Liturgical Week,* December 11–13, 1945 (Peotone, Ill.: The Liturgical Conference, Inc., 1946), 12–13.

34 *Philosopher's Chronicle,* February 1938.

35 Hillenbrand to Haas January 21, 1938, quoted in Robb.

36 I have interviewed Higgins, Cantwell, Killgallon, McManus, and Wycislo, and they have also cited Hillenbrand as one of their primary inspirations. Scores of other Chicago priests active in social or liturgical ministries invoked his name almost reflexively when asked about the origins of the interest in their work.

37 See Barbara Warne Newell, *Chicago and the Labor Movement* (Urbana, Ill.: University of Illinois Press, 1961).

38 "Noted Speakers on Economics at the Cathedral," *The New World,* March 18, 1938; "Cathedral Sermons on Labor Arouse Widespread Interest," *The New World,* April 1, 1938.

39 "Eleven Catholic Labor Schools Open Sessions," *The New World,* November 1, 1940.

40 Reynold Hillenbrand, "The Family and Catholic Action," *Proceedings of the National Liturgical Week* October 14–17, 1946 (Highland Park, Ill.: The Liturgical Conference, Inc., 1947), 129–30.

41 I would maintain most educated Catholic priests and laypersons during the neoscholastic era held a common ideology. Differences that emerged were often personality clashes or over means rather than ends.

42 Stritch to John J. Clifford, S.J., March 10, 1945, Box 2964, Chancery Files, Stritch Papers, Archives of the Archdiocese of Chicago. (Hereafter cited as AAC.)

43 Stritch to Ducey, July 14, 1947, Chancery Files, Stritch Papers, AAC.

44 I can only deduce this from Stritch's opposition to the activities of the Grail on Doddridge Farm. Debra Campbell reports that "the local chancery" voiced opposition to a Grail program that aimed at "developing a strong, dynamic, living faith." "Faith is an infused supernatural gift," the Chancery corrected, "which we do not develop." In all likelihood this was written by Clifford who was the chief theological consultant for Stritch and the Chancery. See Debra Campbell, "The Struggle to Serve: From the Lay Apostolate to the Ministry Explosion," in Jay P. Dolan et al., *Transforming Parish Ministry,* 241.

45 Hillenbrand participated in arbitration cases with some of the following companies: Universal Statuary, Manganese Steel, Campbell Soup, and Artcraft Statuary. His deliberations are found in his papers at AUND.

46 Hillenbrand to Stritch, November 16, 1941, Box 2943, Chancery Files, Stritch Papers, AAC.

47 Edward M. Kerwin to Stritch, May 9, 1941, Box 2943, Chancery Files, Stritch Papers, AAC.

48 Hillenbrand to Cantwell, April 3, 1950, Cantwell Papers, Box 1, Folder 1–8, Chicago Historical Society.

49 Kantowicz, *Corporation Sole,* 125.

50 Andrew Greeley makes this assertion in *The Catholic Experience,* 253. Msgr. John Egan concurs in this.

51 Reynold Hillenbrand, "The Priesthood and the World," in *Proceedings of the National Liturgical Week,* August 20–23, 1951 (Conception, Mo.: The Liturgical Conference, Inc., 1952), 167.

52 Cantwell interview; Russell Barta, interview with author, October 25, 1987. Cantwell and Barta formed the Adult Education Program that introduced modern biblical studies into the Archdiocese of Chicago beginning with a week of scriptural study for priests at the Maryknoll Seminary in Glen Ellyn, Ill.

53 Tuzik describes these theological differences on 262–63.

54 Dennis Geaney, O.S.A., "From the Editor's Notebook," *Upturn, Association of Chicago Priests Newsletter* (June–July 1985): 9.

Chapter 5. The Rise and Fall
of Bernard Sheil

[1] Msgr. James Hardiman, interview with author, June 28, 1988. Copy in Archives of Archdiocese of Chicago. (Hereafter cited as AAC).

[2] For biographical details see Roger L. Treat, *Bishop Sheil and the CYO* (New York: Julian Messner, Inc., 1951) and Steven M. Avella, *This Confident Church: Catholic Leadership and Life in Chicago, 1940–1965* (Notre Dame, Ind.: University of Notre Dame Press, 1992), 22–30, 109–49.

[3] Memo of Tommy Corcoran to Franklin D. Roosevelt, Presidential Personal Files, 5177, Franklin D. Roosevelt Library, Hyde Park, N.Y.

[4] Franklin D. Roosevelt to Honorable Frank Knox, October 4, 1939, Presidential Secretary File, "K," Franklin D. Roosevelt Library.

[5] Harold Ickes, *The Lowering Clouds: The Secret Diary of Harold L. Ickes* (New York: Simon and Schuster, 1955), 110.

[6] Memo of Ralph C. Leo, 1942, George Drury Papers, AAC.

[7] James O'Gara, "Chicago's Catholic Times Square," *America* 82 (January 28, 1950): 492–95.

[8] "Church Must Battle for Negro Rights, Bishop Sheil Tells Catholic Convention," *Chicago Sun,* September 29, 1942, Daniel Cantwell Papers, Box 28, Folder 28–9, Chicago Historical Society, Chicago.

[9] "Labor's Bishop," *Newsweek,* July 15, 1946.

[10] "Why Bishop Sheil Left the CYO," *Chicago Daily News,* January 24, 1955.

[11] George Drury, interviews with author, December 1987–January 1988. Copies in AAC.

[12] James Francis McIntyre to Samuel A. Stritch, April 30, 1947, Box 2971, Stritch Papers, AAC.

[13] Bernard Sheil to John F. Noll, May 26, 1945, William Campbell Papers, Box 6, April–June 1945, Chicago Branch National Archives.

[14] "For Joe: 'Phooey!', " *Time,* April 19, 1954.

[15] Mary Elizabeth Carroll, "Bishop Sheil: Prophet Without Honor," *Harper's,* November 1955, 45–51.

[16] Drury interviews, AAC.

Chapter 6. Cardinal Meyer and
the Era of Confidence

I am grateful to Dr. Richard Thompson and Rev. F. Paul Prucha, S.J., for their comments on this essay. Much of this material is drawn from my doctoral dissertation, "Meyer of Milwaukee: The Life and Times of a Midwestern Archbishop" (University of Notre Dame, 1984).

[1] The following account is drawn heavily from Xavier Rynne's *The Third Session: The Debates and Decrees of Vatican Council II* (New York: Farrar, Straus, and Giroux, 1965), 257–61; Vincent A. Yzermans, "Declaration on Religious Freedom, Historical Introduction," in *American Participation in the Second Vatican Council* (New York: Sheed and Ward, 1967), 617–42. Rynne's and Yzermans's descriptions of the events of November 19, 1964, are substantiated by letters to the author from Bishop Francis Reh (January 21, 1982) and Paul Emile Cardinal Leger (July 15, 1983).

[2] Rynne, 257.

[3] Vincent A. Yzermans, "The Reluctant Leader: Albert Cardinal Meyer 1903–1965," *Chicago Studies* 5 (Spring 1966): 10.

[4] Quoted in Cletus F. O'Donnell, "Albert Cardinal Meyer. The Prince and The Priest," *Chicago Studies* 5 (Summer 1966): 118.

[5] Yzermans, "Reluctant Leader," 15–16.

[6] Much of this information can be found in James Hennesey, S.J., *American Catholics: A History of the Roman Catholic Community in the United States* (New York: Oxford University Press, 1981), 280–306; Jay P. Dolan, *The American Catholic Experience: A History From Colonial Times to the Present* (Garden City, N.Y.: Doubleday, 1985), 349–420.

[7] Dolan, 417.

[8] Philip Gleason makes use of the term *maelstrom* in his public lectures; James Hennesey describes the era as a "revolutionary moment" in the last chapter of *American Catholics.*

[9] Gerald A. McCool, S.J., *Catholic Theology in the Nineteenth Century: The Quest for a Unitary Method* (New

York: Seabury, 1977) is the standard account of the more theoretical aspects of neoscholasticism. Its use as a distinctive Catholic ideology is discussed in William M. Halsey's *The Survival of American Innocence* (Notre Dame, Ind.: University of Notre Dame Press, 1980); Philip Gleason "Neoscholasticism as Preconciliar Ideology," *U.S. Catholic Historian* 7 (Fall 1988): 401–12; and Steven M. Avella, "John T. McNicholas in the Age of Practical Thomism," *Records of the American Catholic Historical Society of Philadelphia* 94 (March–December 1986), 15–25. Edward Kantowicz's *Corporation Sole: Cardinal Mundelein and Chicago Catholicism* (Notre Dame, Ind.: University of Notre Dame Press, 1983) does not directly allude to his subject's ideological background but strongly implies that Mundelein's effective leadership had a strong basis in Church teaching.

[10] Robert Bellah et al., *Habits of the Heart: Individualism and Commitment in American Life* (New York: Harper and Row, 1985), 39.

[11] Robert Massey, *St. Francis Seminary, 1955–1981: One Hundred and Twenty-Five Years of Continuity and Change* (Milwaukee: St. Francis Seminary Memorial Publication, 1981), 31, 33–41.

[12] See Anthony F. Kuzniewski, S.J., *Faith and Fatherland* (Notre Dame, Ind.: University of Notre Dame Press, 1980) for the account of Sebastian Messmer's wrangling with the Poles.

[13] "New Biblical Institute at Rome," *America* 1 (June 5, 1909): 197; William J. McGarry, S.J., "The Pontifical Biblical Institute," *Catholic Mind* 19 (October 8, 1931): 456–64. The best discussion of biblical scholarship at the time of Meyer's studies is found in Gerald P. Fogarty, S.J., *American Catholic Biblical Scholarship: A History from the Early Republic to Vatican II* (New York: Harper and Row, 1989), 171–98.

[14] The service of Muench and Haas as rectors of St. Francis Seminary is recorded in Colman Barry's *American Nuncio: Cardinal Aloisius Muench* (Collegeville, Minn.: St. John's University Press, 1969), 22–31 and Thomas E. Blantz, C.S.C., *A Priest in Public Service: Francis J. Haas and the New Deal* (Notre Dame, Ind.: University of Notre Dame Press, 1982), 125–34. Moreover, Muench's diary in the Archives of the Catholic University of America gives additional insights into his dealings with Archbishop Stritch. See Steven M. Avella, "Samuel Stritch and Milwaukee Catholicism, 1930–1940," in *Milwaukee History* 13 (Autumn 1990): 70–91.

[15] Steven M. Avella, " 'We Will Do Our Duty': The World of Moses E. Kiley," *Salesianum* 80 (Fall/Winter 1985): 12–17.

[16] Fr. David Ross King to Fr. Daniel Cantwell, March 18, 1945. Cantwell Papers, Box 1, Folder 1-5, Chicago Historical Society, Chicago.

[17] Minutes of the Meetings of the Board of Consultors, October 21, 1953; December 14, 1953; March 15, 1954; May 7, 1954 and *passim,* Archives of the Archdiocese of Milwaukee.

[18] This dynamic growth is described by Frederick I. Olson, "City Expansion and Suburban Spread," in Ralph Aderman, ed., *Trading Post to Metropolis: Milwaukee County's First 150 Years* (Milwaukee: Milwaukee County Board of Supervisors, 1987), 47–68.

[19] Meyer to Msgr. Joseph Emmenegger, March 21, 1956, Archives of the Archdiocese of Chicago. (Hereafter cited as AAC.)

[20] Thomas T. Brundage, "Devotional Prayer in the Archdiocese of Milwaukee, 1945–1980" (Master of Divinity thesis, St. Francis Seminary, 1987).

[21] *Catholic Herald-Citizen,* November 15, 1958.

[22] Former Mayor Frank Zeidler, interview with author, July 14, 1987.

[23] The original Catholic Action movements in Milwaukee had begun under Archbishop Stritch in the 1930s and included a highly energized Holy Name Society as well as an active Catholic Youth Organization. Specialized Catholic Action groups had also begun at about the same time and had been especially fortunate in the leadership of Fr. John Russell Beix. Beix, a minor seminary professor, had become thoroughly committed to the Jocist methodology and had secured enough popular support to open a Catholic Action headquarters in 1949, appropriately named the Cardijn Center. The Cardijn Center offered programs of adult education to the cells of Young Christian Students and Young Christian Workers formed by Beix as well as the participants in the Christian Family Movement in Milwaukee.

[24] "Blessing of St. Luke Church," September 14, 1958. Notecards, Meyer Papers, AAC.

[25] Quoted in "The Church and Neighborhood Conservation in Chicago: The Experience of a

Group of Chicago Pastors," *National Conference of Catholic Charities,* 1955, 5.

[26] "The Catholic Church and the Negro in the Archdiocese of Chicago," Clergy Conference Report, September 20–21, 1960, Meyer Papers, AAC.

[27] "Report to the Archbishop: The Conservation Committee of the Archdiocese," November, 1958. Meyer Papers, AAC.

[28] Little of substance has been written on this influential and controversial prelate. For a long time the primary source for the life of Bishop Sheil was Roger L. Treat, *Bishop Sheil and the CYO* (New York: Julian Messner, Inc., 1951) and Philip A. Grant, "Bishop Bernard J. Sheil's Condemnation of Senator Joseph R. McCarthy," *Records of the American Catholic Historical Society of Philadelphia* 97 (March/December 1986): 45–60. Kantowicz devotes considerable attention to the prelate in *Corporation Sole,* 173–88. Avella's *This Confident Church* continues where Kantowicz left off.

[29] "National Labor, Civic Leaders on '48 Series at Sheil School," Clipping scrapbook, Edward V. Cardinal Papers, Viatorian Archives, Arlington Heights, Illinois. James O'Gara, "Chicago's Catholic Times Square," *America* 82 (January 28, 1950): 492–495. "Sheil School of Social Studies On Its Tenth Anniversary," *Today* (March 1953).

[30] "Education for Catholic Adults: Interview With Russell Barta," *Ave Maria* 87 (April 12, 1958): 5–10.

[31] Steven M. Avella, "The Life and Career of Monsignor Reynold Hillenbrand" (unpublished seminar paper). Dennis Robb, "Specialized Catholic Action in the United States, 1936–1945: Ideology, Leadership, and Education" (Ph.D. diss., University of Minnesota, 1972) contains much valuable information on Hillenbrand.

[32] Msgrs. Daniel Cantwell and John Hayes to the author.

[33] Charles Harbutt, "Chicago," *Jubilee* 4 (September 1956): 8.

[34] Msgr. John Egan to author.

[35] "Cardinal Meyer's Statement to the President's Commission on Civil Rights," May 6, 1959. Meyer Papers, AAC.

[36] Daniel Cantwell to Bernard Dauenhauer, October 8, 1959, Cantwell Papers, Box 4, Folder 4-3, Chicago Historical Society, Chicago.

[37] "The Mantle of Justice" in *The Catholic Church and the Negro in the Archdiocese of Chicago,* Clergy Conference (September 20–21, 1960), 25, 29.

[38] See P. David Finks, *The Radical Vision of Saul Alinsky* (New York: Paulist Press, 1984), 111.

[39] Msgr. John Egan to author; Fr. Anthony Janiak to author.

[40] Fr. Barnabas Mary Ahern to author; Fr. Francis McCool to author.

[41] "Mother Church Rejoices," *Council Daybook,* vol. 1 (Washington, D.C.: National Catholic Welfare Conference, 1965), 26–27.

Chapter 7. The Beginning and the End of an Era: George William Mundelein and John Patrick Cody in Chicago

[1] *Chicago Tribune,* October 3, 1939, 1, 10; October 6, 1939, 3; October 7, 1939, 7.

[2] *The Chicago Catholic,* May 7, 1982, 6–12; Andrew M. Greeley, "The Fall of an Archdiocese," *Chicago* 36 (September 1987): 128–31, 190–92; William Clements, Gene Mustain, and Roy Larson, investigative series on Cody, *Chicago Sun-Times,* September 10, 1981, 1–7; September 11, 1981, 1–5; September 12, 1981, 1–4, the *Sun-Times* charged Cody with nepotism in the purchase of insurance from the son of his stepcousin and also with the diversion of large sums of money to support that stepcousin, Helen Dolan Wilson. It was never stated, but always strongly implied, that Cody was having an affair with Mrs. Wilson. The nepotism is undeniable. Cody did channel substantial insurance business through David Dolan Wilson's agency in St. Louis. Whether this nepotism is improper, however, can be debated. No one ever charged that the insurance purchased was inadequate. Some of Wilson's plans were quite innovative. To paraphrase Mayor Daley, who should the cardinal have given the business to, his enemies? That Cody helped support Mrs. Wilson, a childhood friend whose widowed father had married Cody's aunt, has also been clearly established by investigative reporters. The crucial question, however, is whether Cody gave Mrs. Wilson his

own money, which would be perfectly legal, or diverted Church funds to her, which would violate the Church's tax-exempt status. This has never been established nor has it been proven that Cody had an affair with Mrs. Wilson. The U.S. attorney dropped all investigations after Cody's death.

3 Too many surveys of American Catholic history lump the early twentieth century in with the nineteenth century, characterizing the whole span of years from the 1830s to the 1960s as the immigrant period. See, for example, James Hennesey, *American Catholics* (New York: Oxford University Press, 1981). The most recent survey history, Jay P. Dolan, *The American Catholic Experience* (Garden City, N.Y.: Doubleday, 1985), recognizes the first half of the twentieth century as a period with distinct characteristics.

4 These points are developed in Edward R. Kantowicz, "Cardinal Mundelein of Chicago: A 'Consolidating Bishop'," in *An American Church,* ed. David J. Alvarez (Moraga, Calif.: St. Mary's College of California, 1979), 63–72; and Edward R. Kantowicz, "Cardinal Mundelein of Chicago and the Shaping of Twentieth Century American Catholicism," *Journal of American History* 68 (1981): 52–68.

5 For background on John Bonzano, see Brendan A. Finn, *Twenty-Four American Cardinals* (Boston: Bruce Humphries, 1947), 309–23. Biographical details on Mundelein are drawn from Edward R. Kantowicz, *Corporation Sole: Cardinal Mundelein and Chicago Catholicism* (Notre Dame, Ind.: University of Notre Dame Press, 1983). See, especially, the chronology of his life on pages ix–xi. The book was based on archival sources and extensive interviews. Comments on Cardinal Cody later in this paper, however, are based solely on the public record, as presented in the secular and religious press, for the Cody papers are not yet open for research at the Archives of the Archdiocese of Chicago.

6 Kantowicz, "Cardinal Mundelein of Chicago and the Shaping of Twentieth Century American Catholicism," 52.

7 Ibid., 59–60.

8 Kantowicz, *Corporation Sole,* 166–68; Milton Fairman, "The Twenty-Eighth International Eucharistic Congress," *Chicago History* 5 (Winter 1976/1977): 202–12.

9 Kantowicz, *Corporation Sole,* 166–68.

10 The two standard works on Spellman erroneously attribute the invention of diocesan central banking to him. See Robert I. Gannon, *The Cardinal Spellman Story* (Garden City, N.Y.: Doubleday, 1962), 249–72; and John Cooney, *The American Pope* (New York: New York Times Book Co., 1984), 95–101.

11 Biographical details on Cody can be found in Joseph B. Code, *Dictionary of the American Hierarchy* (New York: Joseph F. Wagner, 1964). Charles Dahm, *Power and Authority in the Catholic Church: Cardinal Cody in Chicago* (Notre Dame, Ind.: University of Notre Dame Press, 1981), though not a full biography, is the only book-length study devoted to him. For background on Glennon and St. Louis, see Nicholas Schneider, *The Life of John Cardinal Glennon* (Liguori, Mo.: Liguori Publications, 1971).

12 *The New World,* July 1, 1977, 15.

13 For a reasonably full account of Cody's pre-Chicago career, see *The New World,* July 1, 1977, 13, 25–29.

14 Dahm, 1–2.

15 Jeff Lyon and James Robison, "Cody of Chicago," *Chicago Tribune Magazine,* November 9, 1975, 25; *New York Times,* June 17, 1965, 20; John Conroy, "Cardinal Sins," *Chicago Reader,* June 5, 1987, 14.

16 Roy Larson, "Cody—The Man in the Middle," *Chicago Sun-Times,* September 24, 1978, 9; A. E. P. Wall, "Chicago's Cardinal," *The Chicago Catholic,* August 24, 1979, 11.

17 Dahm gives the fullest account of the founding and subsequent history of the ACP. See 103–8 for the censure vote.

18 Quoted by Larson, 9.

19 Kantowicz, *Corporation Sole,* 6–8, 49–64.

20 *New York Times,* November 29, 1970, 47.

21 Dahm, 19–20, 64, 183.

22 Kantowicz, *Corporation Sole,* 203–16.

23 Schneider, 164.

[24] *New York Times,* April 17, 1962, 1, 16; August 19, 1962, 73; September 1, 1962, 1, 20; September 5, 1962, 1, 22; September 6, 1962, 22; June 17, 1964, 1, 20.

[25] David J. Garrow, *Bearing the Cross: Martin Luther King, Jr. and the Southern Christian Leadership Conference* (New York: William Morrow, 1986), 461, 491, 508; Bill Gleason, *Daley of Chicago* (New York: Simon and Schuster, 1970), 45–46.

[26] Dahm, 113–14, 176–80, 227–57; Lyon and Robison, 25; Larson, 9; "The Sharing Years," *The New World,* May 14, 1976, 2–4.

[27] *Chicago Sun-Times,* September 17, 1981, 4; *New York Times,* September 17, 1981, II, 11; September 19, 1981, 8.

[28] Dahm, 315–16; Andrew M. Greeley, William C. McCready, and Kathleen McCourt, *Catholic Schools in a Declining Church* (Kansas City, Mo.: Sheed and Ward, 1976).

[29] Kantowicz, *Corporation Sole,* 150–64.

[30] Lyon and Robison, 52–54; Larson, 9; Greeley, "Fall of an Archdiocese," 130–31.

[31] *Chicago Sun-Times,* September 11, 1981, 1, 3; September 12, 1981, 1,4.

[32] *New York Times,* April 2, 1975, 34.

[33] Dahm, 219.

[34] Robert B. Beusse et al., "Observations on the Media Organizations of the Archdiocese of Chicago submitted to Joseph Cardinal Bernardin," *The Chicago Catholic,* September 2, 1983, 1a–8a. I calculated the subsidy amount from the financial reports of the archdiocese printed annually in *The Chicago Catholic.*

[35] Kantowicz, *Corporation Sole,* 126.

[36] Quoted by Conroy, 32.

Chapter 8. Sacred Space: Parish and Neighborhood in Chicago

The author gratefully acknowledges the assistance of Andrea M. Crofton, Amy Desmond, Mary Claire Gart, managing editor, *The New World,* Mary Kennelly, Joan Radtke, Nancy Sandlebach, assistant archivist, Archdiocese of Chicago, and David F. Schwartz, associate director of research, Archdiocesan Office of Research and Planning.

[1] Bessie L. Pierce, *A History of Chicago,* 3 vols. (New York: Alfred A. Knopf, 1937–57), 1: 180.

[2] "An Irish Relief Society," *Chicago Tribune* editorial, November 23, 1857.

[3] Alfred T. Andreas, *History of Chicago,* 3 vols. (Chicago: A. T. Andreas Co., 1884–1886), 1: 289.

[4] Perry Duis, *Chicago: Creating New Traditions* (Chicago: Chicago Historical Society, 1976), 14.

[5] Daniel Bluestone, *Constructing Chicago* (New Haven, Conn.: Yale University Press, 1991), 65–71.

[6] J. W. Norris, *General Directory and Business Advertiser of the City of Chicago, For the Year 1844* (reprint ed., 1933), 68.

[7] Excerpts from Bishop William J. Quarter's diary, quoted in James J. McGovern, *Souvenir of the Silver Jubilee in the Episcopacy of His Grace The Most Rev. Patrick Augustine Feehan, Archbishop of Chicago, 1890* (Chicago: privately printed, 1891), 64; and in Dr. John E. McGirr, *Life of Rt. Rev. William Quarter* (1849; reprint ed., 1920), 46–47.

[8] McGovern, 69; *Chicago Democrat,* October 15, 1845; McGirr, 48.

[9] Quarter to Purcell, September 2, 1844, Catholic Archives of America, University of Notre Dame, quoted in Gilbert J. Garraghan, *The Catholic Church in Chicago, 1673–1871* (Chicago: Loyola University Press, 1921), 109–10.

[10] Quarter to Archbishop of Vienna, December 20, 1845, translated and quoted in Rev. Francis J. Epstein, "History in the Annals of the Leopoldine Association," *Illinois Catholic Historical Review* 1, no. 2 (October 1918): 231.

[11] Quarter to Archbishop of Vienna, January 26, 1846, *Illinois Catholic Historical Review,* 232.

[12] A Sister of Mercy, "The Sisters of Mercy: Chicago's Pioneer Nurses and Teachers, 1846–1921," *Illinois Catholic Historical Review* 3, no. 4 (April 1921): 342–43.

[13] Ibid., 346.

[14] Joseph J. Thompson, ed., *The Archdiocese of Chicago: Antecedents and Development* (Des Plaines, Ill.: St. Mary's Training School Press, 1920), 701.

[15] "Our Religious Orders. The Jesuits in Chicago," March 27, 1875, St. Ignatius College Prep Archives.

[16] *Daily Chicago Tribune*, May 25, 1857.

[17] Quoted in Garraghan, *The Jesuits of the Middle United States*, 3 vols. (New York: America Press, 1938), 3: 402, 406–7.

[18] Contract between Patrick O'Connor and Arnold Damen, May 23, 1860; *Jesuits* 3: 410.

[19] *Chicago Tribune,* July 17, 1860.

[20] See dedication program in Bro. Thomas Mulkerins, S.J., *Holy Family Parish: Priests and People* (Chicago: Universal Press, 1923), 30–31; *Chicago Times,* December 25, 1863; and program for the "Inauguration Concert of the Largest Church Organ in the United States," in Mulkerins, 98–100.

[21] *Chicago Times,* August 23, 1857.

[22] Quoted in *Jesuits*, 3: 419.

[23] "Our Religious Orders," March 27, 1875.

[24] Rev. Joseph P. Conroy, S.J., *Arnold Damen, S.J.* (New York: Benzinger Brothers, 1930), 127; *Chicago Times,* April 25, 1869; excerpts from Rev. Thaddeus J. Butler's 1869 lecture appeared in *Sceal,* the newsletter of the Chicago Irish Folklife Society 4, no. 2 (Winter 1987): 1, 4; "Our Religious Orders."

[25] Catharine E. Beecher and Harriet Beecher Stowe, *American Woman's Home* (reprint ed., 1991), 17, 451, 455, 458.

[26] *Chicago Evening Journal,* October 9, 1872.

[27] Bluestone, 63.

[28] Mary Foote Coughlin, *A New Commandment: A Little Memoir of the Work Accomplished by the Good Shepherd Nuns in Chicago During a Half Century, 1859–1909* (Chicago: Privately printed, 1909), 62.

[29] *Chicago Times,* June 22, 1873.

[30] Austin Morini, O.S.M., "The Foundation of the Order of Servants of Mary in the United States of America (1870–1883)," trans. Conrad Borntrager, O.S.M., *Scrinium Historiale* XIX (Rome: Edizioni Marianum, 1993).

[31] Morini, 81, 85, 84, n. 179.

[32] Ibid., 103, n. 157, n. 186.

[33] George A. Lane, S.J., and Algimantas Kezys, *Chicago's Churches and Synagogues: An Architectural Pilgrimage* (Chicago: Loyola University Press, 1981), 66–67.

[34] J. L. Spalding, *The Religious Mission of the Irish People and Catholic Colonization* (New York: The Catholic Publication Society Co., 1880), 116.

[35] "They'll Never Sign Again," *Goodall's Daily Sun,* May 14, 1888. My thanks to John E. Corrigan for directing me to this controversy.

[36] *Goodall's Daily Sun; Chicago Times; Chicago Tribune,* May 28, 1888.

[37] *Goodall's Daily Sun,* May 28, 1888.

[38] For a discussion of the Edwards Law, see Charles Shanabruch, *Chicago's Catholics: The Evolution of an American Identity* (Notre Dame, Ind.: University of Notre Dame Press, 1981) and James W. Sanders, *The Education of an Urban Minority: Catholics in Chicago, 1833–1965* (New York: Oxford University Press, 1977).

[39] McGovern, *Silver Jubilee,* 276, 277.

[40] See Joseph John Parot, *Polish Catholics in Chicago, 1850–1920* (DeKalb, Ill.: Northern Illinois University Press, 1981) and John Iwicki, C.R., *The First One Hundred Years: A Study of the Apostolate of the Congregation of the Resurrection in the United States, 1866–1966* (Rome: Gregorian University Press, 1966).

[41] *Chicago Tribune,* September 3, 1893; *Chicago Times,* September 4, 1893.

[42] George W. Mundelein, "Dedication of Church of St. Mary of the Angels," Archdiocesan Archives, Box 23.

[43] "St. Mary's, The Parish of Contrasts," *Chicago Sunday Tribune,* November 19, 1899.

[44] Quoted in Rev. Msgr. Harry C. Koenig, ed., *A History of the Parishes of the Archdiocese of Chicago,* 2 vols. (Chicago: Archdiocese of Chicago, 1980), 1: 772.

[45] *Inter Ocean,* June 18, 1899; Koenig, 1: 375; *Chicago Tribune,* March 19, 1899.

[46] *Chicago Tribune,* November 26, 1899.

[47] *The New World,* October 22, 1904.

[48] *The New World,* December 15, 1906.

[49] *The New World,* July 21, 1906.

[50] *The New World,* May 25, 1907; James F. Bundy, "Fall From Grace: Religion and the Communal Ideal in Two Suburban Villages, 1870–1917," (Ph.D. diss., University of Chicago, June 1979), 305, 310.

[51] Quoted in Koenig, 2: 1437.

[52] George W. Mundelein, *Two Crowded Years* (Chicago: Extension Press, 1918), 72, 76.

[53] Ibid., 44, 48, 49.

[54] Edward R. Kantowicz, *Corporation Sole: Cardinal Mundelein and Chicago Catholicism* (Notre Dame, Ind.: University of Notre Dame Press, 1983) and "To Build the Catholic City," *Chicago History* 14 (Fall 1985): 4–27.

[55] See Charles Fanning and Ellen Skerrett, "James T. Farrell and Washington Park: The Novel as Social History," *Chicago History* 8 (Summer 1979): 80–91.

[56] See James R. Grossman, *Land of Hope: Chicago, Black Southerners, and the Great Migration* (Chicago: University of Chicago Press, 1989).

[57] James T. Farrell, "The Young Manhood of Studs Lonigan," *Studs Lonigan* (New York: The Modern Library, 1938), 240.

[58] Steven M. Avella, *This Confident Church: Catholic Leadership and Life in Chicago, 1940–1965* (Notre Dame, Ind.: University of Notre Dame Press, 1992).

[59] "Re-Thinking Chicago: A New Philosophy and Statesmanship for Chicago" (Proceedings of Three Re-Thinking Chicago Conferences, 2nd ed., 1936), 92A, 92B.

[60] Glen E. Holt and Dominic A. Pacyga, *Chicago: A Historical Guide to the Neighborhoods* (Chicago: Chicago Historical Society, 1979), 124.

[61] Quoted in Avella, 213.

[62] Georgie Anne Geyer, "Powerhouse in Urban Affairs," *Chicago Daily News,* December 15, 1962; "Church Symbolizes Faith in Inner City," *Chicago Tribune,* March 24, 1963; *"Alive at 85,"* history of St. Mark Church (April 21, 1979); and *A History of the Parishes of the Archdiocese of Chicago* 1: 53,341–42, 572–73.

[63] See Thomas M. Gannon and David F. Schwartz, "Church Finances in Crisis," *Social Compass* 39, no. 1 (1992): 111–20; *The New World,* June 2, 1989; June 8, 15, 1990: "Diocese Sees Pride and Pain," *Chicago Tribune,* June 11, 1990.

[64] While most of the churches canonically suppressed were shuttered, five new city parishes were created through a process of consolidation: Assumption, B.V.M./St. Catherine of Genoa; St. Basil/Visitation; St. Casimir/St. Lumilla (renamed Our Lady of Tepeyac); St. Clara/St. Cyril/Holy Cross (renamed St. Gelasius); and St. Francis of Assisi/Our Lady of the Angels. See also *The New World,* January 12, 19, 26, 1990; February 2, 1990; March 9, 30, 1990; May 18, 1990; June 8, 15, 22, 24, 1990; *New York Times,* July 9, 1990.

[65] *The New World,* May 28, 1993.

Suggestions for Further Reading

Avella, Steven M. *This Confident Church: Catholic Leadership and Life in Chicago, 1940–1965.* Notre Dame, Ind.: University of Notre Dame Press, 1992. Examines the Catholic Church in Chicago during the period of its greatest influence, in the 1940s and 1950s.

Frisbie, Margery. *An Alley in Chicago: The Ministry of a City Priest.* Kansas City, Mo.: Sheed and Ward, 1991. A biography of pioneering social action priest Msgr. John Egan.

Holli, Melvin G., and Peter d'A. Jones, *Ethnic Chicago.* 3rd ed. Grand Rapids, Mich.: William B. Eerdmans Publishing Co., 1994. Historical essays on many of Chicago's ethnic and racial groups.

Kantowicz, Edward R. *Corporation Sole: Cardinal Mundelein and Chicago Catholicism.* Notre Dame, Ind.: University of Notre Dame Press, 1983. Analyzes the leadership of the archbishop who "put Catholicism on the map" in Chicago in the 1920s and 1930s.

Koenig, Harry C., ed. *A History of the Parishes of the Archdiocese of Chicago* and *A History of the Institutions of the Archdiocese.* 4 vols. Chicago: Archdiocese of Chicago, 1980. A reference work. A treasure trove of information about Chicago's Catholic past.

Lane, George A., and Algimantas Kezys. *Chicago Churches and Synagogues.* Chicago: Loyola University Press, 1981. Photo essays on notable Chicago places of worship.

McCaffrey, Lawrence J., Ellen Skerrett, Michael F. Funchion, and Charles Fanning. *The Irish in Chicago.* Urbana and Chicago: University of Illinois Press, 1987. Four essays that examine the ethnic, religious, political, and literary dimensions of Irish Chicago.

Pacyga, Dominic A., and Ellen Skerrett. *Chicago: City of Neighborhoods.* Chicago: Loyola University Press, 1986. Historical essays and neighborhood tours.

Parot, Joseph John. *Polish Catholics in Chicago, 1850–1920.* DeKalb, Ill.: Northern Illinois University Press, 1981. Describes the Catholic priests and parishioners of Chicago's Polonia.

Sanders, James W. *The Education of an Urban Minority: Catholics in Chicago, 1833–1965.* New York and Oxford: Oxford University Press, 1977. An interpretive history of the largest Catholic school system in the United States.

Shanabruch, Charles. *Chicago's Catholics: The Evolution of an American Identity.* Notre Dame, Ind.: University of Notre Dame Press, 1981. Describes the rich mosaic of European immigrant groups that laid the foundations of the Catholic Church in Chicago before 1920.

Index